Imprisoned or Missing in Vietnam

Imprisoned or Missing in Vietnam

*Policies of the Vietnamese
Government Concerning
Captured and Unaccounted For
United States Soldiers, 1969–1994*

by LEWIS M. STERN

McFarland & Company, Inc., Publishers
Jefferson, North Carolina, and London

British Library Cataloguing-in-Publication data are available

Library of Congress Cataloguing-in-Publication Data

Stern, Lewis M.
    Imprisoned or missing in Vietnam : policies of the Vietnamese
government concerning captured and unaccounted for United
States soldiers, 1969–1994 / by Lewis M. Stern.
        p.   cm.
    Includes bibliographical references and index.
    ISBN 0-7864-0121-4 (lib. bdg. : 50# alk. paper)
    1. Vietnamese Conflict, 1961–1975 — Missing in action — United
States.   2. Prisoners of war — United States.   3. Vietnam —
Foreign relations — United States.   4. United States — Foreign
relations — Vietnam.
DS559.8.M5S73   1995
959.704'37 — dc20   95-115
                                                                            CIP

Manufactured in the United States of America

McFarland & Company, Inc., Publishers
  Box 611, Jefferson, North Carolina 28640

This book is for my mother,
Sylvia C. Stern,
for making me do my homework

TABLE OF CONTENTS

PREFACE AND ACKNOWLEDGMENTS

I began this writing project with the intention of outlining the history of Vietnam's postwar response to U.S. government efforts to focus Hanoi's attention on the matter of accounting for missing American service personnel. During 1992 the Senate Select Committee on Prisoner of War and Missing in Action (POW/MIA) Affairs organized several public hearings featuring the testimony of the senior-most U.S. government officials responsible for policy decisions during the 1960s and 1970s. The committee declassified millions of pages of documents concerning this issue, and this enabled me to utilize some very unique documents and testimony in my effort to sort out the complex trajectories of U.S. and Vietnamese negotiations during 1969–1973. The main goal which I set for myself was to draw some conclusions about Vietnamese negotiating and decision-making regarding the POW/MIA issue. I have reserved those comments for the concluding chapter.

Much of this writing focuses on what the Vietnamese were saying publicly or privately about this issue and is therefore dependent upon their prodigious output of media statements, official proclamations, and broadcast commentary. Some of the chronology I have attempted to provide utilizes remarks by Vietnamese officials made to me directly or to Western journalists, humanitarian assistance workers, government officials, and academics who either shared their comments with me directly or included their valuable insights in their own publications about the Vietnamese views of the POW/MIA issue. In many instances I have refrained from naming the officials whose remarks were central to my understanding of the Vietnamese perspective on this issue. At those junctures I have provided as accurate a description as possible of the individual's proximity to the information and his or her position in the government or party hierarchy to allow readers to make judgments regarding the reliability and knowledge of the cited source.

I was involved in Department of Defense policy-making on the POW/MIA issue from at least September 1989 to early 1994 as country director for Indochina in the Office of the Assistant Secretary of Defense for International Security Affairs. I accompanied General John W. Vessey, the presidential emissary for POW/MIA Affairs, to Hanoi five times between October 1989 and April 1993. I provided analytical and policy support to several principal advisers to the secretary of defense on POW/MIA Affairs from 1989 until January 1992, when the secretary of defense named a deputy assistant secretary of defense for POW/MIA affairs and created a special policy office distinct from the entity in the Office of the Assistant Secretary of Defense for International Security Affairs which had been responsible for this issue since the early 1980s. I continued to provide input on this issue through the new office, and directly to the assistant secretary of defense, throughout 1993 and 1994. I participated in three technical sessions with the Vietnamese during 1990–1992, traveled to Vietnam with Deputy Secretary for Veterans Affairs Hershel Gober and Assistant Secretary of State Winston Lord in July 1993 and June 1994, and escorted a Senate delegation to Hanoi and Ho Chi Minh City in January 1994.

I learned a great deal about this issue from our military's technical specialists, whose dedication and expertise have long served the U.S. government. I owe a great deal to Joe Harvey, former commander of the Joint Casualty Resolution Center (JCRC), whose friendship and insights I prize equally. I learned much about the issue, and about Vietnam, from a decade-long friendship with Robert Destatte, who was assigned to the Joint Task Force–Full Accounting's detachment in Hanoi during 1993 and 1994. A succession of Defense Intelligence Agency (DIA) and JCRC specialists with whom I have worked have impressed me, taught me, and helped me to gain a better understanding of how the Vietnamese formulated their positions on this issue. Paul Mather, Chuck Trowbridge, Bill Bell, Bill Gadoury, Joe Schlatter, Bob Sheetz, Gary Sedow, and Tom McKay helped me learn about the process, the personalities, and the politics. All should be absolved of any responsibility for the manner in which I have come to understand the history of this issue and the way I have interpreted Vietnamese motives, intentions, political aims and goals, and policy decisions.

Many academics and journalists contributed in one way or another to this study, either by providing moral support and encouragement, their own insights, or their critical perspectives on my views. Over the past ten years William Turley allowed me to turn many of our conversations toward this issue. I take full responsibility for the manner in which I have interpreted the viewpoints we discussed that have, in one form or another, worked their way into this text. Elizabeth Becker pushed and prodded me to think these issues through and urged me to think in terms of this kind of a study, though she is also blameless for the way I have handled the views of the Vietnamese leaders we have discussed over time. Nayan Chanda, Virginia Foote, Nguyen Manh Hung, Bill Herod, Fred Brown, Robert Mueller, Bob Dalton, Doan Van Toai, Pham Duc Kien, and Bui Tin allowed me to explore their thoughts on the subject, and engaged me in debate over the central themes in this writing. I thank them for the advice they gave and suspect I will regret rejecting the advice I ignored.

Others in the U.S. government deserve mention for the support they provided, the manner in which they encouraged me to think about the more enduring questions, or the way they tolerated my hypothesizing in the midst of struggles to prepare negotiating points, brief senior leaders, and organize technical and policy meetings. General John Vessey, General Frank Libutti, General Tom Wilkerson, General Robert Kingston, Colonel Bill Jordan, Lieutenant Colonel Jim Caswell, Lieutenant Colonel Arthur Gorman, and Mr. Frank Light were among those who were either charitable with their time or with kind words as I groped for explanations of "why they behave like Vietnamese." Andre Sauvageot was a good friend throughout the years we worked together on this issue and helped me put my ideas to some strict, tough tests, including his razor-sharp logic and profound understanding of the Vietnamese. Richard Armitage, Karl Jackson, Charles Twining, Chris La Fleur, Ken Quinn, and Carl Ford allowed me to think through certain odd turns to an argument, were patient with my efforts, and helpful with their experience.

I owe thanks to the many Vietnamese with whom I spoke about this issue. Some are mentioned in the text. They helped me to understand important aspects of a complex puzzle. Throughout the text I cite a variety of individuals, including Vietnamese officials and Western nongovernmental organization officials, who in private conversations or correspondence between myself and the individuals cited provided information that I thought shed light on the issue.

Finally, I want to thank my family for allowing me the reprieve from household chores necessary to complete this writing, for enduring long absences during my travel overseas, and for asking some of the more difficult questions about this sensitive and often disturbing issue.

The views expressed in this book are those of the author alone and do not represent the positions of any part of the United States government.

INTRODUCTION

From the earliest discussions of the terms under which the captured and detained American military and civilian personnel would be returned to the United States, to the increased cooperation in searching for witnesses and wartime archival data and investigating crash and grave sites two decades after the end of the war, Vietnam's decisions were calculated to extract advantages, maximize negotiating leverage, manipulate symbols, and garner international sympathy and support.

The initial post–1975 position taken by the Vietnamese on the POW/MIA issue was fundamentally uncooperative and inflexible. In part it may have been a visceral response to the thought of assisting American invaders to account for their missing in the face of so much devastation inflicted on Vietnam by the United States. It was also, in part, postwar hubris. Vietnam intended to stand up to the American machine, to flex its muscles and display its strength and independence. Hanoi did not yield to good sense in 1978 when confronted with the opportunity to come to an agreement with an American administration not at all averse to normalizing relations. When the Carter administration offered a chance to end Vietnam's isolation, the Vietnamese government sought to leverage Washington into underwriting postwar reconstruction. The Vietnamese invasion of Cambodia closed the door on any possibility of rapprochement. Another decade would pass before significant internal political changes, shifting regional alignments, changing Western interests, Sino-Soviet rapprochement, and progress toward a nonmilitary settlement of the Cambodian conflict would bring Hanoi to the point of rethinking its regional equities, recognizing the importance of mending fences with the West, and realizing the need to take steps to resolve the POW/MIA issue.

The manner in which the Vietnamese leadership arrived at decisions should shed light on the alignment of interests and opinion involved in formulating Vietnamese policy on this issue and the relative strength and influence of individual decision-makers. If Vietnamese policy-makers were above all else practical, then why did they persist in seeking reparations as a condition for discussions regarding the MIAs? Why did they continue to seek leverage over the U.S. by using an issue that ultimately afforded them no advantage and merely served to galvanize increasingly vocal anti–Vietnamese interests in the U.S., the Congress, and the executive branch? Did they really calculate that they would be able to win sympathy and press the U.S. to lift the

1

embargo? Why were the Vietnamese so stubbornly unable to realize the strength and influence of the congressional POW/MIA caucus and to understand that American public opinion on this issue militated against their ever being able to divide and weaken the various U.S. interest groups focused on the POW/MIA issue?

If Vietnamese foreign policy decisions were reached on the basis of establishing consensus positions at the highest levels of leadership, then why was the Ministry of Foreign Affairs (MFA) not able to hold the Ministry of Interior (MOI) and the Ministry of National Defense (MND) to agreements struck by the MFA to implement various aspects of the commitment to cooperate with the U.S. in seeking information about missing Americans during 1989 to 1991? Why was the MOI so much of a problem for the minister of foreign affairs, especially in the late 1980s when the Foreign Ministry sought to undertake joint investigations, comply with American requests for information about specific cases of missing Americans, and produce witnesses to incidents of loss and captivity? Why was the Defense Ministry only marginally involved and basically disinterested in the early 1980s? How was the foreign minister able to function according to his own agenda on the POW/MIA issue and to associate that agenda closely with the goal of broadening and diversifying foreign relations and restoring the basis for relations with the West for so long?

Once the decision was taken to improve Vietnam's image and to rebuild relations with the West, Vietnam became more reasonable, flexible, and cooperative on this issue. In this context there was a persistent gap between (1) the ministerial-level decision to agree to U.S. policy proposals regarding the modalities of joint investigations, access to witnesses and wartime archival information, and the means by which cases could be resolved, and (2) working-level actions to implement those decisions. Vietnamese technicians and experts and middle-level ministerial personnel involved in the practical aspects of managing the POW/MIA issue often acted in a manner that did not serve to turn policy-level decisions into operational plans agreed to by senior Vietnamese officials. If Vietnamese decision-making was centrally controlled and based on top-to-bottom transmissions in the spirit of "democratic centralism," then why did the department-level officials have significant enough authority to essentially undermine agreements struck between U.S. and Vietnamese senior officials? Controlling for individual characteristics of particular bureaucrats and inefficiency, why were middle-level officials able to frustrate efforts of U.S. counterparts to implement agreements? Was the entire system primed to drag its heels on this issue, or was there significant working-level unwillingness to implement rapidly and efficiently the agreements of senior officials as the result of differing perceptions and interests or clashing convictions regarding the relative importance of keeping promises to the U.S. on this issue?

This book will attempt to answer these and other questions in a preliminary manner, based on an analysis of official Vietnamese statements about the issue; observations of and participation in the negotiating process during the period from 1989 to 1994; discussions with middle-level Vietnamese officials associated with Hanoi's MIA policy; assessments of Vietnamese media commentary, Vietnamese scholarship, and political tracts on the issue; discussions with U.S. government officials involved in the formulation and implementation of the POW/MIA policy; and discussions with nongovernmental organization representatives with an interest in this issue.

This study begins with an account of Hanoi's negotiating position on the POW/MIA issue during the course of the Paris peace talks and ends with the final U.S. government decision to lift the embargo against trading with Vietnam.

CHAPTER ONE

POW/MIA Negotiations from the Paris Peace Talks to the Fall of South Vietnam, 1971–1975

Negotiating the Peace Agreement

From the beginning of the plenary peace talks which convened in Paris in early 1969, the Democratic Republic of Vietnam (DRV) took the position that the complete withdrawal of U.S. troops from Vietnam was the condition for the release of U.S. prisoners. The DRV saw the issue of missing Americans as a bargaining chip which could be used to pry concessions from the U.S. government. During the war the Vietnamese sometimes indicated to the U.S. that they had shot down and captured U.S. pilots when in fact those claims were false. That may have been a tactical military decision, or it may have been an organized propaganda ploy intended to demoralize America on the very vulnerable home front, but in either way it demonstrated Hanoi's willingness from the start to utilize the POW issue as a means of achieving military and political advantages.[1]

Negotiators for the United States consistently maintained the position that the release of prisoners should be unconditional. Henry Kissinger rejected repeated efforts by Hanoi to tie the release of American POWs to the issue of postwar reparations and to the question of the timing of the release of political prisoners held by the South Vietnamese government (GVN). Three issues emerged as the key to negotiating the resolution of the POW question: the timing of the releases of military prisoners, the timing of the exchange of civilian prisoners, and the matter of guaranteeing the return of U.S. personnel captured in Laos and Cambodia.

On 31 May 1971, Kissinger expressed willingness to agree on a deadline for the complete withdrawal of U.S. troops in return for the repatriation of U.S. POWs. Between May and October 1971, the U.S. and Hanoi negotiators wrestled with the question of the timing of the release of the prisoners. Washington proposed that the return of POWs begin once the date for the withdrawal of U.S. troops was set. This was rejected by Vietnam. In late June 1971, Le Duc Tho proposed a nine-point plan to end the war. The second point proposed that "the release of all military men and civilians captured in the war should be carried out in parallel and completed at the same time as the troop withdrawals." On 1 July, the Provisional Revolutionary Government (PRG) of South Vietnam representative in Paris proposed a seven-point plan for settlement of the conflict in South Vietnam that tied the unconditional withdrawal of American forces, which was to be completed by the end of 1971, to the release of all military and civilian prisoners.

Le Duc Tho took the position in private talks that the nine-point plan would be the basis for any and all discussions of peace and that none of the nine points could be discussed in isolation from the others. Tho pressed Kissinger to establish a specific withdrawal date in return for an agreement to release the POWs. Kissinger committed to a 1 August 1972 date for withdrawal if a peace agreement could be reached by 1 November 1971. The Vietnamese had publicly offered to treat the total withdrawal of U.S. forces and the prisoner exchange as separate matters, though in the secret talks Tho held firmly to the link established in the nine-point plan. At a 13 September session, Hanoi made it clear that the nine-point plan represented its view of what should result from the talks, not a negotiating starting point. In October the U.S. offered to withdraw all of its forces, except for a small technical and advisory presence needed to sustain logistics and observe the ceasefire, within seven months of the signing of a statement of principles. In that context, American prisoners and "innocent civilians" would be released at the same time. The ceasefire and political settlement would be negotiated afterwards.

Tho turned down an offer to convene again in November 1971. In private sessions, Tho repeatedly stated that the offer had been made for a prisoner exchange in return for a U.S. troop withdrawal. He accepted Kissinger's proposal for another secret meeting in mid–March 1972 and ultimately met with Kissinger again on 2 May 1972, the day before Quang Tri Province fell to the People's Army of Vietnam (PAVN). In May, Kissinger proposed that U.S. forces in Indochina would withdraw no later than four months after the signing of an agreement if Hanoi agreed to a ceasefire in place and returned U.S. POWs. Tho rejected that formulation. The next day the plenary sessions in Paris were suspended. On 9 May, President Richard Nixon announced the failure of the secret talks, the decision to mine Haiphong Harbor, and the initiation of other interdiction measures. Washington restated its willingness to withdraw its forces completely within four months of the acceptance of a ceasefire in place and a POW exchange.

In July, Kissinger briefed South Vietnamese President Nguyen Van Thieu on the results of his meetings with Le Duc Tho and reassured Thieu of the U.S. government's continued commitment to Saigon's security and well-being. Kissinger sought to address Thieu's concerns regarding the risks of a ceasefire in place, the formation of a coalition government, and Hanoi's insistence that the Thieu regime resign before any agreement was signed. Tho and Kissinger met twice in August. In September, the PRG issued a statement accepting the principle of agreeing to a ceasefire prior to defining the resolution of internal political problems, including the nature of the coalition arrangement and the transition period prior to a general election. Kissinger met Tho on 15 September and registered Washington's concern over the implication of the PRG proposal that Thieu would be removed by the U.S., rather than the South Vietnamese people themselves. At a 26 September meeting, Tho proposed the establishment of a tripartite National Council of Reconciliation and Concord that would not be considered a government and would operate on the principle of unanimity.

On 8 October 1972, Tho proposed an immediate ceasefire and prisoner exchange, the withdrawal of U.S. forces, cessation of war against the DRV, and the prohibition of augmentation of the armed forces operating in South Vietnam. Tho agreed that the ceasefire could come before the political reconciliation between the PRG and the GVN. In October, after long negotiations, Washington agreed to a complete withdrawal of U.S. forces within six months of the agreement and the parallel release of captured military personnel and "innocent civilians" in the three countries of Indochina. By mid–October a 58-page draft emerged, and it became the subject of vigorous and contentious U.S. efforts to convince Thieu to accept the terms of the agreement and a rigorous and combative effort to deal with the technical, procedural, and linguistic differences between Hanoi and Washington. By late October, among the remaining issues that required some additional smoothing over was the relationship between the release of U.S. POWs and the release of Vietnamese civilians who had been incarcerated in GVN facilities for political transgressions. Additionally, Hanoi refused to agree to the U.S. position that the DRV should accept responsibility for ensuring that Vientiane and Phnom Penh would turn over all U.S. POWs. According to a variety of participants, including Nixon and Kissinger, in late 1972 Hanoi gave its "private assurances" that no POWs were held in Cambodia and that those held in Laos would be returned to the U.S. by the DRV. Hanoi would not provide a formal written provision to this effect, however, either as part of the agreement or as a protocol.[2]

The draft peace agreement that emerged in late 1972 from years of secret negotiations between Le Duc Tho and Kissinger called for the return of captured and detained military and civilian personnel and provided for the establishment of commissions and teams to implement the accords and attendant protocols. The final negotiations also addressed the issue of Americans who were still missing and unaccounted for. Article 8(a) provided for the return of "captured military personnel and foreign civilians" simultaneous with and not later than the completion of the withdrawal of U.S. troops and required the U.S. and Hanoi to exchange complete lists of POWs on the day of the signing. Article 8(b) of the Paris Accords stated:

> The parties shall help each other to get information about those military personnel and foreign civilians of the parties missing in action, to determine the location and take care of the graves of the dead so as to facilitate the exhumation and repatriation of the remains, and to take any such other measure as may be required to get information about those still considered missing in action.[3]

Article 8(c) stipulated that within 90 days of the start of the ceasefire, the two South Vietnamese "parties" would "do the utmost" to resolve the issue of Vietnamese civilian personnel captured and detained in South Vietnam. The article spoke of prisoners held "by the parties" to the conflict and did not specifically address the question of POWs held by Laos and Cambodia.

According to the accords, the Four Party Joint Military Team (FPJMT) would continue to function beyond the 60-day limit imposed on the existence of the Four Party Joint Military Commission (FPJMC) by the peace agreement. In fact, the team remained active in Saigon until the fall of the GVN in 1975. The Joint Casualty Resolution Center (JCRC) was activated in January 1973 in Saigon to serve as the FPJMT's operational element. The unit, under the command of General Robert C. Kingston, was assigned the mission of resolving the status of U.S. missing personnel and locating and investigating crash and grave sites throughout Southeast Asia. The JCRC was authorized to utilize air and ground search teams to locate grave sites, grave registration specialists from the U.S. Army's Central Identification Laboratory, and crash site investigators. In January 1972 the U.S. delegation to the FPJMC provided the DRV with 14 case summaries recounting the details of Americans who remained unaccounted for in Vietnam. In April, Ambassador William Porter presented the Vietnamese with information about 14 U.S. personnel who were identified by Hanoi as having been captured, but who were not on the "complete list" provided by Hanoi in late December 1970.

In November the U.S. proposed protocols on the ceasefire, the joint military commission, mine clearance, the role of the International Commission for Control and Supervision (ICCS), and the return of prisoners. In response to clear indications that Washington was backing away from certain aspects of the agreement as a result of Thieu's strong concerns, Tho informed Kissinger that the Politburo had instructed him to reopen issues that had been agreed to in October. Washington and Hanoi continued to disagree over the size of the ICCS. Hanoi was reluctant to accept Washington's insistence that the ceasefire extend to all of Indochina. Additionally, Hanoi and Washington differed over the military status of the demilitarized zone. Hanoi reintroduced demands that Thieu be removed and again insisted that political prisoners be released simultaneously with America's POWs. Hanoi's goal was to force

Washington to return to the October draft, while Washington sought to accommodate the Thieu government by insisting on major conceptual and textual changes.

During 4–11 December, after presenting the case for serious changes in the October draft, the U.S. government altered its positions on the regroupment of PAVN main force units to enclaves and troop reduction and settled for assurances from Hanoi that it would influence the Pathet Lao to obtain a ceasefire within two weeks of the signing of the Paris Accords. Kissinger was not able to move Tho to make a parallel guarantee for Cambodia, however. The remaining disagreements revolved around Washington's demands for strict regulation of civilian movement across the demarcation line, major alterations in the concept of the reconciliation council, and changes in the preamble and text of the draft agreement to expunge references to the PRG.

Throughout December, Kissinger told Tho that if Hanoi persisted in actions which seemed likely to scuttle the agreement, President Nixon would be under inordinate pressure to bring to bear decisive force to drive Hanoi to embrace the principles of the October draft. Tho and Kissinger met on 13 December. The next day, in response to what the U.S. negotiators perceived to be clear indications that the Vietnamese were not prepared to stop withdrawing agreed-upon positions and insisting on linguistic changes, Washington cabled Nixon's warning to Hanoi that grave consequences would result if negotiations failed to resume by 17 December. On 15 December, at a subdelegation meeting on drafting the protocols, Hanoi reintroduced the demand that the release of all POWs be linked to the release of political detainees in Saigon. Hanoi hoped that the retraction of several earlier concessions would convince the U.S. to back away from demands for significant changes in the draft documents. Specifically, Hanoi wanted the U.S. to abandon the position that changes needed to be made in the draft documents regarding the character of the council of national reconciliation and concord, the legal status of the demilitarized zone, the nature of the elections provided for in Article 9, and the provision of ceasefires in Laos and Cambodia.

On 8 January, following intensive bombing that destroyed Hanoi's surface-to-air missile defense system and vital military supplies that had been stockpiled with difficulty in the face of the naval blockade, Tho returned to the conference table. Hanoi reiterated its position that the release of American POWs should be accomplished simultaneously with the return of civilian POWs. Following three weeks of discussions and counterproposals, the protocols were initialed on 23 January 1973. The protocol concerning Article 8(b) required that all captured U.S. and allied military and civilian personnel be returned to U.S. authorities, that the rate of return of POWs be no slower than the rate of withdrawal of U.S. and allied forces, and that U.S. and allied POWs be returned at places convenient to the concerned parties and approved by the FPJMC. The protocol required that the safety of personnel engaged in facilitating the return of captured personnel be guaranteed, that the return of captured personnel not be delayed for any reason, and that the captives be treated in a humanitarian manner prior to return. The protocol stipulated that the FPJMC must agree to the modalities of the return of the U.S. POWs and be allowed to field joint teams to observe the repatriation. According to the protocol, the FPJMC would assume responsibility for accounting for missing personnel and for the investigation of violations of the protocol. Finally, the protocol text had to be distributed to each prisoner within five days of the signature of the agreement in protocol. On 23 January 1973, after months of discussions and wrangling over the issues raised in the proposed protocols, Kissinger and Tho initialed the Agreement on Ending the War and Restoring the Peace in Vietnam. On 27 January the formal agreement was signed.[4]

Implementing the Agreements and Protocols

During the 30 January 1973 meeting of deputy delegation chiefs to the FPJMC, Brigadier General John A. Wickham, Jr., representing the U.S., proposed that the commission establish a subcommission on POWs. The PRG representative, Colonel Dang Van Thu, agreed and proposed the formation of a parallel two-party subcommission to deal with captured South Vietnamese civilians. The FPJMC agreed that the subcommission on prisoners should commence operations on 3 February. General Wickham requested that Hanoi reply quickly to U.S. requests for information about U.S. POWs and about individuals not on those lists. He also asked that death certificates be provided to the U.S. representatives to assist in accounting for missing personnel and that Hanoi undertake to return the remains of the missing.

During early February the POW subcommission worked out the modalities of the release of prisoners held by the North Vietnamese and the PRG, Red Cross access to detention facilities, and the release of POWs held by the South Vietnamese government. The subcommission and the FPJMC managed the release operations, including the arrangement of dates and places for the release, transportation of reception teams, coordination of the Red Cross inspections of the last sites of captivity for the released prisoners, and negotiating procedures for each proposed prisoner release. The subcommission and the FPJMC also coordinated with the Saigon government's delegates to ensure that their side lived up to its responsibilities regarding the release of civilian detainees, prodded the PRG and the DRV delegates to provide prison release information, including lists, in a manner that comported with provisions of the Paris Accords, and negotiated the release of Americans captured in Laos.

On 27 January 1973, the DRV and the PRG provided the U.S. delegation with separate lists of individuals who had died in captivity. The U.S. negotiators protested that the list did not include the names of any of the 350

Americans captured in Laos. On 1 February, Vietnamese officials in Paris gave U.S. representatives a list of nine Americans and one Canadian who had been captured in Laos. On 25 June 1992, Dr. Roger Shields, deputy assistant secretary of defense in the early 1970s, told the Senate Select Committee on POW/MIA Affairs:

> Some lists were passed to U.S. citizens by representatives of the DRV . . . and in one case to representatives of Senator Kennedy showing a number of U.S. military as having been captured or having died in captivity. These lists were never considered to be official and complete lists. They were not transmitted by official representatives of the DRV to the U.S. government. The information the lists contained did not conform to the requirements of the Geneva Convention relative to the treatment of prisoners of war. And we believed the lists, with good reason as it turned out, to be incomplete. Statements by the enemy that they held an American prisoner were accepted by the U.S. as confirmation of POW status and were welcome. Statements relating to those who died in captivity were not accepted as a basis for a status change. . . . Another significant list is the one passed by the DRV to representatives of the U.S. government in Paris in January 1973, as required by the Paris peace accords. That list was official in the sense that it represented for the first time an official statement by the other side about Americans they were holding and those whom they reported as having died in captivity. This list was not accepted by us as a complete accounting for those held prisoner or for those who died in captivity. First, that list did not include the names of those prisoners missing in Laos. It also omitted the names of men we knew to have been in captivity at one time. The list of those reported as having been captured in Laos passed to us a short time later by the DRV was viewed in the same way.[5]

At the same time the U.S. representatives provided a private letter from President Nixon to Prime Minister Pham Van Dong in which the principles that would govern U.S. participation in the postwar reconstruction of North Vietnam were spelled out. The letter stated that "the Government of the United States of America will contribute to postwar reconstruction in North Vietnam without any political conditions" and noted that preliminary U.S. studies indicated that "the appropriate programs for U.S. contribution to post-war reconstruction will fall in the range of $3.25 billion of grant aid over five years." The letter also proposed the formation of a Joint Economic Commission to develop programs for the U.S. contribution to reconstruction of North Vietnam. On 2 February the U.S. side expressed its concern over the fact that only ten names appeared on the list of American POWs held in Laos. In a letter to Prime Minister Dong, President Nixon wrote:

> The list of American prisoners held in Laos which was presented in Paris on February 1st is unsatisfactory. U.S. records show that there are 317 American military men unaccounted for in Laos and it is inconceivable that only ten of

these men would be held in prison in Laos. There can be no doubt therefore that the implementation of any American undertaking is related to the satisfactory resolution of this problem. It should also be pointed out that failure to provide a complete list of prisoners in Laos or a satisfactory explanation of the low numbers thus far presented would seriously impair the mission of Dr. Kissinger to Hanoi.

During his 10–12 February meetings in Hanoi, Kissinger provided the Vietnamese with folders on unaccounted for personnel. On 12 February, Hanoi released 135 U.S. POWs, and on 18 February Hanoi freed an additional 20 U.S. POWs. On 14 February, Hanoi and Washington announced an agreement to establish a Joint Economic Commission. The communiqué specifically noted that an agreement had been struck concerning the necessity of systematically determining the fate of the U.S. MIAs.

In February 1973, following the signing of the Paris Peace Agreement, Prime Minister Pham Van Dong signed a decree establishing the Vietnam Office for Seeking Missing Personnel (VNOSMP, Co Quan Viet Nam Tim Kiem Ti Tuc Nguoi Mat Tich Trong Chien Tranh Viet Nam). The office, according to the decree, was empowered to collect information from local administrative committees, regular army units, local forces, and security units pertaining to MIAs"; "determine the location and take care of graves of the dead" and "direct the exhumation, recovery (thu hoi) and preservation of remains of MIAs; systematically record information on recovered remains; and manage the repatriation of remains. The decree stipulated that the VNOSMP would be composed of "permanent representatives" from the Foreign Ministry, Defense Ministry, Ministry of Public Security, and the Health Ministry. The Office of the Prime Minister was given the authority to determine the VNOSMP's budget and responsibility for implementing the decree along with the Foreign Ministry, Ministry of Public Security, Ministry of Health, and the chairmen of the provincial and municipal administrative committees.[6]

The Vietnamese insisted that there were no additional prisoners beyond those on the lists and those scheduled for release in the agreed-upon 60-day period. In late February 1973, Hanoi had still not provided the list of Americans to be freed on 27 February and had begun to suggest that the freeing of the U.S. POWs would be tied to the release of the "political prisoners" in South Vietnam, a link the U.S. had strongly rejected throughout the discussions of the peace agreement terms. In response, Washington suspended troop withdrawals and mine-clearing operations. Hanoi relented and went on to free the U.S. prisoners on schedule.

Hanoi continued to maintain that it could not guarantee that the Pathet Lao would comply with the arrangements for the release of U.S. service personnel captured in Laos by the agreed date of 28 March 1973, the end of the 60-day period specified in the Paris Accords. The Vietnamese regarded the U.S.

demand for the release of POWs captured in Laos as being beyond the jurisdiction of the Paris Accords. In late March the Vietnamese urged that Washington understand that the withdrawal of U.S. troops and the release of prisoners should proceed "with no relation to the POWs held by the Pathet Lao." The question of "U.S. persons captured in Laos" was "within the sovereign power of Laos" and was "beyond the competence of the FPJMC," according to Hanoi's chief representative to the commission, General Tran Van Tra. Hanoi released 135 U.S. POWs on 12 February, 20 on 18 February, 133 in early March, 108 on 14 March, and 134 on 28 March. On 16 March the PRG released 32 Americans. On 27 March, Hanoi released the seven U.S. military personnel and two civilians on the list of POWs captured in Laos. On 1 April the last U.S. POW captured by PRG forces was released in South Vietnam. In a 28 March 1973 memorandum to the national security advisor, Secretary of Defense Elliot Richardson stated that "there has been no accounting of U.S. personnel missing in Laos other than the 1 February 1973 list of ten who were probably all captured in Laos by North Vietnamese rather than the Pathet Lao." Richardson recommended that following the recovery of the last prisoners from North Vietnam, Hanoi be "advised unequivocally that we still hold them responsible for the return of all POWs being held in Indochina."[7]

In late March, following the agreement to the arrangements for the final release operations with the North Vietnamese delegation, the Hanoi representative raised the issue of assigning 30 individuals from its delegation to the FPJMT which, according to the provisions of the Paris Accords, was to remain in Vietnam following the termination of the Joint Military Commission to deal with the issue of MIAs. Before the date of termination of the FPJMC, the U.S. delegation informally discussed with the DRV representatives and the PRG delegation the issue of prisoners whose names did not appear on the lists received from Hanoi in Paris and who had not been released. The questions raised about the unaccounted for prisoners were not resolved through these informal approaches. On 4 April the U.S. delegation to the FPJMT passed complete lists and detailed folders on MIAs to the Vietnamese representatives and informed the Vietnamese delegations that the U.S. believed that the DRV and the PRG had information on the fate of these individuals who were not returned during Operation Homecoming.

On 19 April, Washington reacted to Hanoi's violations of the Paris Accords by suspending Joint Economic Commission meetings and publicly criticizing Hanoi's failure to provide information on U.S. MIAs. In a new round of Paris talks which began in May, Washington pressed Hanoi to stop the hostilities in Cambodia as the condition for economic assistance to postwar reconstruction. During those sessions the U.S. and the DRV agreed to promote a settlement in Cambodia, strictly observe the ceasefire in South Vietnam, and resume Joint Economic Commission talks. Those talks resumed on 19 June.

From mid–May to June, during a total of 12 days of discussions with the

Vietnamese, Kissinger raised the question of a good faith effort to account for MIAs. Hanoi, according to Kissinger, sensed that Washington's leverage was eroding, in large part as a result of congressional efforts to prohibit the use of funds for military activity in Southeast Asia. As a consequence, Hanoi was confident that the U.S. administration could not apply strong measures such as air strikes because of popular and congressional opposition to such moves. On 5 May the PRG delegation "privately" informed the U.S. delegation that it was unable to obtain information in response to a 9 April request regarding a particular case that was part of a U.S. died-in-captivity list. In early May the U.S. formally presented a list of 1,114 U.S. and foreign persons who were missing in Vietnam to the delegates of the FPJMC and repeatedly pressed the PRG and the DRV for information about U.S., Korean, and Australian MIAs.

Throughout May, the U.S. government pressed the matter of Vientiane's responsibility to provide explanations for the discrepancy between the number of POWs the U.S. believed had been held in Laos and the nine who had been returned. Hanoi feared that the question of U.S. aid to Vietnam would become submerged to this issue and made this preoccupation clear during FPJMT meetings. By early May, Hanoi was convinced that the U.S. government was seriously crippled by the consequences of the Watergate break-in and was thoroughly focused on pressuring Hanoi to compel the Pathet Lao to comply with the demand to return and account for POWs. Hanoi was also convinced that Washington would not expedite reconstruction assistance. From that point, Vietnamese cooperation with the FPJMT diminished.

In late May, in a meeting with Le Duc Tho, Kissinger emphasized the importance of Nguyen Co Thach's commitment to Ambassador William Sullivan to help the U.S. coordinate with Laos to obtain information concerning U.S. personnel MIA in Laos and requested that Hanoi refrain from contradicting the U.S. position and public statements that Article 8(b) applied to all of Indochina. Kissinger also asked Tho for a written statement by the DRV that "there are no prisoners being held in Laos, that all the prisoners held in Laos have been released." Tho told Kissinger that he had acknowledged that all the POWs had been released, but gave no indication that he would acquiesce to Kissinger's request for a written statement to that effect.

On 13 June 1973, the U.S. and the DRV issued a joint communiqué reiterating the obligations established by the Paris Accords to release remaining POWs, to provide a full accounting for MIAs throughout Indochina, and to make information about those who died in captivity or in their incidents of loss accessible to the U.S. Point 8 of the communiqué stated that "In conformity with Article 8 of the Agreement, (a) any captured personnel covered by Article 8(a) of the Agreement who have not yet been returned shall be returned without delay, and in any event within no more than thirty days from the date of the signature of this Joint Communiqué." To accomplish this, the communiqué included an agreement that the parties would, in conformity with Article 8(b):

help each other to get information about those military personnel and foreign civilians of the parties missing in action, to determine the location and take care of the graves of the dead so as to facilitate the exhumation and repatriation of remains, and to take any such other measure as may be required to get information about those considered missing in action. For the purpose, frequent and regular liaison flights shall be made between Saigon and Hanoi.

Hanoi, however, failed to comply with these provisions and sought to blunt U.S. efforts to press for the implementation of the accords on the basis of its confidence that Washington was stymied by congressional prohibitions against military actions in Vietnam. In September 1992, George H. Aldrich, former legal adviser to the State Department, told the Senate Select Committee:

> To the extent that those provisions were not carried out, the causes, I believe, are to be found in the general breakdown of the settlement, particularly in the reluctance of the Vietnamese parties to respect the cease fire and the national reconciliation provisions, the . . . inability to achieve a mutual cease-fire in Cambodia while the United States ceased its involvement pursuant to U.S. legislation, our consequent inability to offer North Vietnamese the benefits . . . of economic aid and normalization of relations and, of course, the consequences of the unfolding scandal called Watergate.[8]

During 1973, in close coordination with the RVN delegation, the U.S. delegation researched and provided information on 100 PRG dead and missing. The U.S. also responded to the requests of third countries concerning their dead and missing. The position the U.S. delegation took in raising these cases was that the majority of third country missing personnel were engaged in humanitarian work, their governments were not actually parties allied in the conflict, and most of them were not signatories to the Paris Accords. The U.S. delegation also made similar overtures to attempt to determine the fate of 17 newsmen from seven different countries. These requests were all rejected by the PRG. The U.S. explained that, with the exception of the repatriation of the remains of 23 U.S. personnel listed on a died-in-captivity list in March, the DRV and PRG refused to meet any of their obligations stipulated in Article 8(b), while proclaiming that they had in fact scrupulously implemented those responsibilities. On 23 July the DRV and the U.S. delegations issued a joint statement that the Joint Economic Commission meetings had been suspended. They were never resumed. In a late July diplomatic note, Washington protested that Hanoi had failed to provide information on "more than 1,300 Americans listed as missing, and on those who died but whose bodies had not been recovered." The PRG simply refused to respond to any of the inquiries by the U.S. or the GVN concerning requests for information on the dead and missing. In a July 1973 memorandum, the DRV Foreign Ministry took credit for creating "favorable conditions" for the FPJMT to visit the graves in the north and "exhume and repatriate remains." In an early August memorandum, the Vietnamese Foreign Ministry accused the U.S. of cancelling seven liaison flights and argued that the responsibility for the delay in the implementation of Article 8(b) of the Paris Accords and Article 10 of the protocol, which provided for the return of captured personnel and the exhumation and repatriation of the remains of U.S. personnel who had died in the DRV, was the fault of the U.S.[9]

In early August 1973, the U.S. initiated the "folder program," a formal and organized attempt to assemble information from the Defense Intelligence Agency (DIA) and JCRC files for passage to the Vietnamese. On 27 August the DRV returned one folder with the explanation that Hanoi would not take responsibility for accounting for personnel lost outside of northern Vietnam. From September to November, the U.S. sought to deliver folders concerning American MIAs to the PRG and the DRV. During this period Vietnam continued to link the repatriation of DIC (died in captivity) list remains with the release of Communist prisoners held by the GVN.[10] In a September 1973 statement, the Foreign Ministry once again claimed credit for having returned "ahead of time" all captured U.S. personnel and for having "created favorable conditions for the U.S. side to visit the graves of U.S. pilots who died in northern Vietnam and to make preparations for the exhumation and repatriation of remains," even though the four participants had not yet, from the DRV viewpoint, defined general principles and operating guidelines for such activities.[11] In December 1973, Communist soldiers ambushed a U.S.–South Vietnamese team searching for bodies of missing Americans, killing one American and one South Vietnamese. Ambassador Graham Martin ordered the cessation of JCRC operations in the south.[12] Hanoi argued that the ambush was a direct result of America's refusal to acknowledge that South Vietnam was not controlled by the government in Saigon and that the safety of JCRC teams in the field could be guaranteed only by cooperating with the PRG. In March, the DRV made it clear that further cooperation on MIA searches would be permitted only when America ceased providing assistance to the Saigon government.[13]

Throughout 1973, Hanoi rebuffed JCRC requests to assign a liaison officer to Hanoi, permitted Americans to enter the DRV to visit grave sites on only two occasions despite repeated requests, and refused to permit repatriation of the remains of American personnel that were interred in the grave sites visited. Hanoi argued that Article 8(b) called for the construction of cemeteries and memorials for Vietnamese who died in the south in the service of the DRV, and it took the position that there would be no progress toward the resolution of the issue until those terms were met.[14] DRV opposition to JCRC casualty recovery operations during the early 1970s may have been a product of Hanoi's concern that such operations could be used to challenge PRG control over certain regions or could be trumpeted by the GVN as indication that they held sway over and could conduct operations in specific areas.[15]

Through mid–1974 the U.S. and RVN delegations continued to meet regularly at the scheduled plenary session and repeatedly invited the DRV and PRG to the negotiating table. On numerous occasions the GVN attempted to exchange lists of missing with the PRG and gave them lists of DRV and PRG dead in an effort to enhance progress. According to U.S. government accounts, the U.S. continued to provide a weekly Saigon-Hanoi liaison flight even though the primary purpose of this flight, which was to exchange information on missing and dead, was never fulfilled. The U.S. also continued to provide vehicular support to the DRV/PRG, and the GVN continued to supply billeting, electricity, water, and other supplies to the DRV/PRG and to extend privileges and immunities as agreed upon by the four parties. The GVN allowed the PRG to conduct a weekly press conference for the PRG, even though it was frequently used to call for the overthrow of the South Vietnamese government.[16] In February, DRV delegates to the FPJMT told their U.S. counterparts that Saigon had made progress in releasing political prisoners and that as a consequence, the repatriation of the remains of the 23 Americans who had died in captivity could proceed. In March 1974, Hanoi repatriated the remains of the last 11 personnel on the DRV list of 23 personnel who were on Vietnam's 27 January 1973 DIC list.

Hanoi refused to repatriate a 24th set of remains on the grounds that the service member died in a crash incident, not in captivity, and therefore was not part of the DIC category of losses. After a GVN crew member was killed by PRG ground fire during a prisoner exchange, the Saigon government cancelled privileges and immunities for the PRG team. Hanoi responded by cancelling plans to repatriate 47 additional sets of remains. Between April and June 1974 the U.S. provided folders on missing American service personnel to the DRV and PRG delegations. In June 1974 the GVN offered to restore privileges and immunities, but the PRG rejected the proposal.[17] During early June the PRG delegation repeatedly claimed that heavy hostilities and alleged GVN "land grabbing" and bombing operations prevented the FPJMT from entering PRG-controlled areas for the purpose of carrying out the search for MIA information and pursuing crash site investigations. Curiously, those were areas touted by Radio Hanoi as model liberated areas, including Quang Tin, Quang Ngai, Binh Dinh, Ca Mau, Soc Trang, Tra Vinh, Vinh Long and Ben Tre Provinces.[18] The DRV and PRG delegations initiated a boycott of working sessions on June 1974 and brought U.S. and RVN attempts to implement Article 8(b) to a halt, except for the weekly Saigon-Hanoi liaison flight, official correspondence between delegations, and meetings between the Communist delegations and concerned U.S. citizens groups facilitated by the U.S. delegation. In a 21 January 1975 letter to Senator Kennedy, Hanoi's foreign minister, Nguyen Duy Trinh, stated that Vietnam would not release information on missing Americans until Washington stopped providing military assistance to South Vietnam and forced President Thieu from office.[19]

In February 1975, the U.S. delegation passed 13 new folders on 20 missing Americans to the DRV and PRG representatives. In April 1975 the U.S. provided the DRV and PRG delegations with lists of all missing U.S. military and civilian personnel, as well as lists of missing Third Country Nationals. In April 1975, the Vietnamese released to Senator Edward Kennedy the names of three U.S. aircrew reported to have died in North Vietnam. By the end of April 1975, the Communists had completed their military takeover of South Vietnam. In May, Radio Hanoi announced that there could be no progress toward the resolution of the problem of missing and deceased Americans until the U.S. signaled its willingness to undertake favorable consideration of financial compensation to rebuild northern and southern Vietnam.[20]

At the time of the termination of active U.S. involvement, there were 2,583 unaccounted for service personnel, of whom 1,919 were lost in Vietnam. Over 80 percent of the 571 men missing in Laos were lost in areas under the control of the PAVN. Over 1,100 of the 1,919 service personnel were reported dead at the time of their loss, but the remains of those personnel could not be recovered at the time. Four hundred were categorized as "over water" losses — individuals believed to have been lost at sea in a crash or otherwise (drownings, etc.).

CHAPTER TWO

Postwar POW / MIA
Contacts and Conflicts, 1975–1981

In the aftermath of the Communist victory, the U.S. government regarded the 1973 Paris Accords as still binding, especially in regard to the responsibility of accounting for MIAs. Hanoi took the position that the responsibilities regarding MIA information and repatriation spelled out in Article 8(b) were "no more binding than the fulfillment of Article 21 [of the Paris Accords] on reconstruction aid," which stipulated that the U.S. "will contribute to healing the wounds of war and to postwar reconstruction of the DRV and throughout Indochina."[1] In February and April 1975, the U.S. passed folders on missing American personnel and updated lists of U.S. military, civilian, and third-country nationals who were MIA to the DRV and PRG. On 15 April, DRV officials informed Senator Edward Kennedy that the remains of three Americans would be repatriated in late August 1975 as the direct result of his request for information on unaccounted for personnel and appeals by the families of the MIAs. In a June 1975 letter to U.S. congressmen, Prime Minister Pham Van Dong pointed to Vietnam's long humanitarian tradition and feeling of sympathy with the families of missing U.S. soldiers as motivating factors behind Hanoi's "unilateral" decision to "allow repatriation of remains of those Americans who died in captivity," and to direct "the responsible services to endeavor to seek information about those Americans considered as Missing in Action, in accordance with Article 8(b) of the Paris Agreement."[2] In early July, in public statements rebuffed by the U.S. government, Dong offered normalization on the basis of U.S. compliance with obligations articulated in Article 21 of the Paris Accords. On 30 October 1975, the DRV released nine Americans and an additional five foreign nationals who had been taken prisoner in April 1975. Arlo Gay, a U.S. civilian who was captured on 30 April 1975 in South Vietnam and released in late September 1976, told DIA officials that on 27 August 1976 a North Vietnamese lieutenant colonel told him that "there is some problem with the United Nations which is why we are holding some Americans." According to Douglas Clarke:

> On 10 August — just before the question of North and South Vietnam's admission to the United Nations was to be considered by that organization — the North Vietnamese embassy in Paris notified the State Department that Hanoi was ready to deliver the three bodies. Concurrently with contacting the Government officially, the North Vietnamese sent a telegram to Cora Weiss, an anti-war activist of long standing . . . informing her of their intentions.

The U.S. veto of Hanoi's application for United Nations membership prompted the DRV to cancel publicly the repatriation of the three sets of remains. In early December 1975, during a visit to Paris by members of the House Select Committee on Missing Persons in Southeast Asia, the Vietnamese again offered to return the same three sets of remains. In late December, following a public announcement of Hanoi's intention to repatriate the remains, the United Nations High Commission for Refugees turned the remains over to the House Select Committee on Missing Persons in Southeast Asia on Hanoi's behalf.[3]

During the early December 1975 trip to Paris, House Select Committee members met with members of the PRG and DRV delegations and requested that U.S., third country, or international teams be permitted to search for the remains of missing American service personnel. The committee also asked for the return of the remains of the two marines killed during the evacuation of Vietnam, whose bodies were inadvertently left behind during the chaotic departure from Saigon. The Vietnamese ambassador agreed to return the remains of the three previously identified U.S. MIAs, to continue to search for other missing personnel including the two marines, and to return Americans who had been stranded in Saigon following the April 1975 Communist victory.[4] In late December, four House Select Committee members traveled to Hanoi to receive the remains of three U.S. personnel. The members reiterated the importance of conducting grave and crash site investigations, turned over "representative files" on U.S. MIAs, and proposed the opening of a U.S. or third country mission to work with Hanoi's MIA agency. Twenty-eight file record summaries concerning 40 U.S. MIAs were provided to the Vietnamese, along with case summaries regarding five Americans lost in Laos. Vietnam's prime minister and deputy foreign minister told the Select Committee members that the U.S. was committed by Article 21 and President Nixon's letter of 1 February 1973 to provide reconstruction assistance. According to Douglas Clarke, the members of the House Select Committee were "stunned to learn, from the Vietnamese, of the letter to Premier Pham Van Dong of 1 February 1973. [Congressman Montgomery] emphasized to the Vietnamese that, in their opinion, the Nixon letter notwithstanding, any form of grant aid for Vietnam was out of the question."[5]

The U.S. continued intermittent and largely unproductive contacts with the Vietnamese on this issue in 1976. In January, Senator George McGovern visited Saigon and Hanoi for discussions concerning the MIA issue and the question of reunifying Vietnamese families separated at the end of the war and to pursue the issue of Vietnam's postwar international role. Pham Van Dong told McGovern that Vietnam shared the senator's concern regarding accounting for MIAs, as well as the reunification of families, and agreed as a matter of principle to the importance of a safe return to Vietnam of Vietnamese who were evacuated when the Americans departed Saigon in April 1975, though Dong made no firm commitment to the latter proposal. Xuan Thuy told McGovern that Hanoi considered the provisions of Article 8(b) to still be binding and that Hanoi continued to conduct unilateral MIA investigations. The Vietnamese restated their view that the U.S. was responsible, under the Paris Accords, for providing postwar economic assistance. Upon his return, McGovern told the Senate Foreign Relations Committee that withholding diplomatic recognition, blocking UN membership, sustaining the trade embargo, and freezing Vietnamese assets could only serve to insult and offend the government of Vietnam, whose cooperation was essential to efforts to resolve the MIA issue. He urged that those policies be changed.[6] In February the PRG returned the remains of the two marines killed during the evacuation of Saigon. In a March 1976 diplomatic note, Henry Kissinger invited Hanoi to start discussions "looking toward eventual normalization of relations." The exchange of notes that followed culminated in formal talks at the embassy level in Paris in mid-November at which U.S. representatives highlighted the central importance of the MIA issue and Vietnamese representatives politely restated their basic position on Article 21. The Vietnamese communiqué summarizing the meeting stated that Hanoi was "disposed toward an exchange of views on the problems which preoccupy the American side and to meet fully its obligations under Article 8(b)."[7]

Washington maintained that a complete accounting for the MIAs was the "absolute precondition" for any real steps toward normalization. In an 8 May 1976 diplomatic note, the State Department made its position clear:

> Talks on the basis of the selective application of past agreements would not be fruitful. . . . The United States believes it would be more useful to discuss issues affecting future relations between our two countries. The humanitarian concern for a full accounting of our missing men will be one of the primary issues of the United States in such discussions. Until this issue is substantially resolved, there can be no real progress toward normalization of relations.

Vietnam responded by agreeing to a meeting in Paris as a means of settling postwar issues, including the matter of postwar reconstruction and the problem of U.S. MIAs. Hanoi reiterated its position that the U.S. needed to honor the pledges made as a result of signing the 1973 agreement, especially Article 21, and that reneging on its commitments while demanding that Vietnam implement Article 8(b) ran counter to international laws and practices. Washington agreed to the meeting in Paris and restated its basic positions. A 19 July diplomatic note stated that: "A full accounting for those Americans missing in action and the return of the remains of those killed in action is a matter of primary concern to the United States. . . . United States does not consider that it has an obligation to provide reconstruction assistance to Vietnam."[8]

On 31 July 1976, Hanoi announced its intention to repatriate 48 Americans stranded in Vietnam after the fall of Saigon, in keeping with Vietnam's "strictly humanitarian" policies. One month later, in a 27 August diplomatic note, the Vietnamese Foreign Ministry proposed that steps be taken to schedule a first meeting in Paris to discuss the modalities of normalization, as offered in the 19 July diplomatic note from Washington. In mid–September, the Vietnamese Foreign Ministry expressed its concern that its 27 August note had gone unanswered, publicized the text of previous notes on the subject of the proposed Paris meeting, and denounced Washington's criticisms that there had been no progress in bilateral contacts. On 6 September the DRV provided the U.S. with the names of 12 Americans who were unaccounted for, indicating only that the 12 had died. Also in September, a U.S. civilian captured on 30 April 1975 was released by the PRG. Nevertheless, on 13 September the U.S. vetoed Vietnam's application to the United Nations because of what the U.S. ambassador to the United Nations, William Scranton, described as Hanoi's continued failure to provide a full accounting of the MIAs. The Vietnamese retorted that the veto was an election-year play by the president that concealed the real progress on the issue and that the U.S. accusation that Vietnam remained uncooperative was just one more effort by Washington to manipulate the issue at the expense of the MIA families. Hanoi criticized the U.S. government for not replying to the call for a liaison committee meeting for the purposes of renewing diplomatic negotiations on unresolved bilateral issues.[9]

On 24 October the U.S. and Vietnam agreed to a meeting which was held on 12 November. Tran Hoan, the Vietnamese representative, reiterated Hanoi's basic position:

> We are ready to carry out fully, and I repeat fully, our obligations regarding the provisions of Article 8(b) of the Paris Accord . . . but, the American side must also assume its obligations regarding the contribution to healing the wounds of war and to post-war reconstruction in Vietnam and to carry out what was agreed at Paris in 1973 in the Joint Economic Commission. It is not only a question of law or of legality, but also a question of honor, responsibility, and of conscience.

The Washington representative responded by indicating the U.S. government's desire to look to the future, but the talks reached an impasse, with the Vietnamese side arguing that the U.S. had as much of a humanitarian obligation to provide reconstruction assistance as Hanoi had to comply with the provisions of Article 8(b).[10]

In the first months of 1977, Hanoi continued to call on the U.S. government to fulfill its obligation to "contribute to binding the wounds of war and the reconstruction of Vietnam" and to carry out the commitments to which the Joint Economic Commission agreed in 1973. In early February, Vo Van Sung, Vietnam's ambassador to Paris, expressed his country's willingness to meet once more for discussions concerning issues of importance to both Vietnam and the United States. To the Vietnamese, the implementation of Article 8(b) and Article 21 were "interrelated."

In March 1977, Leonard Woodcock, president of the United Automobile Workers, headed a visit to Hanoi by the Presidential Commission on Americans Missing and Unaccounted for in Southeast Asia, which was appointed by President Carter in February 1976. This commission, composed of former senator Mike Mansfield, Ambassador Charles Yost, Congressman G. V. Montgomery, and Marian Wright Edelman, director of the Children's Defense Fund, traveled to Vietnam and Laos with the authority to reach agreements necessary to obtain information and recover remains. In Hanoi the commission was received by Prime Minister Pham Van Dong. The Vietnamese committed themselves to providing "all available information" on missing U.S. personnel and to returning remains as they were recovered and exhumed and told the commission that the VNOSMP budget had been increased. The Vietnamese offered to turn the remains of 12 U.S. airmen over to the commission, declared that all living U.S. military POWs had been returned to the custody of the United States, and asserted that all U.S. civilians who remained in South Vietnam after 30 April 1975 and who had registered with the Vietnamese authorities had departed Vietnam. Hanoi agreed to provide information about missing Americans to the U.S. through diplomatic channels, rather than through various nongovernmental organizations, private citizens, and elected representatives. They continued to make the case that the U.S. had an obligation to provide assistance to Vietnam under the terms of Article 21. On the final day of the commission's stay in Hanoi, the Vietnamese provided the remains of 12 U.S. servicemen whose deaths had been reported to Washington by the Vietnamese prior to the September 1976 vote on the issue of Vietnamese membership in the United Nations. The Vietnamese also provided information about two Americans who had stayed behind after the fall of Saigon in April 1975 and subsequently died, and they agreed to return the remains of both those Americans. One of those two individuals was Tucker Gougelman, a one-time Central Intelligence Agency employee. Finally, Hanoi proposed that Washington resume talks in Paris on bilateral issues.

Upon its return, the Presidential Commission reported that there was "no evidence to indicate that any American POWs from the Indochina conflict" remained alive. Further, the commission judged that "no accounting will ever be possible for most of the Americans" lost in Indochina as a consequence of terrain, climate, circumstances of loss, and passage of time. Finally, the Commission emphasized that the Vietnamese had given "clear formal assurance" that MIA information and remains would be provided to the United States. The Presidential Commission also expressed the view that the Lao would provide information and remains as they were found and noted that though the commission had been unable to meet with representatives of the Cambodian government, Phnom Penh had repeatedly denied that it held foreign prisoners. On that basis, the commission concluded that it was unlikely that further information on missing Americans would be provided by the Cambodian government. The commission drew the conclusion that improved relations with the governments of Vietnam and Laos was the "best hope for obtaining a proper accounting for our MIAs." Although the commission report made the case that little further information on the fates of missing Americans could be expected from the Vietnamese, or the Lao, the report argued that both governments had already provided only a minimal response and were clearly in possession of additional information on missing Americans.[11]

In April the U.S. presented Vietnamese representatives in Paris with negotiating folders pertaining to missing U.S. service personnel and identification records pertaining to the remains received by the Presidential Commission on 18 March 1977. In a 19 April letter to Deputy Assistant Secretary of State Frank Sieverts, Vu Hoang provided the identity of an American serviceman who the Vietnamese claimed had died in December 1972 when his plane was shot down.

In early May, Richard Holbrooke, assistant secretary of state for Asian and Pacific affairs, met with Deputy Foreign Minister Phan Hien. Holbrooke proposed unconditional normalization of relations and the immediate lifting of the embargo. Hien restated Hanoi's views of Washington's "responsibility" to contribute to "healing the wounds of war" and promised that Vietnam would provide additional information on MIAs. In early June, the Vietnamese delegation in Paris informed the U.S. government that they were prepared to return the remains of 20 unaccounted for personnel in August or September. Additionally, Hien evinced flexibility concerning the form and content of assistance expected by Hanoi, but he did not alter Hanoi's position on "reparations," a point underscored by Hanoi's decision to publish the text of the 1973 letter from Richard Nixon to Prime Minister Pham Van Dong in which Nixon wrote that "the U.S.A will contribute to postwar reconstruction in North Vietnam without any political conditions" and identified a preliminary "planning figure" of $3.25 billion of grant aid over five years. Congressional reaction to Vietnam's demands came in the form of an amendment to the House of Representative's State Department Authorization Bill which prohibited any form of reparations and a later Senate amendment requiring U.S. government opposition to International Financial Institution (IFI) loans to Vietnam.

The U.S. government provided negotiating folders to the Vietnamese delegation in Paris throughout June and July. In late September, Vietnam returned the remains of 22 unaccounted for personnel to a delegation of State Department and Department of Defense officials who traveled to Hanoi. Washington continued to provide folders through December.[12] In July 1978 a Vietnamese delegation visited the U.S. Army's Central Identification Laboratory in Hawaii (CILHI) for briefings on technical aspects of remains identification. Fred Brown observed that during the four-day "technical meeting" in Honolulu:

> Vu Hoang, a senior Foreign Ministry official and the delegation chief, made clear in private that Vietnam had dropped its aid precondition and wanted normalization on American terms "by Labor Day or at the latest Thanksgiving." No mention was made of Christmas, the day on which Vietnam invaded Cambodia. Vu Hoang suggested that giant C-5A aircraft be used to bring materials to build a U.S. embassy in Hanoi "with a big commercial section. U.S. Navy Seabees would be welcome to oversee the construction." Although Vu Hoang's statement seemed explicit and unequivocal, it was nonetheless a trial balloon hoisted at the working level and required high-level expression. The message was conveyed immediately to the State Department, where it became enmeshed in the bureaucratic infighting with the National Security Council staff. A Vietnamese proposal shortly thereafter for another Paris meeting in August 1978 was not accepted by the United States.[13]

In late August the Vietnamese returned 11 sets of remains to a U.S. delegation headed by Representative G. V. Montgomery. Vietnam, however, did not relent in its insistence that normalization be accompanied by U.S. assistance, in spite of the hint of flexibility communicated by Vu Hoang during Montgomery's visit to Hanoi. Not until September was Holbrooke able to pry an agreement to normalize without preconditions from Foreign Minister Nguyen Co Thach. By then, in the face of Vietnam's invasion of Cambodia, Hanoi's increasingly close relationship with Moscow, and the flood of refugees, the president had decided to defer normalizing with Hanoi, rejecting a two-track approach which proposed simultaneous normalization with Beijing and Hanoi.[14]

There were few further efforts to draw Hanoi out on the POW/MIA issue during the last year of the Carter presidency. In December 1978, in response to the Vietnamese invasion of Cambodia, the House Subcommittee on Asian and Pacific Affairs cancelled a trip to Hanoi. The trip took place eight months later, in mid–August 1979, under the leadership of Congressman Lester Wolff, who presented the Vietnamese with negotiating folders and reports indicating the possible location of crash and grave sites of American MIAs which the U.S. government wanted to investigate. The Vietnamese were not responsive to requests for active efforts to uncover information on crash and grave sites, but did agree to periodic visits to Hanoi by JCRC personnel for technical discussions.[15] In March 1979, Hanoi returned marine private Robert Garwood to U.S. custody. The Vietnamese described him as an American serviceman who had "voluntarily gone over to the Liberation Armed Forces in 1965 and stayed on in Vietnam at his own will after the war to live a normal life."[16] In October 1979, Vietnam responded negatively to U.S. efforts to schedule a JCRC liaison officer visit to Hanoi, explaining cryptically that Hanoi would inform the U.S. when the time was "convenient" for such a meeting. Hanoi permitted the first technical meeting to take place in late 1980.[17]

In April 1980 the Department of Press and Information of the Foreign Ministry issued a "white paper" entitled "On the Question of Americans Missing in the Vietnam War." The publication jogged quickly through the course of Vietnam's dealings with Washington on the POW/MIA issue, beginning with the "goodwill, serious attitude and humanitarian policy" that informed Hanoi's approach to Article 8(b) of the Paris Accords, and summarized Operation Homecoming and Vietnam's repatriation of Americans who remained in southern Vietnam after April 1975. The white paper charted Vietnam's cooperation in the area of repatriation of remains and efforts to locate information that would assist in accounting for the fate of missing personnel, stressing the 1973 establishment of the VNOSMP and unilateral Vietnamese efforts to locate and identify remains of U.S. servicemen during the mid- and late 1970s. The publication, laden with praise of Hanoi's goodwill and enduring humanity from American politicians and senior leaders, underscored the limitations that rendered a full accounting impossible, including the passage of time and the circumstances of loss in harsh terrain. The paper took the position that Washington had seriously politicized the issue and thereby hampered progress, especially by efforts to "play the China card" against Vietnam.[18] The white paper criticized the testimony of a Vietnamese mortician who went before the U.S. Congress in 1980 and gave an account of his work as an undertaker processing bodies of Americans. In that testimony, the mortician said he had observed a room filled with several hundred sets of remains. He claimed that over 400 remains were "warehoused" in Hanoi and that he had seen "three Caucasians whom he believed to be Americans" in Hanoi. The Vietnamese denounced the testimony as a primary example of "negative attitudes and actions by the U.S. side."[19]

The white paper referred to this as a "story concocted for political ends with familiar political tricks and with fictional details which can confuse public opinion."[20] The white paper dismissed the mortician's testimony and noted that other similar claims made by refugees were accorded an unambiguously skeptical reception by certain U.S. congressmen. The Foreign Ministry concluded by stating that the U.S. had "distorted" Hanoi's sincerely humanitarian inclinations. The ministry also issued a warning:

Such acts could only cause difficulties to the efforts to promote peace and friendship between the two peoples, and certainly could not contribute to creating favorable atmosphere in Vietnam for efforts to account for American MIAs, and by following such a course, the U.S. could be taken in by the insidious manoeuvres of the Beijing expansionists.[21]

CHAPTER THREE

Progress and Accountability During the Reagan Presidency, 1982–1989

In 1982, Vietnam faced political stalemate in Cambodia, diplomatic isolation, a seriously growing dependency on the Soviet Union, and further foreign policy reversals. Vietnam paid a high price to maintain an occupying force of 180,000 troops in Cambodia. Regional antipathy to Vietnam's Cambodia policy stiffened world support for resolutions at the United Nations calling for the withdrawal of foreign forces in Cambodia and elections monitored by the United Nations. The Association of Southeast Asian Nations (ASEAN) and the U.S. were also able to obtain United Nations General Assembly approval of the credentials of the coalition government of Democratic Kampuchea for the fourth straight year by the largest majority since 1979. Vietnam's troop withdrawal plans and proposals for "safety zones" along the Thai-Cambodian border had little credibility in the region. Sino-Soviet rapprochement left Hanoi facing diminishing support for its Cambodian policy from Moscow at a moment when border hostilities with China threatened to escalate. Chinese willingness to begin supporting the Cambodian non–Communist resistance as well as the Khmer Rouge represented a serious challenge to Hanoi's already precarious position. On top of this, Hanoi confronted continued declines in production levels, a mounting $3.5 billion foreign debt, radically steep oil price hikes, and across-the-board failures to meet targets set in the 1976–81 five-year plan.

Under the administration of President Ronald Reagan, the U.S. resumed MIA discussions with Vietnam and expanded the dialogue to include communication about the emigration of Amerasian children, the Orderly Departure Program, and the legal exit of former inmates of Vietnamese reeducation camps.[1] The U.S. government continued, however, to refuse to consider normalization of relations as long as Vietnam occupied Cambodia and otherwise played a destabilizing role in the region. U.S. policy stated that once a political settlement of the Cambodian problem was achieved in accordance with principles of the International Conference on Kampuchea, the U.S. would consider the normalization of relations, which would proceed at a pace conditioned by the progress in accounting for missing U.S. service personnel.

Hanoi's minor flexibility that facilitated the resumption of dialogue on these humanitarian issues was intended to preserve some contact with Washington in the face of the U.S. government's refusal to consider normalization of relations as long as Vietnam persisted in its occupation of Cambodia. By agreeing to expanded POW/MIA discussions, Vietnam hoped to make a slight dent in its diplomatic isolation and to ensure that it did not jeopardize other minor advances in U.S.–Vietnamese bilateral matters, including the refinement of Orderly Departure Program procedures, the development of a system for managing the migration of children of American servicemen and Vietnamese mothers, and Washington's willingness to continue facilitating the mailing of remittances and commercial items by Vietnamese residents of the United States to relatives in Vietnam.

During policy-level talks held in Hanoi in February 1982, the Vietnamese agreed to hold four technical meetings a year between the JCRC and CILHI and the VNOSMP. (The first meeting was not held until December 1982. The second session was held in March 1983.) The Vietnamese also agreed to consider the U.S. proposal to conduct joint U.S.–Vietnamese searches for the remains of missing Americans. In a September meeting in Hanoi with a delegation of the National League of Families of POW/MIAs, Vice Foreign Minister Vo Dong Giang reiterated Vietnam acceptance of the U.S. government proposal to convene four technical sessions each year.[2]

The third in the series of technical meetings with the Vietnamese took place in June 1983. The meeting culminated in the repatriation of the remains of nine individuals and the provision of identification data on three others, the largest number of remains returned since 1978. By July, eight sets of the repatriated remains had been identified as those of American servicemen. Thirteen sets of remains were returned by Vietnam during January–July 1983. During the ASEAN Foreign Ministers Conference in July 1983, Secretary of State George Shultz made an intervention for assistance on the POW/MIA issue to the association's foreign ministers, who responded positively and promised full support. The Vietnamese rejected Shultz's claim that Hanoi held over 400 sets of remains of U.S. service personnel and suspended technical talks.[3]

In October 1983, White House and National League of Families officials met in New York with Vietnamese Foreign Minister Nguyen Co Thach. Thach acknowledged the priority accorded the issue by the U.S. government and urged another high-level mission at a level similar to the 1982 visit to Hanoi led by Deputy Assistant Secretary of Defense Richard Armitage. The U.S. representative suggested that the two countries begin joint crash site searches, emphasized the importance of the live prisoner issue, urged that Hanoi unilaterally repatriate remains in its possession, and brought up the issue of Hanoi's knowledge of the fates of U.S. servicemen, especially those who crashed in the Hanoi/Haiphong area in the vicinity of populated metropolitan areas.[4] In January 1984, a joint communiqué issued by Hanoi, Vientiane, and Phnom Penh pledged "on the basis of humanitarianism, and understanding the American people" that the three Indochinese governments would "try to inform one another about the Americans missing during the war in Laos, Vietnam, and Kampuchea."[5]

In February 1984 a policy-level delegation led by Richard Armitage and composed of officials from the White House, the State Department, the Department of Defense, and the National League of Families, traveled to Hanoi and reached agreement to accelerate cooperation and to stop linking the POW/MIA issue to U.S.–Vietnamese relations in other areas. Hanoi also agreed to focus initial efforts on the "most accessible cases" in the Hanoi/Haiphong area and those listed as having died in captivity in Vietnam. The Vietnamese agreed to an early resumption of POW/MIA technical meetings and provided Armitage with some preliminary information on several U.S. service personnel. The U.S. government made clear that the issue was of great importance to the United States and that the limited progress in resolving the POW/MIA issue heightened the frustration and impatience of the American people. The U.S. delegation urged the Vietnamese to share more information on American MIAs and to respond to proposed dates for technical meetings, which Washington regarded as important vehicles for discussing individual cases of missing Americans. The Vietnamese delegation, led by Thach, promised to accelerate the search for U.S. MIAs, to resume the quarterly technical sessions, to concentrate efforts in the Hanoi/Haiphong area, and to focus on the cases of Americans known to have died in captivity. In August the Vietnamese held a technical meeting in response to a formal U.S. government request.[6]

In October 1984, U.S. government and National League of Families representatives met again with Foreign Minister Thach in New York. Thach renewed and strengthened the commitments he had made in February and agreed to set an early date for the next technical meeting, which was held in Hanoi later that month. Thach stated that his government had considered the proposal for joint crash site investigations and said that an experimental field activity was possible. Thach also agreed that live-sighting cases could be discussed in detail at future technical meetings. He catalogued factors limiting Vietnam's ability to respond to the U.S. government request for information on MIAs and to conduct unilateral searches for the remains of missing Americans. He indicated that Vietnam was focusing its efforts on loss incidents that occurred in the Hanoi/Haiphong area and on the died in captivity (DIC) list of prisoners who had been held in the south by the PRG. The U.S. government representative urged that the proposal for joint crash site surveys and excavations, the costs of which the U.S. was prepared to absorb, be given serious consideration. Washington was prepared to dispatch a technical team to provide details concerning the activities, expenses, and planning requirements that would be involved in such an undertaking. Thach committed himself to presenting the proposal for the consideration of the Vietnamese government and to dispatching field teams to follow-up on reports and locate witnesses who could provide information on MIAs. Thach reiterated Hanoi's intent to pursue those matters in a humanitarian spirit to improve the atmosphere between Hanoi and Washington.

In 1985, Hanoi evinced a new foreign policy flexibility aimed at breaking its diplomatic isolation and counteracting the impact of a steadily deteriorating economy. In January, the Indochinese Foreign Ministers Conference proposed a six-point plan calling for the elimination of the "Pol Pot clique," a simultaneous withdrawal of Vietnamese troops from Cambodia, and free elections under foreign observers. ASEAN responded with pronounced skepticism. China reacted cooly and spoke of the possibility of a "second lesson" meant to evoke the military drubbing Beijing claimed to have administered in January 1979. At the same time, China rejected Hanoi's overtures aimed at reopening bilateral talks.

In the midst of these negative responses to Vietnam's diplomatic initiatives for resolving the Cambodia conflict, Hanoi called on the U.S. to play a responsible regional role and offered reason to believe that Vietnam was prepared to improve cooperation on the POW/MIA issue. In January 1985 during a session in New York with the League of Families executive director, Ambassador Hoang Bich Son, permanent representative to the United Nations, pledged that 1985 would be a "year of progress" on the MIA issue.[7]

In March 1985, National Security Council staffer Richard Childress led a policy-level delegation to Hanoi for further talks. Foreign Minister Thach agreed to increase the number of technical meetings from four per year to six and indicated flexibility on the scheduling of additional technical sessions. He noted that preparations were being made to make five sets of remains available for repatriation to the United States, a decision announced at a February technical meeting. Thach restated his government's position on the live prisoner issue: there were no more American servicemen in Vietnam. Childress stressed the importance of responding to queries on reported sightings. Thach supported the concept of joint crash site searches, but explained that there was not yet agreement to this concept in Vietnam, in part because of the lack of normal relations with Washington. Childress proposed a two-year plan aimed at scheduling bilateral searches and investigations with a view to resolving the POW/MIA issue in an expedited manner. The U.S. delegation stressed the humanitarian character of the issue and noted that the POW/MIA problem could become an obstacle to the future normalization of relations in view of the strong attitudes held by the American people on this issue.[8]

Through mid-1985, the Vietnamese media continued to characterize Washington's position on the POW/MIA issue in strong, inflammatory terms. According to a 6 June article from the military's daily newspaper:

[The U.S.] is trying to capitalize on the concern of many Americans about the MIA issue in order to incite anti–Vietnamese sentiment, in disregard of truth and reason. It is quite preposterous that while Mr. Reagan is imposing on Vietnam the responsibility of seeking American MIAs in Vietnam, that is, those who had come to Vietnam and committed crimes, he is washing his hands of all responsibility of the United States for having caused suffering and death to millions of Vietnamese and its duty to help heal the wounds of war in Vietnam.[9]

In August 1985 a delegation led by Childress returned to Hanoi to discuss Vietnam's announced intention to resolve the POW/MIA issue within two years and to explain the U.S. proposal for joint plans to accomplish that objective. The U.S. plan called for nationwide joint investigations of live-sighting reports and surveys and excavations of grave and crash sites. Vietnamese officials did not react to the joint plan but provided a unilateral plan and requested U.S. reaction.[10]

Acting Foreign Minister Vo Dong Giang outlined a three-phase plan for a two-year intensive effort to resolve the POW/MIA issue. The plan was to prepare local authorities for participation in excavations, which were to proceed through the end of 1985. In 1986 activities would include intensive collection and verification of information. Excavations and repatriations were to take place in 1987. Giang committed to continued unilateral efforts to repatriate remains. He noted that while excavations would "normally" be accomplished unilaterally by Vietnam, joint activity was a possibility. Giang stated his government's interest in defining an accurate data base in conjunction with U.S. government specialists. The U.S. government representative underscored the importance of keeping the priority focus on the died in captivity list and discrepancy cases, organizing regular technical sessions on a more frequent basis, and addressing the live prisoner issue.[11] Hanoi rejected the U.S. proposal to open an office in Hanoi that would facilitate work on the POW/MIA issue and agreed to discuss the case of the "yachtsman" Robert Schwab, who had been arrested and incarcerated in the south after entering Vietnamese territorial waters.[12]

In September 1985 a follow-up meeting was held in New York. Vo Dong Giang made it clear that Hanoi planned to proceed with commitments made in October to intensify the search for remains. Giang reiterated Hanoi's satisfaction with the technical meetings at which the U.S. side provided new data on locations of remains or evidence suggesting where remains might be found. Giang reaffirmed Vietnam's willingness to investigate live sightings and also reaffirmed Hanoi's commitment to make increased progress on the POW/MIA issue without linking it to other issues. The U.S. representatives committed to rapidly building Vietnam's data base on missing Americans by providing case folders on the Hanoi/Haiphong cases, the DIC cases, discrepancy cases, and high probability crash sites. The U.S. representatives also told the Vietnamese delegation that Washington would assist Vietnam in investigations of live POW reports and provide all necessary technical expertise to facilitate crash site surveys and excavations, including forensic support, explosive ordinance disposal, and engineering assistance. The U.S. side was prepared to provide training to Vietnamese personnel involved in unilateral surveys or excavations and to assist in Hanoi's efforts to locate information by canvassing populations in the area of crash sites and broadcasting statements on the Voice of America (VOA) radio to discourage trading in remains.[13]

In January 1986, Assistant Secretary of State Paul Wolfowitz and Assistant Secretary of Defense Armitage led an interagency delegation to Hanoi for another meeting with Foreign Minister Thach. Armitage stressed that the resolution of the live prisoner issue remained the highest U.S. government priority. The U.S. side emphasized the importance of sharing of information in advance of field activities to assist in selecting sites for excavation. The Vietnamese expressed willingness to investigate live-sighting reports and explained how their intensified efforts under the so-called two-year plan had generated information about alleged missing Americans requiring further investigation. The Vietnamese agreed to hold a technical meeting in late February at which time that information was to be passed to American technical experts. Thach agreed to multiple joint excavations and acknowledged the necessity of improving coordination in the selection of sites for excavation.[14]

In the same month, Ambassador Bui Xuan Nhat, who replaced Hoang Bich Son as Hanoi's permanent representative to the United Nations, told the executive director of the League of Families that Hanoi believed Washington was not serious about pursuing a two-year plan.[15] In April 1986, Vietnam made the case in the media that its "goodwill" had been demonstrated through "concrete actions" such as the two-year commitment, the return of 54 sets of remains since July 1985, and the provision of information on 23 others, in addition to Hanoi's consent to allow a U.S. government representative to take part in a joint excavation near Hanoi. Hanoi claimed that in the 7 January talks it had proposed a written understanding aimed at obtaining agreement to accelerate implementation of the two-year plan to resolve the issue. Hanoi agreed to bilateral cooperation to resolve the issue, and to holding additional meetings when necessary, apart from the regular technical discussions. Vietnam accepted the high priority the U.S. government placed on the DIC list. Hanoi warned, however, that the reported U.S. readiness to use force to free Americans who were allegedly under lock and key in Vietnam could hinder resolution of the issue. The Vietnamese took exception to a February statement they ascribed to Armitage to the effect that the United States was ready to use force to free any Americans being held prisoner in Vietnam. On 1 March the Communist Party's daily newspaper complained that threats to use force violated the recent bilateral pledge to create a "favorable atmosphere" for resolving the issue.[16]

Throughout March and April, Vietnam repeated its denial that it was holding U.S. prisoners of war but alluded to the possibility that Americans who "infiltrated" the country after the war were being held in areas outside of Hanoi's control.

The Vietnamese spoke of the MIA issue as a matter that commanded the close attention of the Vietnamese public, warning the U.S. that actions which angered the Vietnamese people, including public statements that characterized Hanoi's intentions in negative terms, would hamper Washington's efforts to resolve the POW/MIA issue. Hanoi vocally denied accusations that it held live Americans in custody and counterattacked by arguing that the U.S. government had infiltrated Americans back into the country at the end of the war. Hanoi characterized live-sighting reports from refugees as misinformation and fabrications, criticized Washington's approach to the issue as "bellicose," and described its own willingness to continue to resolve the MIA issue "on a case-by-case basis." Hanoi argued that since Washington was not satisfied with the level of Vietnamese cooperation, the commitment to carry out a formal plan to resolve the MIA issue should then be the subject of a formal memorandum of understanding between the two governments, a position clearly unacceptable to Washington. In mid–April a Vietnamese diplomat informed the chief of the JCRC Liaison Office in Bangkok that because the "current situation" was not favorable for the conduct of a technical meeting, Hanoi would not participate in the scheduled 23–26 April technical session. At the same time, Reuters quoted Foreign Minister Thach as saying that Vietnam could not hold talks with Washington on a humanitarian issue such as the missing servicemen while Washington carried out "attacks on humanity with its air raids on Libya." The foreign minister stated that Hanoi would decide upon the resumption of talks "in the light of developments and when there are no longer these barbarous acts."[17]

In May 1986, during a meeting in New York, Deputy Foreign Minister Hoang Bich Son announced Vietnam's agreement to resume technical activities and increase VNOSMP personnel and resources dedicated to resolving the issue. Son also reaffirmed Hanoi's intention to repatriate Robert Schwab.[18] Following a May 1986 policy-level meeting with the Vietnamese in New York and a June technical meeting, a U.S. interagency delegation met with Foreign Minister Thach in Hanoi to formulate U.S. commitments to support Vietnam's unilateral two-year plan. Hanoi agreed to conduct technical talks in August and October, to hold at least six such meetings each year, and to provide the U.S. with written results of its investigations into the reports of live sightings. The Vietnamese also agreed to permit U.S. experts to accompany its officials on investigations in accessible areas and to discuss specific crash sites for excavation. Vietnam accepted an invitation to visit the U.S. technical facilities at the JCRC and the CILHI.

Although the August and October technical meetings did take place, and although Vo Dong Giang reaffirmed Hanoi's humanitarian intentions during the October meeting, the Vietnamese began to publicly back away from their commitments during 1987.[19] In January and February 1987, Vietnam rejected U.S. proposals for technical discussions in Hanoi. According to the Reagan administration's *Final Interagency Report*, in an effort to increase momentum, President Reagan named former chairman of the Joint Chiefs of Staff, General John W. Vessey, Jr., as special presidential emissary to Hanoi on the POW/MIA issue. Hanoi accused the U.S. of deliberately making public the contents of the negotiations only five days after Hanoi had been officially notified of the intention to dispatch General Vessey to Vietnam. Hanoi also complained bitterly about a $1 million reward posted for the return of a live American by several Republican congressmen. In early May, Trinh Xuan Lang, then head of the Foreign Ministry's Press and Information Department, attributed the "absence of progress" to the refusal of the Reagan administration to accept Vietnam's two-year program.[20]

Hanoi was initially very tentative about the idea of a presidential envoy.[21] During talks in Hanoi in late May with Richard Childress, the Vietnamese argued that the agenda of the meetings with the special envoy should be "open" and not limited to humanitarian issues. Childress' interlocutor was Dang Nghiem Bai, head of the Foreign Ministry's North America Department. Dinh Nho Liem, first deputy foreign minister, received members of the U.S. government delegation before they departed.[22] In the month before Vessey traveled to Hanoi, the Vietnamese sought to portray their position as reasonable, flexible, and motivated by the loftiest humanitarian principles. Nguyen Van Linh, general secretary of the Communist Party, told Japanese journalists that Hanoi was fully prepared to entertain a U.S. request for placing a liaison office in Hanoi to undertake the daily work associated with the MIA issue, though after being rebuffed in August 1985 the U.S. government had repeatedly rejected the idea of such an office. Nevertheless, Linh was not overly optimistic about the prospects for reaching agreements on the MIA issue that would lead to real improvements in bilateral relations and suggested to the Japanese journalists that real progress would not begin until Reagan's successor was in place.[23] Vietnam vehemently denied that it sought to leverage economic aid from the U.S. in return for information about American MIAs. Hanoi maintained that it was consistent in approaching the issue of missing Americans as a strictly humanitarian matter. Hanoi reiterated the position that the meetings with Vessey should not be limited in focus to humanitarian concerns relevant to the Americans alone, but should take up matters of importance to Vietnam. Hanoi, however, was not at all specific about the items it wanted raised in discussions with the special envoy.[24] In late July, Nguyen Co Thach categorically denied rumors that Hanoi was prepared to allow or was considering allowing the U.S. to open a liaison office in Vietnam.[25]

The Vietnamese were clearly interested in using the first visit by the special envoy as a means of widening the dialogue with Washington. On the eve of the talks, Deputy Foreign Minister Nguyen Duy Nien referred to problems concerning wartime orphans, amputees, victims of chemical weapons, and Vietnam's own wartime missing as the sorts of issues Vietnam would put on the table in discussions of humanitarian problems. In public remarks before the commencement of the sessions with Vessey, Foreign Minister Thach told reporters that if the special envoy requested permission to open a liaison office in Hanoi, Vietnam would ask to open a similar office in Washington. Thach's position represented not so much a well-worked out policy response, but more of a tone-setting statement intended to suggest to Vessey and his delegation that Hanoi would insist on the validity of its own humanitarian claims in the dialogue with Washington and that Hanoi would be unwilling to allow the U.S. to walk away from the table with any advantages that painted the Vietnamese in an unflattering light.[26] Thach told reporters before the start of the meetings that relations with the U.S. must be thought of as "two way traffic and no longer one way traffic." Thach told reporters that he had "many cards in his pocket" going into discussions with Vessey and that he had the authority to guide the discussions toward a range of other areas in addition to the MIA issue.[27]

During May talks in Hanoi with a delegation led by Childress, Vietnam agreed to continue to pursue the issue as a humanitarian problem and accepted the proposed visit by the presidential emissary without preconditions.[28] During the early August meetings, General Vessey obtained agreement to resume and expand cooperation on POW/MIA and other humanitarian issues of mutual concern. The two sides reaffirmed the need to focus first on discrepancy cases and on Americans listed as having died in captivity in the south. The U.S. delegation provided representative case files for consideration by the VNOSMP. Vessey also indicated that the U.S. could not consider direct aid to Vietnam without a Cambodian settlement, but would encourage American nongovernmental organizations (NGOs) to provide prosthetics assistance to Vietnam's disabled.[29] Both Vessey and Thach characterized the meetings in modest terms, suggesting that they were satisfied with the progress that had been made. Thach told reporters following the first session that the meetings had resulted in a "better understanding" between the two sides. The joint statement at the conclusion of the meetings did not go far beyond that, but noted that the talks had been candid and constructive, that both sides agreed to avoid linking humanitarian issues with broader political questions, and that specific steps to accelerate accounting for missing Americans had been agreed to by both sides and would be discussed further at meetings of experts planned for the near future.[30] Two technical meetings took place in Hanoi in late August. One focused on the technical aspects of the MIA issue and the other on the humanitarian needs of Vietnam. In September 1987, Vessey led a delegation to New York for a meeting with Thach to discuss the progress on commitments made during the August sessions. In mid–November, Vietnamese and

American specialists met in Hanoi for further talks about Hanoi's humanitarian needs. In a December session in New York with a U.S. delegation led by Childress, the Vietnamese agreed to more rapid cooperation and to schedule technical talks for January 1988.[31]

Throughout the first quarter of 1988, the Vietnamese worked to discredit the link between U.S.–Vietnamese normalization and the settlement of the conflict in Cambodia and to prod Washington to accept a direct role in providing humanitarian assistance to Vietnam. Foreign Minister Thach periodically chided Washington for its inability to press beyond the congressional prohibition on direct governmental assistance to Vietnam. In March, for example, Thach told a French Press Agency (AFP) reporter that in response to Washington's "refusal" to give direct assistance to Vietnam, Hanoi was compelled to tell the United States that Vietnamese laws forbade giving humanitarian assistance to Washington. Thach's meaning was that Hanoi's disappointment over the indirect nature of the humanitarian assistance program could have implications for continued progress on the MIA issue. Thach staked out the position that Vessey's promise to provide Vietnam with limited humanitarian assistance through NGOs came under the umbrella of the U.S. government. In a mid–April interview with AFP, Thach was very explicit about the link between progress on the MIA issue and direct humanitarian aid from the U.S.: "If the United States wants to leave this problem in the hands of NGOs, we will do the same," which, Thach implied, would seriously slow down cooperation and progress.[32] In January 1988, during technical talks in Hanoi, the Vietnamese side promised to provide the remains of 23 missing Americans, or information concerning their fate, within one month. In March, Hanoi repatriated 17 sets of remains and information concerning 3 additional missing Americans and conducted a technical meeting with U.S. casualty resolution specialists that was followed by the repatriation of 27 sets of remains in April. Many of those remains were either not identifiable or were upon analysis by the U.S. Army's CILHI found to be Mongoloid remains not belonging to Americans.[33]

In June, General Vessey met with Foreign Minister Thach in New York. They renewed the agreement to accelerate cooperation on the POW/MIA question. General Vessey restated Washington's commitment to meet certain of Vietnam's humanitarian needs. Thach repeated his promise to fulfill the August 1987 commitment to resolve the discrepancy cases and agreed in principle to conduct surveys and excavations of grave and crash sites. He also accepted an invitation for Vietnamese technical personnel to visit CILHI and JCRC in Hawaii.[34]

In July 1988, Vietnam agreed to initiate joint field investigations aimed at resolving the "compelling" cases presented by Vessey and to expand their unilateral efforts to account for missing Americans.[35] During the July technical meeting in Hanoi, the Vietnamese presented proposals for the joint activities, and at a subsequent meeting, they agreed to begin the joint investigations on 25 September.[36] The Vietnamese reaffirmed the agreement to define a joint program of activities, including search and excavation work necessary to resolve the 70 "priority" cases presented by Vessey in August 1987. Vietnamese media coverage of a late July specialists' meeting spoke in positive, upbeat terms of the attitudes of both sides at the meeting.[37]

On 31 July, however, Thach wrote Vessey a letter in which he criticized remarks by Assistant Secretary of State Gaston Sigur made before the Subcommittee on East Asian and Pacific Affairs of the House of Representatives on 28 July. Sigur had opposed House Resolution 271, which contended that the establishment of interest sections in Hanoi and Washington "would facilitate the resolution of humanitarian issues (MIAs, the Orderly Departure Program, resettlement of Amerasians, and release of reeducation center detainees) by increasing communication and cooperation between the United States and Vietnam." Sigur argued that because there was "no dearth of cooperation" on humanitarian issues and because the dialogue had resulted in progress on each of these issues, an interests section would not necessarily enhance cooperation or increase communication and would eliminate the ability to separate the humanitarian issues from political questions:

> The establishment of interest sections — regardless of legislative language to the contrary — would be seen in Hanoi as an important political concession directly related to our desire to resolve these humanitarian issues. In this way, a relationship between political and humanitarian issues would have been created, and any future progress on our humanitarian agenda would be affected by the state of our political relations. This would not be in our interest.

Thach wrote Vessey that Sigur's position revealed an attitude and policy aimed at continuing the isolation of Vietnam. In his letter to the presidential emissary, Thach concluded: "Obviously, that statement shows the U.S. Department of State is continuing to pursue a hostile policy against Vietnam. That statement has touched off indignation among the Vietnamese people and hampers implementation of the agreements between you and myself."

Following the 29 July broadcast of Sigur's remarks on the VOA, the party and military daily newspapers echoed Thach's views, in somewhat more strident terms.[38] Hanoi sustained this criticism through mid–August, arguing that any slow-down in progress toward achieving the fullest possible accounting was the result of the obstinacy of the U.S. government, Washington's lingering hostility toward Vietnam, and the U.S. government's own efforts to link the MIA issue to other political matters, especially the achievement of a Cambodian settlement, despite Washington's own protestations that the MIA issue should be treated as a humanitarian question.[39] Senator McCain responded by announcing his suspension of efforts to enact into law the proposal for opening interest sections.

Vessey responded to Thach's letter on 5 August by explaining that Sigur's statement reflected the administration's "longstanding viewpoint" on relations with Vietnam. Vessey pledged to continue the implementation of agreements reached between Vietnam and the U.S. in August 1987 and June 1988, and requested a resumption of activities. According to the Vietnamese media account of the correspondence, Thach answered on 27 August. He reiterated his concern with Washington's unremitting hostility toward Vietnam and challenged "the U.S. authorities declaration that it will make bilateral relations conditional upon the settlement of the MIA issue," a position Thach said was at variance with the agreement between himself and Vessey. He restated Hanoi's commitment to treat the MIA issue in a humanitarian manner, separate from political issues, and agreed to "let the U.S. side participate in joint investigations and survey activities" and to hold meetings of specialists in September. Thach concluded by noting his "high respect" for the agreements reached with Vessey, and he urged the presidential emissary to "create a favorable atmosphere for the realization" of these agreements.[40]

Thereafter, activity resumed. According to the Reagan administration's *Final Interagency Report*, the Vietnamese took several significant steps to implement their July agreement to conduct joint field investigations aimed at resolving specific discrepancy cases. The first two teams conducted ten-day joint operations in areas north of Hanoi in late September and early October. In late October, U.S. teams conducted similar activities in the area west of Hanoi. Between December 5 and 15, three joint teams investigated cases in the areas of Vinh and Dong Hoi, south of Hanoi.[41]

Six technical talks on the POW/MIA issue were held in 1988, and unilateral remains repatriations were significantly increased. A separate U.S. team met with the Vietnamese to address their humanitarian concerns. Further, there were three ten-day periods of joint investigations, along with a visit by a U.S. forensic team to examine remains unilaterally recovered by the Vietnamese. In October, following the first joint investigation, which resulted in the recovery of remains at two locations, Vessey met with Deputy Foreign Minister Tran Quang Co in New York to review progress and press for clearer commitments regarding joint investigative work.[42]

In early January the VNOSMP issued a three-point statement reiterating Vietnam's commitment to carry out the resolution of the MIA issues on the basis of humanitarian principles.[43] Vietnam and the U.S. conducted the fourth joint investigation beginning in mid–January. Additionally, a joint forensic team examined 44 sets of remains, of which 21 were determined to warrant further investigation and analysis. In late January, Hanoi repatriated 25 sets of remains. On 20 January 1989, the Vietnamese released a Japanese who had been detained in southern Vietnam from 1975. Iwanobu Yosida immigrated to

Vietnam in 1966, became a monk, and obtained Vietnamese citizenship in 1973. His 1989 release called into question the credibility of Vietnam's claims to have released all detainees caught in the 1975 collapse of the GVN. Vietnam conducted joint investigations in mid–April and in early June turned over remains on at least two occasions, making much of the arithmetic of repatriation and highlighting Vietnam's cooperation. Vietnam hosted a technical session in March at which planning for the fifth, sixth, and seventh joint investigations was discussed. The fifth investigation was conducted in April. Though no remains were recovered during that investigation, Hanoi unilaterally returned 21 sets of remains which casualty resolution specialists decided merited further analysis. Another technical session in May was followed by the early June commencement of the sixth joint investigations, which were focused on cases north and south of Ho Chi Minh City.[44] Also in early June and July, CILHI observed two separate unilateral Vietnamese field operations that resulted in the recovery of 30 sets of remains, a third of which were identified as being those of missing Americans by early July 1990.[45] In late July, Hanoi repatriated 15 sets of remains, and the seventh joint investigations began. In late August 1989, the JCRC reviewed the results of the investigations into the 70-name list and presented 32 new cases for joint investigation and 30 cases for unilateral investigation. The eighth joint field operation commenced on 20 October, in tandem with forensic team activities which included the examination of approximately 430 sets of remains seized in Hanoi's crackdown on "opportunists" who had during the late 1980s sought to profit from Hanoi's efforts to identify and repatriate the remains of U.S. soldiers killed in Vietnam. These "opportunists," according to Vietnamese media accounts, excavated cemeteries and bought and sold remains in a speculative enterprise that thrived in the south.[46] Five of the 430 sets of remains were selected for return to CILHI for further analysis.

Vessey led another Interagency Group (IAG) delegation to Hanoi in October 1989 for talks that focused specifically on resolving the compelling discrepancy cases initially presented to the Vietnamese in August 1987. The U.S. delegation took the position that the Vietnamese should have information about cases in which there was strong evidence that the unaccounted for Americans survived their incidents of loss and were captured or otherwise came under Vietnamese control. The Vietnamese agreed to increase their efforts to investigate or reinvestigate unresolved discrepancy cases, to research relevant records and provide access to witnesses necessary to case resolution, and to cooperate in resolving cases which occurred in Lao territory where Vietnamese forces were deployed during the war. A technical meeting took place in January 1990, followed by two joint investigations in February and May. During a late November technical meeting in Hanoi, the VNOSMP stressed the importance of "concluding" work on the 70-name list and agreed to investigate jointly four cases. Following that meeting, Deputy Assistant Secretary of State David Lambertson led a delegation to New York for discussions with Vietnam's ambassador to the United Nations, Trinh Xuan Lang, concerning outcome of the technical session.[47]

During February 1989, Hanoi took exception to what it characterized as political stunts by American POW/MIA activists, including the highly publicized reiteration of an earlier offer of a $1 million reward for a live American made by a group that included a former U.S. Congressman. Washington's rapid denial of association with the group and the U.S. government statement that such activities could only prejudice and complicate official efforts to seek the fullest possible accounting was important to Hanoi and helped prevent the activities of the POW/MIA group from becoming a problem for Hanoi.[48] The Reagan administration's *Final Interagency Report* was issued on 19 January. The report stated that "conclusive evidence of the existence of live Americans had not been uncovered." The report went on to say that based on the circumstances of loss and information about some cases, the U.S. government knew "of a few instances where Americans were captured and the governments involved acknowledged that some Americans died in captivity, but there has been no accounting of them." The *Final Interagency Report* noted that resolving these cases had become an agreed priority between the U.S. and Vietnam and emphasized the administration's concern:

> Because of such discrepancies and the lack of knowledge about many cases, the Reagan Administration has concluded that we must operate under the assumption that at least some of the missing could have survived until we can jointly conclude that all possible efforts have been made to resolve their fate. In human terms, return of remains ends family uncertainty and, in terms of the live prisoner issue, it permits us to focus on unresolved discrepancy cases, thus moving us closer to answering the highest priority question. In addition, the United States has placed a high priority on resolving "live sighting" reports received from a variety of sources. Although most have been resolved as correlating to specific individuals returned in Operation Homecoming, necessary priority and resources will continue to focus on such reports.[49]

Hanoi, however, was satisfied with the statement that there was no concrete evidence that live prisoners were still alive in Vietnam and did not publicly make an issue of the administration's "white paper."[50]

In February 1989, the Vietnamese press singled out humanitarian actions by American private voluntary organizations that took place in the context of the "Vessey initative." Hanoi was still not pleased that Washington had chosen to refrain from giving direct assistance to child survival and prosthetics projects. However, in publicizing the work of the NGOs, Hanoi muted that point and praised the value of the individual efforts.[51] Nevertheless, the government of the Socialist Republic of Vietnam (SRV) still felt strongly about the issue. This came out most clearly in the early January statement by the VNOSMP, which addressed in three terse points what were described as queries from cadres and citizens concerning their government's policy regarding cooperation with Washington to recover and repatriate the remains of U.S. casualities. First, the statement said that the work of solving the problem of missing Americans was "humanitarian work" undertaken with respect toward the American people, especially the families of Americans still missing. The U.S. and SRV governments had agreed to pursue this humanitarian work to solve the problems stemming from the war. Second, the VNOSMP had conducted the search for remains and for information about American MIAs without linking this cooperation to any other issue. Third, the statement made the point that the only organization with the responsibility for pursuing the resolution of the problem of missing Americans was the VNOSMP, which drew its staff from the Ministry of Foreign Affairs, the Defense Ministry, the Ministry of Health, and the Interior Ministry. No other officials were invested with the authority to undertake these tasks. This last point was a comment on the multiplicity of U.S. groups, including some with connections to Congress, that had appeared on the scene and proceeded to issue statements, make judgments about Vietnam's cooperation on this issue, and define new courses of action regarding rewards, field searches, and other concrete steps in a manner that impugned what Hanoi had defined as its humanitarian motivation for continuing to cooperate with Washington.[52]

CHAPTER FOUR

Expanding POW/MIA Dialogue and Activity, 1990–1991

Vietnam delivered three central messages in 1990. One was that Hanoi had been more cooperative and forthcoming on the POW/MIA issue during that year than ever before. The second point was that there existed dwindling support for the U.S. government's Indochina policy and that increasing pressure from U.S. businesspeople threatened to render Washington's position untenable. The third was that Vietnam's own bilateral relations with the Asian Development Bank and the World Bank were improving, and the U.S. embargo was losing supporters.[1]

During a mid–January 1990 meeting in Hanoi, JCRC presented a reexamination of the cases on the 70-name list and a summary of the 32 additional discrepancy cases presented to the Vietnamese in October 1989 and 30 Lao-Vietnamese border cases. JCRC categorized the cases as (1) cases that had been concluded, (2) cases requiring further work at a later date, (3) cases in which remains should be recoverable, or (4) cases not yet jointly investigated as well as cases requiring timely additional investigative work. The Vietnamese stood by their position that cases in which the fate of the individual was determined, but no remains were recovered, were nevertheless considered resolved. Hanoi challenged the U.S. conclusions regarding cases where further work was required, arguing that two categories, "killed in action" (KIA) or "MIA/body not recovered" (BNR), were sufficient. Hanoi conducted a unilateral excavation in the presence of a U.S. observer in early February. The ninth joint field investigations were carried out between 16 February and 6 March. Nine cases were investigated and two grave sites were excavated during the ninth field investigations, but no remains were recovered. In mid–April the Vietnamese repatriated ten sets of remains. The tenth joint field investigations were conducted from 20 April to 10 May. A forensic team examined 256 containers of remains recovered by the Vietnamese and sent four sets of remains from this group to CILHI for further analysis. Eight cases were investigated and four sites were excavated during the tenth joint investigations, though no remains were recovered.[2]

In May media commentary, Hanoi expressed its concern with the U.S. government's view that Vietnam's failure to cooperate in efforts to achieve a peaceful settlement of the conflict in Cambodia precluded progress toward normalization. Hanoi argued that Vietnam had cooperated in resolving MIA cases and stated that its "efforts in this humanitarian issue will step by step contribute to normalizing relations with the United States." In Hanoi's opinion, Washington's refusal to acknowledge Vietnam's cooperation represented "actions detrimental to Vietnam's goodwill." Hanoi made two key points in response to Assistant Secretary of State Richard Solomon's reiteration before Congress of the U.S. position that Washington would not normalize relations until the Cambodian problem was solved. First, the Vietnamese argued that the U.S. position ignored trends toward integration and the strong worldwide presumption in favor of establishing normal and proper relations as the key to achieving stability, economic success and peace:

> This is an erroneous and outdated act at a time when international relations have become a law in the world political and economic lives and when extension of economic ties has become an urgent demand of all states irrespective of social and political systems. Mr. Solomon's action also shows that Washington is uncomfortable because many countries including Western ones are setting up economic relations with Vietnam.

Second, the Vietnamese noted that their goodwill had translated into substantial progress:

> For over a year Vietnam has joined the United States in ten major searches for information on the remains of American pilots reported missing during the war. The latest search conducted by joint teams of American and Vietnamese specialists ended on 10 May. It is interesting to note that the Vietnamese government created favorable conditions during the ten searches in 24 provinces. The undertaking also involved investigations into some 100 registered cases of MIA and 6 rounds of identification conducted by the mixed teams. The U.S. highly valued Vietnam's cooperation and assistance in the search for the remains of the MIAs. Over the past ten years Vietnam has handed over to the U.S. side 404 sets of remains, 243 of them have been returned to the U.S. side since September 1987 following the first trip to Vietnam by General John Vessey, Special Envoy of the U.S. President.[3]

In May and June, Washington made it clear that it was dissatisfied with the flagging level of cooperation and the diminished momentum. In late June, Assistant Secretary Solomon told a hearing of the House Foreign Affairs Subcommittee on East Asia that "a relative lack of serious cooperation over the last several months is due, in our view, to the SRV's misplaced perception that the U.S. considers increased activity an acceptable substitute for results."[4]

At that same hearing, Rear Admiral Ronald Marryott, deputy director of the Defense Intelligence Agency, restated the view that Hanoi had stored the remains of U.S. service personnel and that those remains were in the custody of the Vietnamese government:

> Many of you probably remember the Vietnamese mortician who more than a decade ago provided reliable evidence concerning the existence of a warehouse in Vietnam that held U.S. remains. He personally prepared over 260 remains for storage and estimated that the total he saw exceeded 400. His information has been independently verified.
>
> Additionally, forensic experts have found that a substantial number of the remains repatriated by the Vietnamese showed signs of long-term storage. Further, we sometimes get indications that since the war the Vietnamese have made an effort to retrieve American remains buried in locations outside the Hanoi area. Remains showing evidence of storage have been returned from as far away as the Lao border. Therefore, it is logical to assume that other remains, much easier to recover in Hanoi or Haiphong and other accessible areas, were stored and have not yet been repatriated. Precisely how many remains the Vietnamese continue to withhold is hard to judge, but when you take into account their ... record keeping, we must conclude that a serious effort on their part could result in an accounting for many hundreds more of our men.
>
> Recently, the Vietnamese seem intent on convincing us that their citizenry robbed American graves in the hope of using the remains to earn rewards or entry into the United States. Quite frankly, we do not believe the remains of our servicemen are hidden in the homes of private citizens.[5]

On 30 June 1990, the Vietnamese Foreign Ministry rejected the views spoken at the congressional hearing as a "distortion of the facts." The Foreign Ministry's statement, which referred to Marryott's remarks as "slanderous" allegations, noted that these views ran counter to "previous statements of high level quarters in the U.S. administration which highly value the efforts of the government and people of Vietnam in settling the issue of Americans missing in action in the Vietnam war." Hanoi sought to counter the charges that it had delayed progress by arguing that since April the U.S. had twice suspended specialists' meetings scheduled to review the results of the joint searches and discuss plans for the next one. The Vietnamese stressed that they were awaiting a reply from the U.S. side on the time of the meeting and "held the U.S. side fully responsible for retarding the process of settlement of the MIA issue."

On 20 September 1990, Assistant Secretary Solomon led a delegation to New York for a meeting with Deputy Foreign Minister Le Mai and Ambassador Trinh Xuan Lang. The Vietnamese characterized this exchange of views in modest terms, noting that Mai and Solomon agreed that the meeting was "useful" and that it had taken place in an "atmosphere of constructiveness and mutual understanding."[6] On 29 September, during discussions with Nguyen Co Thach in New York, Secretary of State James Baker urged Vietnam to move rapidly to resolve the POW/MIA issue to ensure that this issue would not become an obstacle to improved relations once a comprehensive settlement was reached in Cambodia. Baker also invited Thach to travel to Washington for further discussions with General Vessey and members of the Interagency Group on POW/MIA Affairs (IAG).[7] The Vietnamese were restrained in their public comments on this meeting, calling the session "useful and constructive" in a press communiqué on 30 September. While the Vietnamese press communiqué simply acknowledged the U.S. position that the process of normalization would proceed "alongside" of efforts to achieve a settlement of the Cambodian conflict, later press commentary was more critical of Washington's decision to continue the embargo and the U.S. government's failure to credit Vietnam with significant efforts to solve the MIA issue. In a mid–November interview, General Secretary Nguyen Van Linh spoke of the meeting in quite upbeat terms, noting that the session, though late in the history of postwar relations, "ushered in a new period, letting bygones be bygones" and beginning a "good time" for Vietnamese–U.S. relations. Linh noted that the problem of the remains of American MIAs "has been largely resolved thanks to our goodwill toward the American people."[8]

On 17 October a Vietnamese delegation headed by Thach met with General Vessey and members of the IAG in Washington, D.C. Thach agreed to improve Vietnam's participation in planning joint investigations and to increase unilateral remains repatriations and efforts to locate wartime documentation containing information on missing Americans. Thach agreed to facilitate access to Vietnamese citizens who witnessed incidents of loss and to military units involved in operations in which U.S. personnel were captured, to add more Vietnamese military personnel to the teams participating in the joint activities, and to allow the U.S. teams to stay on-site until thorough investigations of selected cases were completed, thereby lifting the time limit under which the teams had operated in the past. Thach accepted the proposal to create joint information research teams and to host a meeting in Hanoi with a U.S. team for the purpose of discussing access to wartime historical records bearing on loss incidents and the capture and confinement of U.S. personnel. The U.S. team was to be headed by a Department of Defense official and was to include military historians and analysts. General Vessey and Minister Thach discussed the importance of repatriating POW/MIA remains as rapidly as possible in a manner that would facilitate identification. Thach agreed to increase unilateral actions by the Vietnamese to resolve the remaining discrepancy cases and to put in place a mechanism to investigate all unresolved cases. Finally, Thach said he would consider the proposal to establish a temporary U.S. POW/MIA office in Hanoi.[9]

Vietnamese media commentary on the Vessey-Thach session in Washington described the meeting as a "breakthrough" in U.S.–Vietnamese relations and highlighted Hanoi's view of the importance of lifting the embargo and establishing diplomatic relations.[10] Media commentary in early December noted that following the Vessey-Thach meeting, "MIA [cooperation] was accelerated" by both sides:

> After this meeting, specialists of the two countries met in Hanoi to discuss concrete measures in solving the MIA issue. On 20 November, Vietnam handed over to the U.S. the number of American remains collected in the 11th joint search. Eight days later, the U.S. sent a delegation to Vietnam to carry out the 12th joint search, which lasted for 20 days. On 7 December, the Joint Vietnam–U.S. Experts Team for Forensic Medicine and Identification will carry out the third identification of the remains collected in Ho Chi Minh City. At present, the two sides have working plans for the next year. Under their agreement, Vietnam and the United States will carry out their 13th joint search in mid–January 1991.[11]

In an early November technical session, U.S. and Vietnamese specialists discussed plans for the 12th and 13th joint investigations and evaluated Hanoi's unilateral activities. Vietnamese media reports stated that Hanoi had been given high marks for "positive and fruitful" cooperation and that Hanoi had agreed to future joint field activities aimed at "contributing to quickly resolving this humanitarian issue."[12]

Following the Baker-Thach meeting, Ambassador Trinh Xuan Lang provided Washington with information about three Americans allegedly living in Vietnam "outside of government control," men whose names had been mentioned to Baker by Thach. Up to that point, the Vietnamese had been uncompromising in their position regarding live-sighting reports. Hanoi consented to discuss approaches to investigating such reports in 1991 after years of being pressed and moved further toward agreeing to U.S. terms for a "mechanism" that would carry out investigations of these reports in January 1992, though Hanoi balked at the U.S. requirement for unfettered access to areas and facilities and short-notice terms for such investigations. In March 1992, during Solomon's visit, the Vietnamese agreed to facilitate a live-sighting investigation on basically those terms. However, throughout Nguyen Co Thach's tenure, Hanoi's position was that reports of live Americans held against their will by Vietnamese authorities were fabrications and provocations. The Vietnamese refused to budge on the matter of live-sighting investigations. They rejected the U.S. position that reports of Americans "living freely" and reports of Americans in "captive environments" required investigation in order to put allegations and rumors to rest through a transparent, credible effort by specialists to review all evidence, interview witnesses, and visit alleged facilities in which U.S. personnel were incarcerated. Hanoi also rejected the U.S. view that Vietnam's cooperation could enhance the credibility of joint field investigations of discrepancy cases by eliminating the possibility that Americans who survived their "incident of loss" and were captured or detained by Communist forces, but were not repatriated with those who were released in 1973, had in fact remained in Hanoi's jails after the termination of hostilities.

In his October 1990 private discussions with General Vessey, Thach highlighted the case of one American, Walter T. Robinson, who was captured in 1969 and remained in Vietnam after 1975. According to Thach, Robinson had recently expressed the desire to return to the U.S. In Thach's partial, elliptical explanation, Robinson and other Americans were not in Hanoi's custody but were under the control and care of unidentified groups of montagnards in the central highlands. Thereafter, Ambassador Trinh Xuan Lang provided the names of three Americans who were alleged to be living in Vietnam outside of government control, along with some particulars regarding one of these individuals who purportedly was a U.S. serviceman and could be made available to return to the U.S. through the offices of a third party. In November, during a field investigation, the VNOSMP provided JCRC with a list of ten names of Americans who wished to return home. The U.S. government requested access to the individual mentioned by Thach, whose name appeared on the two lists provided by the Vietnamese, and proposed to dispatch a team of specialists to discuss the case and arrange access to the purported American via government-to-government channels. Finally, Washington communicated its interest in rapidly investigating other reports of Americans living in Vietnam under similar circumstances.

In early November, in the face of serious discrepancies and lingering confusion, a U.S. team traveled to Vietnam to investigate these reports. Washington's own investigations had revealed that a Walter T. Robinson had safely returned to the U.S. after a normal tour of duty in Vietnam and that this individual was Caucasian, in sharp contrast to the clearly Negroid or mixed race man identified as Walter T. Robinson in the photographs provided by the Vietnamese authorities. The U.S. team did not gain access to any of the individuals who were purported to be Americans. The team was presented with what the Vietnamese described as overwhelming evidence that remains traders and other undesirables had control of the evidence relating to the individuals on the name lists provided by Lang and the VNOSMP. Hanoi told the U.S. team that some of these remains traders were in Vietnamese custody, but that much of this illegal activity aimed at extracting profit from the MIA issue was beyond the ability of the Vietnamese government to control. The Vietnamese, however, expressed their concern to General Vessey that information on this matter had been made public and had become the subject of a *Washington Times* article prior to any official U.S. government notification to the Vietnamese government. Additionally, the Vietnamese reiterated that Thach had never affirmed that these were Americans still living in Vietnam, in contrast to the claim made by the *Washington Times* article that Thach mentioned Americans living in remote corners about whom the Vietnamese government had no information.[13]

While Foreign Ministry representatives had periodically indicated that Americans could conceivably be living freely in Vietnam and that in such circumstances their existence would not necessarily be known to Vietnamese authorities, that argument had generally been an adjunct to the case that Vietnam held no live Americans against their will. Thach raised the issue in a manner that allowed him to appear helpful soon after his session with Secretary Baker, while at the same time underscoring the established Vietnamese position that the Hanoi government held no Americans against their will. Thach had apparently intended to demonstrate the extreme difficulties that confronted the Vietnamese government's efforts to deal with the various groups of "traffickers" and "outlaws" who sought to exploit the POW/MIA issue for personal gain.

In fact, Hanoi officials did provide the initial reports in a manner suggesting that they wanted to be responsive to Secretary Baker. They did follow up on these reports with high-level correspondence and also provided additional information and photographs. The Vietnamese recognized the high-level U.S. government interest in the issue, accommodated the team that was dispatched from the U.S. Embassy in Bangkok to look into the issue, and provided access to witnesses and facilitated interviews for that team. The Vietnamese were fully cognizant of the sustained public attention to the POW/MIA issue in the United States. In view of this, Thach appears to have drawn the conclusion that the pressure on the administration was sufficient enough to compel Washington to treat seriously the cases Hanoi had mentioned, in spite of prior indications that the particular names represented manufactured stories. Thach's calculation must have been that in the end the episode would serve to legitimize Hanoi's claims that such reporting was bogus and that Vietnam held no live Americans as prisoners.

In practical terms, the Vietnamese were not as helpful as they could have been. They did not comply with the U.S. government request that all transactions on this matter be conducted on a government-to-government basis. They did not grant access to an individual they claimed was the mediator between the government and the group that had control over the purported Americans. The Vietnamese refused to give the U.S. team a copy of the videotape of an interrogation of several Vietnamese who reportedly manufactured information about Americans who were alive in Vietnam. Washington stressed that it was imperative that Hanoi and the U.S. government work together to define a means of handling such reports that would allow U.S. specialists to enter Vietnam to track down the sources of such information and to confirm or deny the reports through interviews with witnesses or individuals with direct knowledge of the whereabouts of purported Americans. Thach rejected the argument that Hanoi and Washington must pursue all live-sighting reports and must therefore develop a mechanism to investigate these reports thoroughly; he asserted that even those reports the U.S. government took to be credible enough to require on-the-ground investigations were false, concocted stories and that Hanoi could undertake those investigations unilaterally and punish perpetrators of schemes to profit from this issue.

The Other MIAs: Vietnam's Missing

The Vietnamese Communist Party held its tenth plenum from 17 to 26 November 1990. The Central Committee discussed three documents at the session: a resolution on the orientations for directing the 1991 socioeconomic development plan, a resolution on a draft report on party building and on the revision of party regulations, and a revised draft of party regulations to be submitted to the Seventh National Party Congress. Beginning in late 1990, party committees at the local, municipal, and provincial levels subjected these documents to detailed criticisms and sought to make significant amendments to the core documents for presentation at the National Congress. During the January 1991 military meetings to review the draft documents, participants in a local military party organization meeting made the point that one of the tasks before the People's Army was to "strive to resolve" the consequences of war, including the search for persons missing as a result of the hostilities, thus making the trauma of unaccounted for wartime casualties a public issue for the Vietnamese military establishment. The participants in the local meeting openly criticized the key documents proposed by the party in late 1990 for neglecting to raise the issue of Vietnam's own missing personnel. Clearly, some military entities were prepared to lobby in order to get this issue written into the documents that were to be put before the National Party Congress.[14]

In late 1990 and early 1991, the issue of Vietnam's MIAs was raised in the context of formal POW/MIA discussions with the U.S. During talks with General Vessey in October 1990 and again in April 1991, Thach suggested that the Vietnamese people were hard pressed to understand why the Vietnamese government was dedicating personnel and resources to look for American MIAs when many Vietnamese were still unaccounted for. During a technical meeting in March 1991, Dang Nghiem Bai, then director of the Foreign Ministry's Americas Department, noted the importance of Vietnam's own efforts to account for its MIAs and suggested that Vietnam was having a hard time convincing provincial officials to be cooperative in efforts to plan joint field investigations and attempts to gain access to provincial archives to research documents that could help resolve cases of unaccounted for Americans. By March 1991 the Vietnamese were phrasing the point in even stronger terms, noting the consequences of widely perceived neglect of Vietnam's MIA issue as resources were diverted to helping the U.S. in the field. For example, in a March 1991 article in *Tap Chi Cong San*, Phan Doan Nam, editor in chief of *The Vietnam Courier*, stated:

From another perspective, in today's world the foreign policy of a country has a strong effect on its domestic situation. The fact that our country is trying to normalize its relations with those countries formerly hostile to us has posed many problems for our domestic affairs. Regardless of its humanitarian character, any issue or gesture of goodwill, such as searching for U.S. soldiers missing in action, if not treated wisely, may also create a negative impact on the domestic situation. This is because during the anti–U.S. war, our country was badly devastated, and we also have between 400,000 and 500,000 soldiers missing in action and unaccounted for.[15]

It looked as though the Vietnamese military, with a certain amount of support from other interests including the foreign policy establishment, was trying to insert a point on the Vietnamese People's Army MIAs into the National Congress documents.[16] In December the Vietnamese received a Red Cross delegation which organized a course on tracing missing personnel. Hanoi, however, did not undertake an appreciably more intense effort on behalf of its missing in Cambodia in response to the minor pressures exerted by the military or as a result of formal Red Cross assistance.[17]

Mounting Congressional Concern

Beginning in late 1990 and throughout 1991, the U.S. government was the target of increasingly intense criticisms from domestic groups that believed the government had failed to pursue aggressively the live prisoner issue, had concealed information, and had relegated the POW/MIA issue to a low level of priority. The late 1990 publication of a book which claimed to reveal evidence of a massive U.S. government coverup and the highly publicized release of the "Interim Report on the Southeast Asian POW/MIA Issue," prepared by minority staff members of the Senate Committee on Foreign Relations, focused considerable attention on the issue. The "Interim Report," released as an enclosure to a 26 October 1990 "Dear Colleague" letter from Senator Jesse Helms, was extremely critical of the executive branch's handling of the POW/MIA policy. The core argument was that following the end of the war in Vietnam, the Department of Defense possessed proof that American POWs were still alive in captivity but chose to ignore that evidence. In the cover letter accompanying the report, Senator Helms said that the summary document represented "a year of intensive investigation, culminating in a major breakthrough in the careful examination of DIA live-sighting reports on POW/MIAs—the first time in 17 years that an independent branch of the government has had an opportunity to make an objective evaluation of the methods used in accounting for those categorized as POW/MIAs in Southeast Asia." In February 1991, the highly decorated colonel who headed the Defense Intelligence Agency's Special Office for POW/MIA Affairs resigned after accusing the government of neglecting the issue, abandoning any real effort to locate and extricate live prisoners in Southeast Asia, blunting the intelligence mission of the DIA Special Office, and covering up this malfeasance. Beginning in early 1991, a variety of interests urged independent investigations of the government's conduct of this policy. The Veterans of Foreign War, for example, proposed the formation of an "independent public commission." Various congressmen proposed the establishment of a presidential commission. In March 1991, Senator Robert Smith introduced legislation to create a Senate Select Committee on POW Affairs, a proposal which received strong endorsement from Senator Helms and from Senator Charles Grassley, who had long advocated a stronger form of congressional oversight for this issue.[18]

First Steps Toward Archival Research

During 3 to 7 January 1991, on the basis of Thach's October 1990 agreement to form a joint research team of American and Vietnamese information specialists, a U.S. government information and research team traveled to Hanoi for discussions with Vietnamese counterparts.[19] At the January meeting, the U.S. specialists from the Department of Defense, DIA, JCRC, and CILHI met with Vietnamese counterparts from the Ministry of Interior (MOI), Ministry of Foreign Affairs (MFA), and the Ministry of National Defense (MND). The Vietnamese agreed to a date for the 13th round of field investigations, which were completed in early February. They also indicated that once the meeting results were reviewed by higher level officials and the U.S. assessment of the 13th field investigations and excavations was received and assessed, the Vietnamese government would be prepared to set a date for the 14th joint investigations. The U.S. specialists provided detailed briefings to define further the type of information necessary to resolve cases of missing Americans. The U.S. team also sought and received Vietnamese agreement to adopt a "geographic approach" to resolving cases and to develop a viable mechanism for investigating selected live-sighting reports which lent themselves to joint investigation. Finally, the Vietnamese side reiterated its agreement to facilitate rapid access to witnesses and information.[20] Uniquely, the Vietnamese media coverage of the sessions noted that the two sides "unanimously held that their meetings had been crowned with high success," a truly effusive evaluation when taken against the more agnostic characterizations the Vietnamese usually employed to describe such technical-level sessions. In mid–January the Vietnamese repatriated 11 sets of remains associated with American MIAs, bringing the total number of repatriated remains to 445, though the number of identifications made by scientific analysis at CILHI was only 247 by mid–1991.[21] The 13th joint activities took place in February, in Quang Binh, Thua Thien, and Quang Nam–Da Nang provinces.[22]

The second information research session was incorporated into expanded technical discussions which took place in Hanoi during 19–23 March 1991. At that meeting, JCRC specialists told the Vietnamese that of the 119 discrepancy cases, 22 sets of remains had been repatriated and identified. Five were repatriated as the result of joint investigations. In the case of four individuals, the U.S. government concluded that their fates were "resolved," but that there was no likelihood of recovering their remains. In 31 additional cases, the U.S. government determined that further joint or unilateral activities were necessary in order to recover remains. In 62 cases, the fates of the individuals remained unknown, and the U.S. side concluded that further joint or unilateral activities were necessary to establish the fate of the individuals and to attempt to recover remains. Hanoi continued to approach case resolution in distinctly different terms from the U.S., emphasizing the determination of death as the end-point for investigations, whereas the U.S. stressed a definition of accountability that went beyond merely confirming the death and required efforts to locate the remains of missing personnel or a convincing explanation of why information on the disposition of remains or the remains themselves could not be produced.

The Vietnamese Foreign and Defense Ministry officials with whom members of the U.S. information research team met maintained steadfastly that it had been impossible to keep systematic records during the war and that climatic conditions wreaked havoc with whatever records did survive the destructiveness of the war. Thach had repeatedly made these points to Vessey, arguing that the assumptions underlying the U.S. argument that Vietnam's wartime archives contained information that could be helpful in resolving MIA cases were simply incorrect. Importantly, though, there were significant differences between the Foreign Ministry, which had committed to improving access to witnesses and archival data, and the Defense Ministry, which had serious objections to providing the kind of access to information requested by the U.S. Underscoring these differences, in late April the military's daily newspaper published a detailed account of the 1966 downing of a U.S. RF-101, complete with the location and times of the downing, the radar screen readings of the missile battalion responsible, the names of the battalion commander and the radar officers, potential witnesses, and an apparent excerpt from a company leader's report, precisely the type of information the U.S. government was requesting and that Vietnam was saying did not exist, was too difficult to locate, or remained strictly controlled and thereby inaccessible to the U.S. government.[23]

The Roadmap

In early April, Assistant Secretary Richard Solomon presented the Vietnamese permanent representative to the United Nations with a description of the four-phased process through which bilateral U.S.–Vietnamese relations would develop in the aftermath of Hanoi's signing the international agreement for a peaceful settlement of the Cambodian conflict and described how cooperation on the POW/MIA issue would influence the pace and scope of the normalization of relations. Phase One was to begin with the signing of the Paris Agreement, which took place on 23 October. Phase Two was to begin with the establishment of the United Nations Transitional Authority in Cambodia (UNTAC) and the initial steps toward a United Nations–supervised election in Cambodia. Phase Three was to begin once Vietnam and the authorities in Phnom Penh had supported the implementation of the Paris Agreement on Cambodia for six months. Phase Four, the final phase, was to begin following a free and democratic election in Cambodia, the establishment of a new National Assembly, and the demobilization of the four Cambodian factions. Thach reacted negatively to the "Roadmap," as the four-phase outline of the future of U.S.–Vietnamese relations came to be called. In Hanoi's view the U.S. government had set conditions that Vietnam would be unable to satisfy as a result of diminishing influence over the Phnom Penh government and trends beyond Vietnam's control.[24] Nevertheless, Thach committed himself to continue cooperation on the POW/MIA issue, while neither accepting nor rejecting the Roadmap.[25]

From the start the Vietnamese argued that the Roadmap was a unilateral document dictating a course of action, not a negotiating position, and was therefore an affront to their sovereignty. Hanoi's position was that bilateral cooperation on the POW/MIA issue should proceed independently of progress toward normalization and that normalization should take place without preconditions. In the third quarter of 1991, the Vietnamese argued that the Roadmap was seriously out of date, given trends toward reconciliation in the region and progress in implementing the peace agreement in Cambodia. Moreover, Vietnam took the position that it had been cooperative because it had repatriated over 400 sets of remains. Hanoi strongly made the case that rapid normalization between Washington and Hanoi would be the best means of guaranteeing the fullest possible accounting for missing Americans. The Vietnamese sought to proceed with MIA cooperation without making formal references to the Roadmap.

Vessey arrived in Hanoi on 19 April 1991 for a two-day visit during which he stressed the importance of improving the planning for joint investigations and urged the Vietnamese to expand their efforts to undertake research in wartime archives for information that could assist in resolving the cases of missing Americans. Vessey also underscored the importance of increasing unilateral repatriations by the Vietnamese. Thach reaffirmed Vietnam's willingness to enhance efforts to provide the fullest possible accounting for missing Americans. Thach committed to improving efforts in information research, in planning of joint investigations, and in following up on live-sighting reports. Both governments agreed that a temporary POW / MIA office should be established in Hanoi in order to facilitate rapid resolution of unresolved cases of missing U.S. personnel and provide an administrative and logistical support base for all POW / MIA activities in Vietnam. The office would also facilitate investigations of live-sighting reports and assist in planning and conducting joint investigations and recoveries, forensic identification activities, and historical and archival research. The office was to be staffed by temporary duty Defense Department personnel. Further discussions on the establishment of the temporary office were conducted during a technical level meeting in Hanoi in early May.[26]

Hanoi was unyielding about the manner in which cases of individual MIAs could be resolved. While the U.S. government required an elaborate chain of evidence to demonstrate that an individual was dead and separated the issue of death from the question of recoverability of remains, Hanoi continued to consider cases "resolved" where evidence of death, short of recovered remains, could be produced. In February 1991, at the conclusion of the 13th joint field investigations, the U.S. and the Vietnamese agreed to assess the first 13 investigations and resulting progress. A March technical meeting revealed substantial differences between the U.S. and Vietnamese specialists regarding the status of individual cases and investigations. During his April meetings in Hanoi, Vessey defended the U.S. assessment, according to which 62 of the 119 discrepancy cases required additional investigative work. Vessey told Thach that in view of the unanswered questions concerning the 62 discrepancy cases, and given the fact that careful investigation of the cases where the U.S. last knew the Americans to be alive could shed important light on the issue of live prisoners, the best course would be to investigate actively those 62 cases on a priority basis.

Thach accepted this argument in principle and indicated that Vietnam would accept the U.S. assessment of the cases requiring additional work and proceed from there. However, as a practical matter the Vietnamese continued to issue challenges to those assessments throughout the rest of the year, arguing that the determination of fate effectively resolved a case.

Hanoi released the "unanimously issued" joint statement following the talks between Vessey and Thach and in a departure from previous post-visit statements refrained from characterizing the talks.[27] On 23 April, however, Hanoi Radio's International Service noted that, in spite of Vietnam's active cooperation with the U.S. government to resolve the MIA issue, "many difficulties still exist on the road to normalization" between Washington and Hanoi. The station commentary clearly laid the blame for slow progress at Washington's feet. Hanoi reiterated its position that no preconditions to normalization should be set by either side.[28] Hanoi felt that Washington's position would become untenable as more American business interests assailed the embargo:

Corporations' representatives, statesmen including the Vietnam war veterans, and even Republican senators, some of them adequately informed of Vietnam's realistic potentials, have come to Vietnam. Many of them have strongly requested that the U.S. administration lift the trade embargo against Vietnam. They demanded that the Cambodian issue be separated from the question of normalizing relations with Vietnam. They believe that the embargo has only barred U.S. corporations from a market full of prospects without any firm justification for its pretext of security.

Hanoi pressed the viewpoint that it had contributed to the resolution of the Cambodian conflict by withdrawing its troops and had participated in the efforts to formulate a peace plan. Hanoi had also committed itself to respect the decisions of Cambodia's Supreme National Council, accept international supervision and control of a ceasefire, and support an enhanced role for the United Nations in administering a free election in Cambodia. Additionally, Hanoi argued that it had cooperated on a range of humanitarian issues, while the U.S. government continued to disparage Vietnam's involvement in efforts to address these issues, including the MIA issue:

> The U.S. Government has made only a small step. It has opened an office to deal with some definite issues. . . . The U.S. side has frequently imposed unilateral conditions considering that the normalization of relations will only benefit Vietnam. How can a unilateral solution promote rapidly and realistically the normalization of relations between the two countries? . . . In the relations with the United States, the Vietnamese side has taken the first step in many issues. Particularly, in the settlement of Americans missing in Vietnam, the Vietnamese side has 13 times or more turned over the remains of American MIAs and allowed American experts to come in to study and propose the best solutions and to establish a U.S. permanent office in Vietnam. [. . .] The Vietnamese side has also begun to agree with the U.S. side to let those who formerly cooperated with the United States to depart legally. Particularly as regards the Cambodian issue—which the United States considers a main condition for settling the normalization of relations—the Vietnamese side has withdrawn all its military force from Cambodia and created basically favorable conditions for a political settlement of the Cambodian issue.

On that basis, the U.S. government's position was weak and contradictory in the Vietnamese view. As a late May *Voice of Vietnam* feature put it:

> In life, goodwill must be manifested by action and absolutely not by empty words. Goodwill to successfully settle a problem or differing views must come from both sides and never from one. It has been publicly known that the U.S. propaganda machinery has thus far held Vietnam responsible for the failure to settle the situation in Cambodia. It has forgotten or intended to forget Vietnam's most basic action in Cambodia which was the withdrawal of Vietnamese troops. On the contrary, it has distorted the event with ill intentions

and has not satisfactorily helped settle the continued assistance of the Khmer Rouge and the prevention of war from recurring there.

Normalizing U.S.–Vietnamese relations is a demand of the peoples of both countries and would benefit both sides. That the U.S. side considers the Cambodian issue a condition for settling the normalization of relations demonstrates that it has not really wanted to normalize the relations as rapidly as large numbers of American people have desired.

If the normalization of U.S.–Vietnamese relations can be achieved first, it will be a condition for reaching a more favorable and rapid political settlement of the Cambodian issue.

These are mainly the premises to accelerate and not to obstruct at all the settlement of the Cambodian issue. On the contrary, this can be achieved only by normalizing the relations and all outsiders also realize that it is time to decide. This is not a favor from the United States but an action which benefits both sides and is more likely to benefit the United States. Hurry up or you will lose your seats.[29]

In Hanoi's view, the "linkage" imposed by Washington as the condition for moving forward had diminishing credibility and made little practical sense, serving only to demonstrate how isolated and out of step the U.S. administration was.

The Seventh National Party Congress and Leadership Changes

The Seventh National Party Congress of the Vietnamese Communist Party, the Congress of "Wisdom, Renovation, Democracy, Discipline and Unity," convened on 24 June. The Congress elected a 146-member Central Committee, which elected a 13-member Politburo, a 9-member Secretariat, and a 9-member Control Committee. The Central Committee named Nguyen Van Linh, Pham Van Dong, and Vo Chi Cong to positions as advisers to the Central Committee and left it to the advisory group and the Politburo to draft a statute outlining the responsibilities of the group and providing for the selection of additional advisers, subject to Central Committee approval. Eight new names were added to the Politburo. Ranks six through thirteen of the Politburo were filled by newcomers whose average age was 60. At the 1986 Congress, nine Central Committee members joined four Politburo members to form the Secretariat. The Seventh Congress chose five Central Committee members and three Politburo members to form the Secretariat.

The new lineup of the Politburo, Secretariat, and Central Committee and Do Muoi's accession to the position of general secretary of the Vietnamese Communist Party represented a net gain for the military and cautious reformers. Muoi was widely regarded as an action-oriented man with considerable experience in untangling Byzantine state bureaucracies. There was some confidence among Vietnamese officials that Muoi would continue the reforms.

Although at first a lukewarm subscriber to the reformist line in the mid–1980s, Muoi quickly became an important voice for sustained economic change and policy flexibility. Seven senior leaders, including General Secretary Linh, "retired" from the Politburo, but Do Muoi, Vo Van Kiet, and Le Duc Anh held onto their positions. Vo Chi Cong, chairman of the Council of State, and Dong Sy Nguyen departed from the Politburo, along with two relatively young members elevated at the Sixth Congress in December 1986: Nguyen Duc Tam, the chair of the Organization Department, and Nguyen Thanh Binh. Minister of Interior Mai Chi Tho also vacated his Politburo seat and was replaced by a deputy, Bui Thien Ngo, who was named minister of interior at the National Assembly meeting in August 1991.

Foreign Minister Nguyen Co Thach lost his Politburo seat. He stepped down from his ministerial post at the August National Assembly session. Minister of Defense Le Duc Anh became the second ranking Politburo member, and Doan Khue moved to the number five slot. Khue replaced Anh as defense minister at the August National Assembly session. Together, the positioning of Anh and Khue represented an important advance in influence for the People's Army, which had been burdened with the need to slim down fast in the face of severe budget constraints and had become embroiled in a debate over new national security requirements, Cambodia, and the role of the peacetime army.

The new Politburo and Central Committee left the Foreign Ministry without Politburo-level representation. Four MFA officials — one ambassador and three vice ministers — were elected to the Seventh Central Committee. Vice Minister Tran Quang Co was elevated to full membership from alternate status. Four MND officials were elected to the Central Committee. All were incumbents. The two MOI vice ministers elected by the Seventh Congress were incumbents. Thus, though the MFA had the same number of seats on the Central Committee as the more conservative MND, the MND officials were experienced second-term members. Additionally, the four MND incumbents coupled with the two incumbent MOI members gave those ministries a slight voting edge over the MFA.[30]

The compelling influence that Thach wielded on foreign policy matters as a result of his Politburo post and his concurrent deputy chairmanship on the Council of Ministers was not duplicated by the appointment of Nguyen Manh Cam, former ambassador to Moscow, as the new foreign minister at the August National Assembly session. Altogether, this was a net gain for the two ministries that had been engaged in frontal combat with Foreign Minister Thach over the issues of national security, the rapprochement with China, diversifying foreign relations, and the U.S.–Vietnamese relationship. The new Politburo was a clear victory for the views espoused by Le Duc Anh in favor of a rapid normalization with Beijing, as well as a negative comment on Thach's approach to Cambodia and the United States.

The Photographs, Mounting U.S.
Domestic Concern and Hanoi's Response

In July and August 1991, several photographs which purportedly depicted Americans in captivity in Indochina were made public by POW activists. The Vietnamese government rapidly agreed to conduct a joint investigation of the photographs and received a delegation of U.S. experts led by a deputy assistant secretary of state which sought to review the photographs and discuss related evidence. Hanoi provided new information and produced witnesses who had recollections of the particular loss incidents in question and promised to publicize the photographs with the aim of uncovering additional information and witnesses. The Foreign Ministry issued a review of their findings regarding one photograph of three individuals alleged to be American pilots who were purportedly still alive in detention in Vietnam and urged the U.S. government to "punish and condemn" those involved in this effort to mislead the U.S. and Vietnamese governments for "purposely prolonging the suffering of the MIA families." After intensive investigations involving the cooperation of the governments in Hanoi, Vientiane, and Phnom Penh, the U.S. government demonstrated that the photographs were not of missing Americans. Some of the individuals involved in surfacing these photographs were implicated in elaborate efforts to concoct evidence that live Americans were being held against their will in Laos and Vietnam.[31]

In the midst of mounting domestic criticism of the administration over the live prisoner issue and the question of stored remains, Vietnam used stronger language to defend its record of cooperation with Washington. Hanoi pointed to the repatriation of 291 sets of remains, the 14 joint field operations that had been conducted through late July, and the priority accorded the investigation of the 119 discrepancy cases as evidence of Hanoi's efforts to resolve the POW/MIA issue. Hanoi also argued more vigorously that with increasing numbers of legislators and business executives visiting Vietnam, the embargo would appear to be more and more "archaic" and the preconditions to normalization imposed by the administration — the political solution to the Cambodian conflict and the resolution of the MIA issue — would be shown to be unrealistic, "regrettable" linkages imposed by Washington's obstinacy.[32]

The photographs ignited a firestorm of American emotions, however, and intensified for Hanoi the problems involved in managing the sensitive live-prisoner issue. The standard positions were not effective defenses against accusations that Hanoi continued to hold American prisoners, manipulate the issue, and conceal evidence concerning the fates of missing Americans. Hanoi had to confront stories, featured prominently in U.S. and Western news media, that after 1973 Vietnam had purposely retained control over those prisoners whose physical or mental condition was especially bad as a result of their wartime confinement or had finally killed prisoners remaining in Vietnamese custody when it was realized that they could not be exchanged in return for money or other advantages. The Vietnamese government attempted to respond with a full-fledged media offensive involving public statements by a higher level of officials than were generally involved in the issue, forceful official representations to the U.S. government disputing the authenticity of the photographs, and press conferences in foreign missions (Bangkok, New York) at which Vietnamese representatives spoke in extremely firm terms about the perfidious exploiters of human emotions. The Vietnamese media described the sustained efforts by Hanoi to examine jointly the evidence uncovered regarding the case of Air Force Major John Robertson, one of the three Americans said to be portrayed in the photograph of Americans purportedly still alive in the custody of the Vietnamese.[33] In early August, Vietnam trumpeted its cooperation with U.S. delegations that visited crash sites and camps where American prisoners were held during the war. The Vietnamese media quoted American specialists who averred that the U.S. had "found no evidence of any American reported as still alive in Vietnam" and described the good cooperation of the Vietnamese in providing wartime documents to U.S. investigation teams. An early August radio broadcast quoted President Bush as having stated at a late July press conference that "there is no clear evidence showing that American prisoners of war are still alive in Indochina."[34]

In August, during a meeting in Bangkok with Assistant Secretary Solomon, Le Mai stressed Hanoi's interest in moving rapidly toward normalization and indicated that from Hanoi's perspective most of the discrepancy cases had been resolved.[35] The 14th joint investigation was completed in mid–August and was hailed by the Vietnamese Foreign Ministry as the biggest investigation to date. The ministry made the point that Hanoi had arranged for an investigation of a photograph of three U.S. servicemen purportedly in Vietnamese custody, including a visit to several detention camps in Quang Nam–Da Nang, which resulted in the conclusion that no foreigner was detained at those facilities. The investigation also included an excavation of the Hai Hung crash site of Colonel Robertson's plane.[36]

On 26 September 1991 General Vessey and members of the Interagency Group for POW/MIA Affairs met with Vietnam's Vice Foreign Minister Tran Quang Co in the Pentagon. Co noted that the Foreign Ministry hoped the remaining discrepancy case investigations could be jointly concluded. Co told General Vessey that Vietnam was willing to undertake more investigations, and he asked Vessey to bring data and details about any other cases requiring investigation so that after the general's visit the Vietnamese could work with the U.S. office in Hanoi to organize such investigations. Co expressed willingness to follow-up on live-sighting reports and agreed that the U.S. and Vietnam should discuss how to conduct investigations on the Lao-Vietnamese border.

Vessey traveled to Hanoi in early October 1991 to "confirm that previous agreements for cooperation on humanitarian matters remained in effect" and to reach agreement on "accelerated cooperation in resolving POW / MIA issues along the lines of the Roadmap." In a statement before the Senate Foreign Relations Committee, Vessey noted that Prime Minister Vo Van Kiet and Foreign Minister Nguyen Manh Cam had pledged "unconditional cooperation" and that six specific agreements had been reached. The Vietnamese agreed to:

> (a) Accelerate cooperation on resolving the discrepancy cases and to put in place the mechanisms, procedures and the physical facilities to pursue fullest possible accounting for all missing Americans.
> (b) Conduct a prompt and diligent search for all historical records which may pertain to missing Americans. (The U.S. would provide technical assistance for the search and would bear a share of the cost of the search.)
> (c) Continue to recover and return promptly remains of Americans missing from the war. The U.S. would continue to provide technical support in the recovery of remains and [to] help facilitate identification of remains.
> (d) Seek cooperation with Laos and Cambodia to resolve the fates of Americans lost in the border areas of those countries.
> (e) Review the cases of all remaining reeducation camp detainees with a view to early release of those detainees and their immediate families consistent with the program established for earlier detainees.
> (f) Explore a joint venture to provide improved civilian helicopter support for the joint field investigations.

Vietnam also agreed to improve support for the Hanoi office, to work with the office to "refine live-sighting investigation proceedings," and to provide liaison with the office.

Vessey agreed to recommend to the president that the temporary office be made permanent and that the U.S. "continue to facilitate humanitarian assistance for the Vietnamese people."[37]

Foreign Minister Cam emphasized his government's intentions to abide by earlier agreements and to pursue cooperation in a humanitarian spirit:

> We have always held that efforts to seek information on, and recover, the remains of Americans missing in action is a humanitarian issue. And also in the spirit of humanitarianism, we have continued to actively cooperate with the U.S. side in the investigation through an MIA office in Hanoi. We are solving the issue with our greatest goodwill, without asking for any attached conditions. This is because we have always regarded this as a humanitarian issue. It is because we are ready to continue to cooperate with the U.S. side in the continued search for, and recovery of, the American remains in order to return them to the U.S. side.[38]

Cam studiously followed his predecessor's line on the Roadmap, rejecting the link between normalization and resolution of the POW/MIA issue and noting that with the signing of the Paris Agreement on Cambodia, the Roadmap had become "obsolete." Vessey maintained that more concrete results were required to demonstrate that Vietnam was cooperating fully. Cam, like Thach before him, was prepared to continue "serious, constructive talks" with Washington in order to settle differences and preferred to proceed without reference to the Roadmap, which Hanoi continued to criticize as an attempt by the U.S. to describe the nonnegotiable terms according to which the POW/MIA issue must be resolved before normalization could proceed. The Vietnamese released the text of the joint communiqué in which "both sides highly valued the results of the unilateral and bilateral investigations" and "confirmed their determination to move quickly toward the fullest possible accounting of Americans missing from the Vietnam war and to continue the recovery and repatriation of remains found."[39] A separate transmission stated that Vessey's meeting with Vo Van Kiet, chairman of the Council of Ministers, took place "in an open and constructive atmosphere" and focused on "remaining issues and prospects for the two countries relations."[40]

In October, in response to the signing of the Paris Agreement in Cambodia, Washington announced the lifting of the embargo on Cambodia, the end to the 25-mile travel restrictions imposed on Vietnamese Foreign Ministry officials assigned to the United Nations headquarters, and the termination of restrictions on group travel to Vietnam. The Vietnamese privately communicated their concern to sympathetic humanitarian organizations that the amount of time it took the U.S. government to implement the decision to lift the 25-mile travel limit and the restrictions on group travel was one more signal that the U.S. government was not really intent on moving forward and was not concerned about keeping promises to Vietnam. In early October, Foreign Minister Cam told a press conference in Hanoi that Washington had "made the MIA issue a condition for normalizing ties," a situation that was not acceptable to the Vietnamese government. Cam resolved to continue to account for missing Americans, whether or not Washington agreed to establish relations, but noted that normalization would "create better conditions to resolve this issue." Cam told the assembled foreign journalists that Vietnam had demonstrated its goodwill by assisting U.S. investigations of the "completely absurd" photographs.[41]

In late November, Assistant Secretary Solomon met with Vice Foreign Minister Le Mai in New York to continue discussions about the modalities of normalization, begun in accordance with Phase One provisions of the Roadmap at the deputy assistant secretary-level in the summer of 1991. Deputy Assistant Secretary Kenneth Quinn and Vietnam's Ambassador Trinh Xuan Lang formed a working group to review claims issues, consular matters, and other issues, including humanitarian matters with a bearing on bilateral relations. In addition to discussing consular and humanitarian issues and the matter of the protection of property, Solomon and Mai reviewed progress on the POW/MIA issue. Mai gave every indication that Hanoi planned to make its best effort to comply with U.S. requirements regarding the accounting for missing American service personnel. He strongly criticized Washington's linking of the issue of normalization and the "very emotional issue of the MIAs" and the implementation of the Cambodian peace agreement. Mai expressed Hanoi's expectation that Vessey would return in mid- or late December to follow-up on agreements reached in April and welcomed the proposed visit of a technical team scheduled to arrive in Hanoi in mid–December to discuss practical aspects of the agreements, including the question of safe, reliable helicopter transportation. The Vietnamese media account of the meeting did not go much beyond the press statement made at the end of the session, in which the two sides characterized the meeting as successful and constructive, noted the basic agenda of the talks, and mentioned the agreement to organize "a number of talks at the expert level" in the following months.[42]

In mid–November the Vietnamese repatriated six sets of remains to the U.S.; in Hanoi's account, this was the 36th repatriation of MIA remains and brought the total number of sets of remains returned to the U.S. to 458. Hanoi media reported the conclusion of joint investigations of live-sighting reports in Hanoi, Ha Tay, and Ha Tinh provinces, which "showed that the information was groundless." The media also mentioned joint forensic examinations of remains that resulted in the selection of 46 sets of remains for further study. The Vietnamese described this as the repatriation of 46 sets of remains identified as Americans. Mid-November radio broadcasts noted that senior U.S. government officials who testified before the Select Committee in early November had acknowledged Vietnam's humanitarian cooperation on the MIA issue and had criticized those who "sought to manipulate and profit from the issue." Vessey, according to the broadcast, "confirmed that there is no evidence of American servicemen still alive in Vietnam and reported on Vietnam's positive efforts toward resolving this issue." In the Vietnamese media account of his testimony, Defense Secretary Richard Cheney "admitted that there was no evidence of live Americans being detained in Vietnam." The broadcast referred to Secretary of State James Baker's meeting in Paris with Foreign Minister Cam and his expression of the U.S. government's "wish to gradually improve its relations with Vietnam." However, the broadcast, and other media reviews of the proceedings of the Select Committee, acknowledged the problems posed by Washington's approach to the issue:

> Despite these political developments there are still . . . obstacles imposed by the U.S. side. On the roadmap for the normalization of the U.S.–Vietnamese relations, according to the U.S., this process mainly depends on the speed of the settlement of the MIA issue, while Vietnam holds that MIA is merely a humanitarian issue and this settlement should be separated by any political issue.[43]

The Vietnamese media passively identified differences within the U.S. administration over this issue, suggesting that though there was general agreement that there was "no compelling evidence that there are any living Americans still held captive in Vietnam," an anti–Vietnamese attitude continued to pervade Washington's management of the issue. According to a mid–November commentary:

> What was clearly prominent in this hearing was that, with its obsolete anti-Vietnamese sentiment, the ultra-rightist force in the United States is striving to cling to the POW/MIA issue as a trump card in their gamble to obstruct the normalization of U.S.-Vietnamese relations. At the hearing, they discussed the need to continue to apply pressure on Vietnam to compel it to cooperate more fully with the United States and provide more information on specific cases. In particular, they emphatically said that the pace and scope of the normalization of U.S.-Vietnamese relations should depend on the progress in resolving the questions of U.S. POWs and MIAs.[44]

The commentary concluded that the "atmosphere at the hearing was overtaken by those who welcomed the great effort Vietnam has made to cooperate with the United States on this issue" and detailed Cheney's views of the fraudulent photographs, Vessey's position regarding Hanoi's "positive cooperation," and the positions of other officials who favored normalization.

In early December, Deputy Foreign Minister Le Mai announced a series of meetings that were agreed to during his November talks with Assistant Secretary Solomon, including a session on live-sighting visits, another visit by the U.S. presidential emissary that would follow up on the agreements reached during Vessey's October visit, a trilateral meeting of representatives from Hanoi, Vientiane, and Washington to discuss the methods for investigating the approximately 400 MIAs lost in areas in eastern Laos along the Ho Chi Minh Trail, and a January meeting on Vietnam's humanitarian needs. Mai pointed out that while Hanoi acknowledged the importance of live-sighting investigations to the U.S. government, Washington needed to acknowledge Hanoi's legitimate security concerns that were raised as a result of U.S. government requests for access to controlled areas and government and military archives. Mai said that the normalization process could be influenced by emotions surrounding the issue, U.S. election year politics, and the situation in Cambodia. He reasoned that Washington's insistence on linking implementation of the Paris Agreement on Cambodia with the MIA issue could derail the process. In Mai's words, Washington had made the normalization process "hostage to the activities of the Khmer Rouge." He criticized Washington's hesitation to lift the embargo and normalize relations and rejected the argument that the sensitivity of the issue required slow and patient efforts: "We understand there are emotions in the United States over Vietnam. But there are emotions in Vietnam too — maybe ten times more because the war was fought on our soil. But we know how to control our emotions in order to overcome the past."[45]

On 9 December, Foreign Minister Cam met with a group of congressional staffers and Defense Department personnel and stressed the importance of normalizing "on the basis of equality, mutual respect and without preconditions." The VNOSMP issued a lengthy position paper on Hanoi's policy toward the MIA issue in conjunction with this visit, in which the Vietnamese side restated its views of the Roadmap. Hanoi, the paper made clear, neither rejected nor accepted the process proposed by the United States in the form of the Roadmap, but refused to acknowledge the Roadmap as a legitimate negotiating position. Rather, in Hanoi's view, it was simply Washington's own "stance" on the issue. The Vietnamese stance started with bilateral U.S.–Vietnamese talks which would "take into consideration the viewpoints of each side." Hanoi took the position that there was high-level agreement to separate the POW/MIA problem from other political issues and made it clear that the Vietnamese government would strive to solve the MIA problem regardless of whether or not relations with the U.S. were normalized.[46] In a separate statement on 9 December, the VNOSMP dismissed the claims of the former KGB official who asserted that he had led a group of Soviet personnel to Vietnam to interrogate U.S. prisoners in the 1975–1978 period, reiterating that after the signing of the Paris Accords in March 1973, Hanoi had returned all U.S. POWs.[47] Four days later, the VNOSMP announced the conclusion of the 15th joint field investigation, which included a joint excavation of the Robertson crash site during which bone fragments were found where the F-4 had crashed in September 1966.[48]

Hanoi was clearly frustrated with the tumult over allegations of nefarious arrangements concocted in Hanoi that allowed Moscow to gain control of U.S. POWs in order to exploit them as slave labor or extract from them intelligence concerning U.S. avionics and aircraft, bombing tactics, and war planes. Hanoi had also drawn the conclusion that the failure of Vessey to travel to Vietnam in December was a result of the U.S. government's clear desire to signal displeasure with the level of cooperation on the POW/MIA issue. Finally, in late 1991 the secretary of defense and senior Defense Department officials and military leadership testified before the Senate Select Committee on POW/MIA Affairs that the U.S. would apply military assets and personnel available within the U.S. Pacific Command to address the POW/MIA issue in much the same way as the assets of the Central Command were utilized in Desert Storm to defeat the Iraqis. The Vietnamese responded edgily to the public statements by senior Defense Department officials to the effect that the U.S. sought to dedicate military forces to this problem with the same will and intensity as had been brought to bear during the conflict in the Persian Gulf. Through the end of the year, Hanoi made clear that it was still concerned with the tone of the Select Committee testimony by the newly designated senior military leadership in charge of the Joint Task Force.

Hanoi's assertions that it would continue to treat the MIA issue as a humanitarian matter and would sustain its cooperation with the U.S. government were given a harsher edge in a signed 7 December commentary in the party's daily newspaper, *Nhan Dan*. In an article entitled "The United States Should End Its Irrational Attitude to the MIA Issue," Tu Thinh argued that Vietnam had invested 600,000 workdays in unilateral and joint search efforts and repatriated 458 sets of remains. Thinh observed that "it is necessary to say that Vietnam has unilaterally solved the MIA issue without demanding any conditions from the U.S. side" and that Washington had taken an "irrational attitude" toward the issue: "Right from the beginning the U.S. side did not consider the MIA issue a humanitarian one. It has linked this issue with the normalization of U.S.–Vietnamese relations, making it one of many other political conditions. It is indeed the U.S. side that has caused setbacks in the settlement of this issue."

Thinh stated that the testimony of senior U.S. officials before the Senate Select Committee damaged the atmosphere of cooperation on this issue: "Some members of the U.S. Congress demand that they be allowed to visit any prison in Vietnam at any time regardless of Vietnam's sovereignty. The U.S. Secretary of Defense even likened the MIA search mechanism to the Gulf War operational command." Thinh observed that "this makes some people question whether the MIA issue is a humanitarian issue or an opportunity for the U.S. to undertake some dark schemes against Vietnam." Thinh also alluded to Washington's efforts to sustain dwindling support for the embargo in private approaches to the Japanese. Thinh referred to differences of views within the U.S. government, noting that "some U.S. circles still persist in their view that some American POWs are still in Vietnam" and concluded that the U.S. "has treated the MIA issue in defiance of its agreement reached with Vietnam that this issue is a purely humanitarian one." He characterized the continuation of the embargo as an "immoral" act and maintained that lifting the embargo and normalizing relations would yield cooperation that was "more favorable and more fruitful."[49]

These hardened positions along with post–National Party Congress assessments of regional issues and relationships were Hanoi's shot across Washington's bow, intended to communicate to the U.S. government that there were limits to Hanoi's forbearance, that the reasoned and civilized approach to this humanitarian issue could not continue while Washington threatened Hanoi's basic interests by keeping the trade embargo in place, and that the highest levels of the Vietnamese government could not defend continued cooperation while the U.S. government so blatantly conspired to enlist the support of other countries to sustain the embargo and treated Vietnam's sovereignty with indifference.[50]

Vietnam made several crucial points throughout 1991, and with increasing vigor toward the end of the year. Hanoi's first message, reinforced by the actions and words of several key ASEAN states, was that the U.S. ran the risk of marginalizing itself in Southeast Asia at a moment when the Southeast Asians were quickly recognizing that Hanoi was serious about changing its relationships with each ASEAN member. Thailand, for example, agreed to consider opening reciprocal consulates, although that was not an altogether uncontentious issue. Thailand also agreed to exchange military attachés with Hanoi and to rapidly resolve the conflicts over disputed fishing waters and incarcerated fishermen from both countries. Thailand also signaled that it could play a significant economic role in the future of Vietnam. Singapore and Malaysia viewed the end of the active military involvement of the Vietnamese in the Cambodian conflict as a turning point, and by late 1991 they had made preparations to change their policies on assistance to the non–Communist resistance.

Another point made more subtly by Hanoi was that the U.S. ran the risk of being seen as pandering to domestic sentiment and extremist strains among the POW/MIA interest groups. Vietnam painted a picture of a U.S. administration trapped in a no-win issue, with a clear need to retain congressional goodwill and to rebuild institutional credibility. Vietnam was willing to be patient and hoped to cast itself in the role of the reasonable, civil player in this issue. Hanoi calculated that the efforts in the U.S. government to throw up obstacles to proceeding with the phases of the Roadmap would receive little support in Congress and from influential business interests. Finally, another subtext from Hanoi was that the U.S. ran the risk of pursuing current policy goals with a target fixation that would result in at best a minimum advantage and at worst a failure to regain the confidence of the American people and resolve the issue of missing Americans. The Vietnamese asserted that they continued to provide access to information, to manifest flexibility on joint investigations, and to take the necessary steps to make the U.S. office in Hanoi a success.[51]

CHAPTER FIVE

Making Promises, Moving Forward: POW/MIA Cooperation in 1992

In early January 1992, the Vietnamese government vigorously denied the claims first made in early 1991 by the former director of the Soviet National Security Committee, Oleg Kalugin, that KGB agents interrogated three American POWs in 1978 and that there were about ten Americans held in Vietnam after 1973.[1] Ambassador Trinh Xuan Lang in New York strongly criticized the reports about the role of the former Soviet Union concerning POWs and denounced them as rumors and fabrications. He stressed Vietnam's independence and sovereignty and suggested that though the Soviet Union helped Vietnam during the war, Vietnam would not have accepted Soviet efforts to gain control over U.S. POWs.[2] A 12 January broadcast noted the media uproar in the U.S., cited a report from Moscow of 9 January in which a second former KGB official said "officially" that he alone and not Kalugin participated personally in a unique interview with U.S. POWs and that this interview took place in January 1973 when U.S. forces were still in Vietnam, and not 1978. The broadcast recounted foreign press speculation suggesting that Kalugin sought to interrupt the trend toward normalization:

> In order to avoid isolation, while nearly all allied countries have normalized their relations with Vietnam, the press and other mass media have diffused sensational news about the so-called evidence of U.S. POWs still living in Vietnam. The FRG "Stade" concluded that Kalugin has disclosed more sensational news in order to turn Vietnam into a United States domestic policy issue in its presidential election and to make U.S. authorities postpone the process of normalizing U.S.-Vietnam relations, at least until after the elections. If so, it is however certainly too late, and then the Vietnam cake is divided up for all countries in the world except the United States.

The official Vietnamese government statement was even more terse: "The constant repetition of Kalugin-type statements is a typical act of those who want to exploit the sufferings of the American people to serve their dark, personal, evil schemes. Following the signing of the Paris agreement in 1973, the Vietnamese Government has handed over to the U.S. Government all the American POWs captured during the war."[3]

A 15 January radio commentary noted that the U.S. State Department had "decided to put an end to investigation" into the reports that American prisoners were being held in the former Soviet Union, and the commentary underscored the extent to which General Secretary Do Muoi's commitment to an "open door policy advocating friendship with all countries irrespective of political system" had improved the atmosphere and POW/MIA cooperation between Washington and Hanoi. The commentary repeated the litany regarding Vietnam's repatriation of over 500 sets of remains, noted "positive steps" taken by the U.S., including the lifting of the ban on American tours to Vietnam and the rescinding of the 25-mile travel limit imposed on Vietnamese diplomats in New York. In addition, the commentator argued that a "broad section of public opinion in the United States" and "other parts of the world" called for lifting the embargo and normalization of relations "in conformity with the common trend for peace, cooperation and development."[4] Another commentary, broadcast on 16 January, criticized the "people who still cling to an outdated hostile policy toward Vietnam," who were responsible for the fabricated reports that Vietnam had shipped American POWs to the Soviet Union. On 20 January the VNOSMP issued a note to the U.S. POW/MIA office in Hanoi describing the results of an investigation which concluded that "there was no such thing as any interrogation of U.S. POWs by KGB officers after the U.S. troop withdrawal from Vietnam in 1973 or after the end of the war in 1975." The note stated:

> The investigation showed that there was only one contact between KGB personnel and an American prisoner of war by the name of Eugene Weaver. Weaver was captured by Vietnam in the city of Hue on 31 January 1968. Upon knowing that Weaver was a Russian-born American the Soviet side asked to meet him and the request was accepted by Vietnam. In January 1973 the KGB officer Oleg Nechiporenko met Weaver only once because of the latter's refusal of another contact. In March 1973 the Vietnamese side returned Mr. Weaver to the U.S. side.[5]

On 20 January the party's daily newspaper stated in strong and direct language that the "U.S. Government and Congress should stop using the MIA issue for political purposes and [as] an obstacle to the process of normalizing relations between the two countries" and sharply criticized "some circles" in the U.S. that continued "their outmoded policy," utilizing the MIA issue to disrupt progress toward normalization. The article, which was summarized in at least two separate radio broadcasts, urged the U.S. government and Congress to "make the American people understand the truth about the MIA issue and be vigilant of allegations." In addition the article stated: "They should take measures to prevent and punish those who make profit of the sufferings of American families. The best way for the U.S. is to promote the process of normalizing relations and to put an early end to the MIA issue. This will surely meet the aspirations and interest of the peoples of both countries."[6]

Vessey returned to Vietnam in late January 1992 accompanied by the newly appointed deputy assistant secretary of defense for POW/MIA affairs and the U.S. Pacific Command–based Joint Task Force Full Accounting (JTFFA) leadership that had been placed in charge of investigating discrepancy cases and last-known-alive cases on a full-time basis, utilizing significantly expanded personnel organized into task force detachments in Bangkok, Hanoi, Vientiane, and Phnom Penh. Vessey met Cam on 30 January. For the first time since the appointment of the presidential emissary in 1987, a vice minister of defense and a senior Ministry of Interior official joined the foreign minister at the negotiating table and the minister of defense received General Vessey following the plenary discussions. Vessey asked Cam for agreement to provide rapid access to information on missing U.S. personnel contained in documents from central archives and military region depositories. He asked Cam to assist in defining a credible procedure for investigating reports of live Americans in captive situations to commit to increased efforts to recover and repatriate remains. He also asked Cam to permit increased joint activities, including preparatory research efforts, technical meetings and longer field investigations and excavations involving larger U.S. teams.

The Vietnamese agreed to strengthen existing mechanisms designed to facilitate access to information on missing Americans and to continue cooperation to resolve problems that hindered forward progress. They accepted the U.S. proposals to field larger teams of field investigators for longer periods with greater frequency, undertake advanced archival research in a more systematic manner, increase the frequency of technical meetings, and enlarge the scope of field operations to include investigations of loss incidents and grave and crash sites beyond discrepancy cases. Additionally, the Vietnamese reviewed the results of the investigations of the 119 discrepancy cases which the U.S. and Vietnam had given investigative priority since 1988 and agreed to hold meetings at the experts level to discuss ways to accelerate resolution of the cases and bridge differences over evidence pertaining to individual discrepancy cases.

In response to Foreign Minister Cam's October 1991 request for a review of the progress made toward resolving the 119 discrepancy cases, Vessey told Cam that in 61 cases, the death of the individual had been confirmed. Seventeen sets of remains had been unilaterally returned by the Vietnamese, and 5 were jointly recovered, resulting in the identification of 22 individuals. Vessey reaffirmed that in 35 cases where death had been confirmed the U.S. was convinced that remains could still be recovered. Vessey told Cam that in 4 other cases the U.S. concluded that the recovery of remains was unlikely, and in 16 other cases the U.S. government analysis was that recovery of remains was possible. In 19 cases in which death had been confirmed, the U.S. judgment was that further joint investigative efforts were required. In 58 of the original 119 cases, fate was still a question. Vessey made the point that the best hope for resolving these cases was through information contained in wartime archives. Additionally, Vessey noted that after another intensive internal review of files, the U.S. had identified 64 additional cases in which analysis of available information indicated that the individual survived the loss incident and might have come into Vietnamese custody and identified 13 additional wartime cases which were listed as POWs not released in 1973 but which had not been included in the original discrepancy case lists provided to the Vietnamese. Vessey told Cam that the U.S. ascribed the same high priority to the additional 77 cases that it placed on the last-known-alive discrepancy cases.

The Vietnamese balked at the presentation of additional cases and strongly reiterated their own view that confirmation of death was sufficient reason to describe a case as resolved. Cam restated the need to accord priority to the original 119 discrepancy cases, but indicated willingness to accept the additional 77 cases as a second group of priority cases. He noted that according to the Vietnamese assessment, 112 of the original group of individuals had died. In 20 cases, remains had been recovered and identified. In 7 cases, remains that were uncovered required further analysis before they could be positively identified and associated with a particular case. In 33 cases, remains could not be recovered, in 51 cases no further search for remains should be required, and in 7 cases there was not enough information to justify further work. In none of the cases, Cam emphasized, was there any indication that the individual involved was still alive. The Vietnamese were hard pressed to abandon their assessment of the results of 15 joint field investigations. However, they were amenable to a joint review of the differing assessments and agreed to put aside their own discrepancy case arithmetic in exchange for working-level discussions that might identify common ground on difficult cases.

The Vietnamese provided Vessey with a copy of an 84-page reference document drawn from archival information that listed downings of American pilots in Military Region 4. The document itself was not an archival item. It was not retrieved from a formal government or military collection, but was a reference document ("tai lieu tham khao"), a summary of air defense actions in MR 4 (Nhat Ky Tac Chien Phong Khong, Quan Khu 4). As such, it represented something one or two steps removed from archival material that was compiled from original sources and after-action reports that were themselves probably closely controlled archival documents. Importantly, the MR4 document was neither controlled nor classified. The Vietnamese facsimile did not bear any indication that classifications or controls had been blotted out in copying the document.

The U.S. government had sought access to this document beginning in mid–1991, when Vietnamese specialists gave U.S. investigators 12 pages of the document during a joint field operation. Those 12 pages provided information relevant to unresolved cases of missing Americans and gave Washington reason to believe that information bearing on additional cases might be contained in the remainder of the document. During 1991 the U.S. government repeatedly urged the Vietnamese to give the Hanoi POW/MIA Office access to the entire original document. General Vessey raised this point in his October 1991 meeting with Nguyen Manh Cam. Assistant Secretary Solomon discussed this matter during the 21 November meeting in New York with Le Mai. In late 1991, the U.S. specialists assigned to the joint research project in coordination with the 15th iteration of joint activities were provided access to a summary of a portion of the 84-page document from MR 4 records. At that point, the Vietnamese information researchers assigned to participate in the 15th joint activities made it clear that they were not authorized to offer more than a synthesis of the pages that had not yet been provided to the U.S. specialists. The U.S. expressed the view that access to the entire document would enable researchers to undertake correlations that did not emerge in the synthesis and summaries which the Vietnamese side had consented to make available. Finally, the U.S. made it clear that following through on the promise to make such information available to the U.S. was a good way of demonstrating Vietnam's serious intent to cooperate, to provide access to information, and to move quickly toward resolving cases. In December 1991 the Vietnamese technicians, experts and local officials demurred when it came to granting access to a military region document promised by a vice minister. The Vietnamese working-level team went to elaborate lengths to suggest it was prepared to be helpful in formulating an approach to the highest levels, where this question had to be answered, but it cautioned that the highest levels were not likely to want to address this question. This was a matter that the Vietnamese clearly sought to contain at the working level.

The Vietnamese were less than forthcoming on the question of exactly what resources might be available in archives that could be of assistance to U.S. efforts to resolve cases. While Vietnamese researchers made the case that exhaustive searches in dozens of provinces revealed no holdings and no documents, U.S. joint teams in MR 4 discovered another document relevant to Haiphong downings. Clearly, through late 1991, the military remained uncomfortable with the promises made by the Foreign Ministry regarding access to wartime archival information. The problem was that though the U.S. government had Foreign Ministery–level agreement to pursue cooperation in the area of wartime records, the Foreign Ministry was obviously functioning in a very different institutional circumstance in which the "national security" bloc, following the Seventh National Party Congress, could easily outvote the Foreign Ministry, and the Foreign Ministry itself was without Politburo-level influence.

By late January 1992, Defense, Foreign Affairs, and the Interior Ministry had arrived at a more stable modus vivendi and had come to the decision, under the auspices of Do Muoi, the general secretary of the Vietnamese Communist Party, that the MIA issue must be rapidly resolved in order to clear the path for normalization. Foreign Minister Cam gave the 84-page document to General Vessey during a private meeting following a call on the defense minister in January 1992. However, though the three ministries achieved some agreement on a course that would allow more rapid progress toward the resolution of the MIA issue in early 1992, the Foreign Ministry proponents of a quick and clean normalization with the U.S. continued to disagree with those who were less inclined to comply with Washington's requests for rapid progress on the MIA issue. In January, Foreign Minister Cam made it clear to Vessey how hard it would be to move beyond the current level of activity and how difficult it would be to obtain military—and popular—support for granting access to documents and archival materials.

In response to Vessey's request, the Vietnamese designated a Ministry of Interior official as the point of contact for live-sighting investigations. That official would meet regularly with the U.S. POW/MIA Office in Hanoi to define an approach to investigations. However, the Vietnamese rejected any public announcement of an agreement to install a mechanism on the grounds that such a statement would be at odds with Hanoi's position that Vietnam did not hold any live prisoners. The Vietnamese also set the date for the next joint field operations, agreed in principle to attend a trilateral meeting with the U.S. that would focus on investigating cases along the Ho Chi Minh Trail, in Lao territory that was under the wartime control of the Vietnamese People's Army, and on the Vietnamese-Cambodian border.

The Vietnamese made it clear that they wanted an assistant secretary to travel to Vietnam to discuss their humanitarian requirements and that it would be their preference to have Solomon and his counterpart, Le Mai, serve as the live-sighting investigators. While the latter demand might have been the result of a misunderstanding concerning Washington's interest in having live-sighting reports handled expeditiously and at an appropriate level, clearly the Vietnamese were looking for a unique visit at a sufficiently high level before they would agree to Washington's basic requests concerning information, remains repatriations, live-sighting investigations, and the 24-month plan for field investigations. Hanoi officials strongly rejected the accusation that they had custody of remains which they were withholding. It was clear, however, that there was agreement between the Foreign Ministry and the Ministry of Defense that there were things that could be done that would comply with American requests for information on wartime systems for transporting and collecting remains and on wartime information regarding the fates of Americans.[7]

The 1 February 1992 joint statement issued at the conclusion of the meeting did not characterize the session. A 7 February Vietnamese News Agency station commentary noted that there were "still numerous obstacles to friendly relations between the U.S. and Vietnam imposed by the U.S. The biggest of these concerns was the MIA [issue]." The commentary quoted General Secretary Do Muoi's view that "Vietnam had always shown its goodwill toward the U.S.," and in recent years had "cooperated with the U.S. to solve the humanitarian questions left behind by the war waged by the U.S. in South Vietnam." The commentary concluded that "public opinion in both Vietnam and the U.S. supports the lifting of the embargo against Vietnam and the normalization of U.S. relations with Vietnam in the interests of the two peoples and of peace, cooperation, and development throughout the world."[8] Several days later, in an interview conducted with foreign journalists, Foreign Minister Cam stated that he had told Vessey that Washington could improve efforts to account for missing U.S. service personnel by lifting the embargo, though Hanoi would continue to cooperate "with or without normalization" because of the humanitarian nature of the issue. Cam explicitly drew a connection between the pace of progress on accounting for MIAs and the scope of U.S. "attention to humanitarian aid in Vietnam" and argued that the lifting of the embargo, which was "abnormal and inhuman" and had "worsened the destruction wrought by the war," would have an immediate positive impact on the "atmosphere" in which Vietnam sought to cooperate with Washington on efforts to account for missing service personnel. Cam stressed that Washington's humanitarian efforts were not equivalent to Hanoi's attempts to resolve the MIA issue and "not proportional to the grave consequences of the economic embargo."[9] Cam reiterated these points in a press conference at the conclusion of a three-day state visit to Manila in the company of Prime Minister Vo Van Kiet.[10]

Vietnam showed its impatience in a 20 February Foreign Ministry statement which dismissed French television reports of 13 February concerning 72 Americans allegedly still detained by Vietnam. The Foreign Ministry spokesperson denounced this story as an "ill-intentioned act toward Vietnam" and an "irresponsible act toward the American people" and stood by the 1980 "White Book" on the MIA issue published by the Foreign Ministry, which stated that the 72 individuals who were stranded in southern Vietnam following the end of the war were not prisoners and had been returned to the U.S.[11] A 21 February station commentary, quoting a 19 December 1991 report from the Russian Federation's Ministry of Security to the effect that no archival evidence could be found that U.S. POWs had been sent to the Soviet Union, tersely dismissed these claims as "fabrications." The station commentary concluded that "any attempt to invent fabrications about, distort the truth or negate Vietnam's goodwill with regard to the POW/MIA issue so as to obstruct the normalization of U.S.–SRV relations for personal gain will produce no results and will instead be condemned by the public."[12]

During late February the Vietnamese expressed concern over conflicting messages from the U.S. regarding the accomplishments of the Vessey visit.

A senior Vietnamese official stationed overseas stated that some members of the delegation that visited Hanoi in late January had publicly expressed their satisfaction with the achievements of the visit and emphasized the importance of Hanoi's decision to hand over the 84-page document, but others had disagreed and described the visit as unproductive and unsatisfactory, which left the Vietnamese perplexed. A senior Vietnamese Foreign Ministry official privately stated that within the SRV government there remained serious disagreements over how to conduct relations with the U.S. and how to respond to what they saw as infinitely escalating American demands for "cooperation" on the MIA issue. According to that official, while the Foreign Ministry seemed willing to go to great lengths to establish normal relations with the U.S., the Defense and Interior ministries regarded the Foreign Ministry's approach as tantamount to a surrender. For that reason, by early 1992, it had become very important to the Vietnamese to get something in return for further concessions on MIA cooperation.

In one sense, the long-standing argument that Hanoi needed an end to the embargo in order to obtain cooperation from the people concealed the real point: the pragmatists in Hanoi who were inclined to favor quick normalization with the U.S. required some gesture from Washington which could be used to strengthen their position in the internal debate over U.S.–Vietnamese relations. The view that the U.S. was making successively more intrusive demands of the Vietnamese was a serious one, not merely a VNOSMP argument used with great theatrical flourish to win leverage in negotiations with U.S. counterparts, according to a senior Vietnamese official. To a lot of Vietnamese, it appeared as though the U.S. was asking Vietnam to act like a defeated country, which prompted some to say that they would not seek normalization at any price. For example, during the last two years of his life, Le Duc Tho made it clear that Vietnam should not scramble in an embarrassing manner to reap the benefits of normalization. Rather, Vietnam should go about this process in a way that maximized its leverage, acknowledged that regional realities were most important to Vietnam, and recognized that normalization did not promise real and major dividends for which the Vietnamese should make major sacrifices.

Clearly, by early 1992, Vietnamese policymakers had decided that they did not need to do anything more than what they were already doing in the area of POW/MIA cooperation. Significant U.S. business pressure and congressional opposition to the U.S. government's Indochina policy would allow them to muddle through until the administration's hand was forced or a new administration was elected. In the Vietnamese view, the U.S. needed to decide whether it was serious about normalization. Vietnam intended to stick firmly to the position that lifting the embargo was the next logical step, and the U.S. needed to decide whether it was prepared to discuss POW/MIA issues and other humanitarian concerns in the context of a normal, proper relationship.

In response to Hanoi's desire that the next discussions concerning the humanitarian needs of Vietnam be conducted at the assistant secretary level, Richard Solomon traveled to Hanoi in early March for the first contact at that level since Assistant Secretary Paul Wolfowitz's 1986 visit to Hanoi. Solomon announced that the U.S. would provide about $1 million in additional prosthetics assistance, $1.5 million of new assistance for displaced children, and $250,000 worth of excess Veterans Administration equipment. The U.S. also agreed to conduct military-run Medical Care Projects (MEDCAPs) during POW/MIA field operations and announced Vietnam's eligibility for free transport for NGO-sponsored humanitarian assistance on a space-available basis aboard U.S. military aircraft directed to support POW/MIA efforts in Vietnam, in accordance with the provisions of the Denton Amendment. During Solomon's visit, the Vietnamese agreed to establish a mechanism for investigating live-sighting reports on short notice and actually conducted the first such investigation. Hanoi also agreed to expand access to wartime archival information that could be helpful in shedding light on the cases of missing Americans. Hanoi consented to a two-year plan to accelerate joint investigations and continued trilateral cooperation with Laos and Cambodia on the POW/MIA issue. Finally, the Vietnamese agreed to renew efforts to recover remains, and in response to a request made by General Vessey during his January visit, they agreed to share information on the system used during the war to move the remains of Americans from battlefields and crash sites to the hands of progressively more senior military and government echelons.[13]

By early 1992, then, the Vietnamese had agreed to the 24-month plan for resolving as many cases as possible according to an approach that placed a primacy on larger teams doing more intensive work over longer periods in agreed-upon regions. Hanoi had also agreed to establish and activate a live-sighting investigative method, to grant real access to archival information, and to take steps to provide the U.S. government with information that could help clarify the "remains" issue. In response to the initial implementation of these agreements and other encouraging trends indicating that Vietnam was intent on improving cooperation on the POW/MIA issue, Solomon told the Vietnamese that the U.S. government agreed to take additional "confidence-building measures" intended to "lead to additional and substantial improvement" in U.S.–Vietnamese relations.[14]

Hanoi, however, took a restrained view of the meetings. Deputy Foreign Minister Le Mai was quoted in media reports following the visit as having "welcomed" the results of the trip, and he acknowledged that the process of normalization had maintained its pace. This was a clear contrast to statements in January and February which indicated Vietnam's impatience with the lack of progress. Mai was also quoted as having described the U.S. humanitarian aid package as "modest in comparison with the great material needs of Vietnam" and not quite proportionate to Hanoi's efforts to comply with Washington's requirements regarding the POW/MIA issue.[15] A station commentary repeated these points and emphasized the need for "further action" in meeting Vietnam's humanitarian needs: "it is what happens next that will decide the true meaning of American aid." The Foreign Ministry took the familiar position that some of the things the Americans were requesting had important security implications which would make Vietnamese compliance impossible. Mai was quoted as having strongly criticized the embargo and Washington's efforts to prevent ASEAN "from helping Vietnam pay its debts to the International Monetary Fund and World Bank." At roughly the same time as Mai was making these remarks, Ambassador Trinh Xuan Lang was emphasizing Hanoi's points on the counter-productiveness of the embargo. During a trip to Washington in early March, he told reporters that "the U.S. embargo has not only caused difficulties for Vietnam, but also harmed U.S. businesses."[16] Nevertheless, Mai characterized what had been achieved during the Solomon visit as an important step forward and said that the meetings had been conducted with "sincerity."[17] Following the visit, the Vietnamese media accorded prominence to the short-notice live-sighting investigation that was jointly conducted in response to Solomon's request.[18] In late March, Vietnam's media described a technical meeting convened to evaluate the 16th joint field investigations and to plan the 17th field activities as having yielded positive results.[19] Hanoi media reports highlighted the 16th joint investigations, which resulted in the location of six sets of remains that were sent to the CILHI for further analysis and stressed Hanoi's "conscientious" efforts to implement the joint agreements on the POW/MIA issue.[20]

An unusually long article in the 7 April issue of the military's daily newspaper reiterated the customary basic points about Vietnam's dissatisfaction that the embargo remained in place and Vietnam's commitment to building a new relationship. The article stated that Vietnam had returned all remains and treated the POW issue as a humanitarian one, whereas the U.S. had politicized the issue with linkages that complicated forward progress. The article argued quite strongly that Vietnam was intent upon continuing its path to socialism in spite of "outside interference," including U.S. efforts to get Vietnam "to depart from this path."[21] At about the same time, a radio broadcast gave an account of a major effort by the Nghe An Province Military Command to repatriate the remains of over 8,000 People's Army casualties from burial grounds in three Lao provinces, a massive undertaking that had proceeded for eight years in a difficult, mountainous environment. This activity underscored the extent to which the army was central to efforts to locate grave sites and organize repatriations and was seriously committed to addressing Vietnam's own MIA problem.[22]

On 13 April 1992 the State Department announced that the U.S. would grant an exception to the economic embargo with Vietnam to allow telecommunications links with Vietnam to be established. On 29 April the State

Department announced that the U.S. government would lift all embargo restrictions on the activities of all nongovernmental humanitarian and nonprofit
organizations and simultaneously grant an exception to the economic embargo
with Vietnam to permit commercial sales to meet basic human needs. The U.S.
government position was that these decisions were taken in recognition of Vietnam's cooperation. However, though certain of the actions fell into Phase Two
of the Roadmap, Washington made it clear that it would be wrong to say that
Phase Two had begun because the U.S. government still expected more cooperation from Hanoi on the issue of U.S. remains and access to wartime archival
information on missing Americans.[23]

In an initial reaction, a Foreign Ministry spokesperson said that the U.S.
decisions were small steps in the right direction toward improving bilateral
relations.[24] Following the U.S. government announcement of the partial exceptions to the embargo on 29 April, a department-level Foreign Ministry
official stated privately that Vietnam had pursued this issue in its humanitarian
tradition and recognized its responsibilities to help the United States account
for its MIAs. He pointed out that Hanoi had asked the U.S. to lift the embargo, which it regarded as an act of hostility against Vietnam, and he noted
that the Vietnamese people were hard pressed to understand why their government needed to provide assistance to the U.S. POW/MIA effort when Vietnam's needs were ignored. Before the exceptions to the embargo were granted,
this official had taken a slightly lower-key approach to this issue. In the aftermath of the U.S. government policy change, the message was tightened in
what seemed to be a retreat to rhetoric that was favored in January, during the
Vessey visit and temporarily stowed during the Solomon trip in March.

In late April, the Senate Select Committee traveled to Vietnam for ex-
tensive discussions and met with General Secretary Do Muoi, who told the
senators that Vietnam would provide whatever help the U.S. government
requested and that Washington had only to be precise in its requests to elicit
a Vietnamese response.[25] The committee identified five areas of concern: (1)
continuing credible investigations of live sighting reports, (2) gaining improved access to wartime archives and records, (3) obtaining access to personnel
who served in the Vietnamese military, in particular PAVN personnel who
served in the system involved in taking American servicemen into custody during the war, (4) providing sufficient logistical support for joint field investigations, and (5) receiving Vietnamese assistance to eliminate the confusion
surrounding the "warehousing of remains" issue.[26] Upon its return from Vietnam, the committee defined resolution of the live-prisoner issue as the over-
riding priority and spoke of the matter of recovering remains as an activity that
could proceed as a long-term process. Individual members spoke of arriving at
closure on this issue by the end of 1992, in the event that cooperation regarding
the five areas of concern continued.[27] The Vietnamese media accounts of the
Senate Select Committee visit highlighted Do Muoi's statement and featured

Senator Kerry's remarks in which he stressed that quick results on the POW/MIA issue could lead to immediate normalization.[28]

In May, during the 17th joint field investigations, the U.S. team enjoyed significant cooperation in crash site investigations, obtained access to eyewitnesses to the capture of several U.S. servicemen, and conducted productive grave site excavations.[29] In early May, Le Mai told a delegation of businesspeople representing the American Chamber of Commerce in Hong Kong that Vietnam categorically rejected the position that Vietnam's cooperation in the implementation of the Paris Agreement on Cambodia should be an obstacle to forward movement toward bilateral normalization. Mai called for the complete end of the embargo and the immediate establishment of formal and proper relations as a means of encouraging continued cooperative efforts to account for missing American service personnel.[30] In late May, Vice Foreign Minister Tran Quang Co echoed these views in private statements to the effect that Hanoi wanted Washington to authorize U.S. businesspeople to travel to Hanoi to open offices, conduct meetings, and negotiate contracts that they would be able to execute when the embargo was finally lifted. According to Co, Hanoi also wanted Washington to cease efforts to persuade other nations to observe the terms of the embargo. Co met with Under Secretary of State Alan Kanter and Under Secretary of Defense Paul Wolfowitz on 26 May 1992. Both U.S. officials separately stressed the importance of access to wartime archives and information pertaining to missing U.S. service personnel, as well as the need for Vietnam to accelerate unilateral repatriations of remains. Co's message to his Washington interlocutors stressed Hanoi's desire to turn a new page in the U.S.–Vietnamese relationship and repeated the basic position on the embargo.[31] On 28 May the Vietnamese media highlighted the meeting with Secretary Kanter and reported the session with Secretary Wolfowitz, characterizing both meetings as frank exchanges of information. A 30 May transmission briefly covered a 28–30 May "specialists" meeting. In early June, Foreign Ministry officials privately stated that Hanoi intended to take some dramatic step in June to keep the momentum going on U.S.–Vietnamese dialogue.[32] Nevertheless, Hanoi's view in late May 1992 was that Washington's responses were important but not sufficient, given Vietnam's cooperation on the POW/MIA issue.[33]

Between June and October 1992, the Vietnamese continued to cooperate with efforts to work out the modalities of a live-sighting investigative process. The cooperation was not always altogether satisfactory to the U.S. government, however. At times, U.S. government efforts to expand the process and make provisions for short-notice investigations elicited strong and negative Vietnamese responses. For example, on 8 August, Trinh Xuan Lang, Vietnam's permanent representative to the United Nations, told *New York Times* reporter Barbara Crossette that the U.S. had made "excessive demands" of Hanoi in its efforts to account for U.S. MIAs. Lang suggested that Vietnamese officials had begun to believe that the ulterior motive for Washington's insistence on following through on live-sighting reports by visiting prison sites and archives was to actively collect intelligence on the internal situation in Vietnam.[34]

In mid–September, Vietnam reacted critically to Washington's decision to renew the embargo. Vietnamese media commentary stressed congressional and business opposition to the U.S. government's approach to the issue of U.S.–Vietnamese normalization, quoting testimony before two subcommittees of the House Foreign Affairs Committee. Vietnamese media reports highlighted Hanoi's "goodwill" toward the U.S. efforts aimed at resolving the POW/MIA issue. A 25 September broadcast quoted a string of prominent U.S. newspaper editorials, letters, and commentary criticizing the embargo and urging normalization as a means of obtaining a quick solution to the POW/MIA issue.[35] A 16 September commentary stated: "Vietnam's attitude is crystal-clear. We hope and are striving to normalize Vietnamese–U.S. relations. But we will not tolerate any pressure. The U.S. administration's decision to extend its trade embargo against Vietnam for another year shows a lack of goodwill and a move unsuitable to the present international situation."[36]

On the same day the media carried a feature on the downing of the first B-52 on 17 September 1967 by the 84th Battalion of the Ha Long Missile Unit, quoting the battalion political cadre, the spotters, their commanding officer, the battalion commander, and message traffic exchanged on the targeting and destruction of the U.S. aircraft, noting exact times during the five-minute interval between the spotting and the destruction of the aircraft.[37]

By the third quarter of the year, approximately 5,000 photographs of the wreckage of U.S. military aircraft, the bodies of American crewmen, Geneva Convention cards, dog tags, other identification cards, and personal weapons had been quietly provided to the U.S. government by an independent researcher who was combing the holdings of the Museum of the People's Army in Hanoi. According to a 28 October assessment by the Defense Intelligence Agency, 1,750 of the 4,785 photographs, were of particular interest. This number included wartime photographs of live POWs (272), casualties and body parts (63), crash sites and wreckage (710), identification cards (325), media reports (265), personal effects (105), and letters (10). The remaining photographs were duplicates or multiple photographs of the same items or remains. Of the 272 photographs of live Americans, approximately 173 depicted POWs who had been returned in 1973. Two photographs were of live POWs who had subsequently died and whose remains had been returned. In late October, two of the live POWs pictured had not yet been identified. Sixty-three photographs showed the bodies of 31 U.S. service personnel, 24 of which had been tentatively identified by late October. Five of those whose bodies had been identified were previously listed as MIA, 6 as KIA/BNR; 13 sets of the remains in the photographs had been returned. Seven of the casualties had not been identified by late October.[38]

The photographs were clearly from a systematic collection maintained by Vietnam's central army museum. The quantity, the annotations on the majority of photographs, and the sequential serial numbering system suggested that the military had a very deliberate standard operating procedure for making photographic records of the bodies of American military personnel and had intended to retain those records. The basic consistency of the items photographed in each instance indicated that PAVN had a rule or a procedure governing the manner in which dead American aircrew should be photographed and some process of routing the photographs to a repository.

It was not entirely clear whether the photographs were provided to the independent researcher as the result of a carefully orchestrated, centrally controlled initiative by the Vietnamese government; through an end run against the bureaucracy by the military, born of their frustration with a slow-moving policy controlled by entrenched interests in the Foreign Ministry; or by the independent, unauthorized efforts of an enterprising, low-level military officer who saw an opportunity to turn a profit in the context of increasingly freer market activities and ever-increasing economic need.

Throughout the 1980s and the early 1990s, access to central and provincial museums by U.S. teams engaged in joint field activities was controlled by the VNOSMP. Although U.S. joint team casualty resolution specialists were occasionally able to gain access to provincial and subprovincial tradition houses, U.S specialists were not granted systematic access to the holdings and records of the museums. The VNOSMP, which considered the question of access a policy matter requiring senior ministerial discretion, brokered access on a case-by-case basis with appropriate military authorities and determined the extent of the access to holdings that would be enjoyed by the U.S. specialists. Importantly, the central military museum operated under the authority of the Defense Ministry's General Political Directorate, which was also responsible for the management of a variety of subordinate institutes, including the PAVN documentary film archives and the Film Institute. It was unlikely that the leadership of the directorate retained such lax and loose oversight over its subordinates that the museum was able to function in an unsupervised and independent manner. According to Western observers familiar with the Defense Ministry, however, by the early 1990s military institutes and other military entities subordinate to directorates had, in at least certain instances, been instructed to begin to generate independent incomes and to become less dependent on directorate-level budgets and support. In this context, the museum may have entered into the relationship with the outside researcher as a potentially lucrative opportunity to become self-supporting.

Nevertheless, given standard operating procedures, the military museum would not have been allowed to operate in this manner without some senior-level guidance and supervision. By 1989 certain military museums had indeed made their libraries and collection catalogues available to foreign academics, but apparently under a rigorous set of rules and restrictions and close supervision, suggesting that the model for relationships with external researchers was already well established by 1992. Further, the museum took deliberate steps to formalize the relationship with the researcher in a manner that would result in a record of the relationship. The relationship between the museum and researcher did not emerge as a clandestine one. Nor did the relationship develop at the outset as the means by which Hanoi would signal its readiness to provide the U.S. with access to wartime records, although it may have been exploited to telegraph that readiness well after the researcher had begun work on the history-writing project that had been the cause for his approach to the museum.

The use of the independent researcher as a means of channeling photographs to the U.S. government may have emerged as a result of the institutional differences between the VNOSMP and the military over the question of wartime archives. The VNOSMP had responded to U.S. efforts to increase access to wartime documents and develop joint cooperation in archival research in a desultory manner as the result of a long-standing Vietnamese Foreign Ministry strategy intent on offering minimum concessions to the U.S. and prolonging negotiations over basic principles of humanitarian cooperation and technical approaches to uncovering information. The Foreign Ministry's hope was to wear down U.S. resolve and elicit from Washington increasingly significant concessions in return for minor POW/MIA cooperation. By early 1992 the military had become more directly involved in decisions concerning access to witnesses and wartime archives, and it quickly grew concerned with certain aspects of the manner in which the POW/MIA issue had been managed under Nguyen Co Thach, including the authority of the Foreign Ministry–controlled VNOSMP over issues such as archival access in which the military had significant interests. The military leadership seemed somewhat impatient with the VNOSMP approach and by early 1992 had concluded that Vietnam's interests could be more effectively served by providing answers to questions concerning wartime processes for collecting and storing remains and granting controlled access to wartime archives.[39]

On 8 October 1992, during his visit to New York for the United Nations General Assembly session, Foreign Minister Cam was invited to Washington for talks with Secretary of State Lawrence Eagleburger and Defense Secretary Richard Cheney, who told him that the U.S. government had obtained copies of 5,000 photographs of American casualties from an official Vietnamese repository and that Washington required direct and systematic access to the entire collection of photographs and to any other similar documentation that would assist in resolving the cases of missing American service personnel. According to at least one account, Cam reacted with surprise and chagrin and reiterated his country's basic commitments to handling this issue as a humanitarian matter.

Shortly after that meeting, Hanoi agreed to receive General Vessey and to determine the means by which the photographs and other identification media would be made accessible to U.S. specialists. Just days before Cam's meeting in Washington, the Vietnamese media carried a terse summary of a 3 October Voice of America interview with the foreign minister, which stressed that the Vietnamese government had handed over all prisoners to the U.S. government after the war and pursued a policy that sought normalization without preconditions. Two days after the meeting in Washington, the Vietnamese media acknowledged the meeting with a brief report that "the two sides exchanged views on the prospects for establishing normal relations between the two countries, and on the settlement of issues of common concern, particularly the POW/MIA and Vietnam's humanitarian issues."[40]

Following an early October meeting in Hawaii between VNOSMP and JTFFA officials, Vessey visited Hanoi during 17 to 19 October in the company of Senator John McCain, a member of the Senate Select Committee on POW/MIA Affairs, and representatives of the IAG. Prime Minister Vo Van Kiet, Defense Minister Doan Khue, Foreign Minister Cam, Vice Foreign Minister Le Mai and senior foreign, interior, and defense ministry personnel met with the U.S. delegation. Hanoi had clearly decided to respond to the situation with candor. In a reversal of the customary protocol, the Vietnamese insisted that a private meeting between Vessey and Cam precede the usual plenary session and preemptively announced at the first session their intention to cooperate by providing access to the photographs, by scouring wartime archives for relevant documents, and by collecting the documentation in the central military museum, where it would be made available to U.S. specialists. The Vietnamese told Vessey that they had been "conducting a country-wide search of all archives for documents, photographs and other materials related to American POW/MIA cases" and that the material uncovered by the searches would be forwarded to Hanoi's military museum. The joint statement at the end of the visit by Vessey, which the Vietnamese broadcast on 19 October, noted that "the two sides agreed that a joint information research team should be formed to examine all the materials collected." The statement indicated that the team had already begun to work and had provided important information on MIA cases to the U.S., some of which was reviewed by Vessey during a visit to the central military museum. According to the joint statement, "the two sides also agreed on the importance of using this new archival information to seek the prompt and early recovery, and repatriation of remains of U.S. personnel." The statement also acknowledged that the mechanism for investigating live-sighting reports had performed in a satisfactory manner and that the accelerated pace of joint field investigations, which accorded priority to resolving the remaining last-known-alive discrepancy cases, had "already resulted in important information on specific MIA cases being provided to the U.S." The joint statement highlighted the mutual interest in rapid strides toward normalization of relations "in the context of accelerated cooperation to resolve the MIA issue" and summarized new steps by Washington to address Vietnam's humanitarian needs.[41]

Vessey briefed the president on the results of the mission to Hanoi on 23 October 1992. According to one account, President Bush reflected the view that the U.S. government should examine ways to move forward on this issue. In a Rose Garden press statement following the meeting, President Bush reaffirmed the importance of the Roadmap, noted the mutual importance of moving rapidly toward normalization of relations, and pointed out that Hanoi's agreement to provide access to documents, photographs, and personal effects of U.S. service personnel would lead to a review of American policy toward Vietnam. "Today," he declared, "finally, I am convinced that we can begin writing the last chapter of the Vietnam war."[42] The Vietnamese press acknowledged President Bush's remarks in a low-key fashion, stating that if the U.S. government's determination to move forward was true, and if President Bush's remarks that the last chapter of the war could now be written, then it would be "beneficial to both sides."[43] On 4 November, the day after the U.S. presidential election, Deputy Prime Minister Phan Van Khai told a press conference in Hong Kong that Vietnam was "ready to build relations with the United States on the basis of equality, mutual respect and reciprocal interest."[44]

In the weeks following General Vessey's visit, the Vietnamese agreed to establish three joint teams that would operate out of the military museums in Hanoi, Da Nang, and Ho Chi Minh City. According to the agreement worked out by the deputy director of the Foreign Ministry's Americas Department and the commander of the JTFFA, the Vietnamese specialists attached to the teams were to search relevant archival holdings of the Ministry of Defense to identify information bearing on unaccounted for Americans and were to make those records available to the U.S. specialists via the museum-based joint research teams. The Defense Ministry's General Political Department, which retained authority over the archives of military units, branches, and Defense Ministry departments, designated the director of the army museum as the executive authority for the research activities. The first joint team began its activities at the army museum in Hanoi on 2 November 1992. The second joint team began to operate out of the Military Region Five museum in Da Nang in early December. The third team commenced activities in early January 1993 in Ho Chi Minh City. Additionally, the Vietnamese committed to establishing unilateral teams at the Armed Forces museum and the Air Defense museum in Hanoi, the Military Region Four museum in Vinh City, the Military Region Five museum in Da Nang, the Military Region Seven museum in Ho Chi Minh City, and the Military Region Nine museum in Can Tho. Those teams were to search the archives of main force units and commands, as well as regional and provincial commands, for information bearing on U.S. MIAs.[45]

Hanoi did not react publicly and officially to the flurry of activity in the wake of the agreement to establish archival research teams. Privately, Vietnamese officials associated with the effort to organize archival research took the position that Vietnam had sought to be helpful by making museum holdings available to U.S. government specialists several years prior to the 1992 agreements, but that U.S. officials were not interested in that access and instead pressed for access to the repositories of military units, commands, and regions. Le Van Bang, then director of the Americas Department, told reporters that the Department of Defense had rejected access to the material in the museums, choosing instead to conduct investigations on a case-by-case basis. Bang claimed that the material had always been available to U.S. specialists and that Hanoi was not hiding anything.[46] Through early December, Vietnamese middle-level officials and specialists privately made the case that they did not realize the importance and value of the photographs and artifacts in the museum and that for the most part Vietnamese officials were unaware of what was in the various central and provincial museums, which were generally large, sprawling, and uninventoried holdings. Vietnamese specialists privately stated that much of the identification media, personal effects, and aircraft artifacts to which the U.S. had requested access following the Vessey visit were actually in private hands, in the homes of peasants or in the possession of retired veterans, civilian government officials, or their families. As such, those materials were beyond the reach of the central government, and it would take extraordinary acts of goodwill to prompt a nationwide effort to turn those items into officials in a systematic manner. The records were incomplete, a consequence of wartime circumstances that often intervened to prevent compliance with centrally articulated regulations requiring written reporting on wartime incidents and field burials involving U.S. soldiers killed in action. Finally, Vietnamese officials privately claimed that the U.S. had consistently emphasized the issue of live Americans and downplayed the importance of accounting for KIA/BNR servicemen via artifacts, personal effects, and identification media of the sort lodged in the museum and tradition house collections.[47]

The disingenuous character of Vietnamese statements on this subject was in large part a function on Hanoi's nervous preoccupation with the possibility that the U.S. public's response to the photographs might set normalization back another decade, expose Hanoi to criticism for wartime barbarism and postwar inhumanity, and open the way for serious attacks of Hanoi's management of the POW/MIA issue. Hanoi was aware that any combination would blunt the meaning and practical impact of Hanoi's decision to be forthcoming and cooperative about missing Americans. U.S. assurances that Washington did not intend to launch a "witch-hunt" did not go far toward convincing Hanoi that it would not be punished for the wartime past, pilloried in the Western press, or denounced by the American public for revelations concerning battlefield procedures.

Hanoi's statements regarding its long-standing willingness to comply with requests for information in its museum holdings were also, in part, the result of a slightly overplayed role as the willing, compliant negotiating partner. Hanoi was confident that well-timed concessions to Washington could only reinforce its appearance as the reasonable, accommodating partner in the POW/MIA negotiations, an appearance which would be used by congressional supporters of an early, rapid normalization to pry a change in position from the more cautious administration.[48] The image of Vietnamese military officers turning over diaries, documents, and personal effects to the visiting U.S. senators during a mid–November visit to Hanoi by members of the Senate Select Committee was compelling and effective in media terms. Ultimately, these images left the U.S. government to explain why Washington was not able to elicit this cooperation years in advance of the 1992 breakthrough. The public debate that emerged in late November–early December in the United States, in part as the result of the last days of the Senate Select Committee hearings, did not focus on Vietnamese behavior, but rather fixed on Washington's approach to the issue and the effectiveness of efforts to sustain Vietnamese cooperation by using pressure and the embargo.[49]

During the course of the mid–November visit to Hanoi by the Senate Select Committee, Vietnam "reaffirmed its consistent policy" in very familiar terms, showcased the cooperation and the bilateral agreements regarding the POW/MIA issue that had emerged in October and November, and committed to solving the issue and helping to alleviate the suffering of MIA families. In this context the senior-most leadership of the Vietnamese government stressed that early normalization "conforms to the interests of stability and development in the region and the world over." President Le Duc Anh acknowledged a letter from President Bush conveyed by Senator Kerry in which Bush "expressed his wish to promote cooperation in the coming time" and affirmed the U.S. government's commitments to accelerate the normalization process. Media accounts noted that Anh asked Kerry to "convey his thanks" to President Bush and to express appreciation for recent U.S. government humanitarian assistance. Prime Minister Vo Van Kiet assured the visiting senators of Hanoi's cooperation and "recommended that both sides should show their positive attitude, look forward, and help each other on solving humanitarian issues." Hanoi refrained from characterizing the visit of the Select Committee and broadcast the entire press statement by Senator Kerry at the end of the visit. Several media commentaries that followed the visit spoke glowingly of the goodwill of the senators and repeated Kerry's endorsement of continued easing of embargo-imposed restrictions by the U.S. government.

In late November–early December, Vietnamese diplomats and officials posted abroad were privately expressing dismay over the U.S. government's hesitancy to move forward by lifting the embargo. According to NGO officials with direct knowledge of Hanoi's views, Vietnamese officials were preoccupied with developing the groundwork for relationships with American businesses and apparently assumed that the U.S. government would at least drift toward the view that Hanoi had taken significant steps forward which required reciprocal actions on Washington's part. These Vietnamese officials regarded the spectacle of the Senate Select Committee hearings as a ritual having more to do with internal U.S. politics than with bilateral U.S.–Vietnamese relations. They were not overly concerned with the views that were expressed by the senators and witnesses and believed that the Senate Select Committee's final report would reflect domestic debates over historical decisions to a greater degree and would not have a strong impact on the process of U.S.–Vietnamese normalization. These diplomats and their colleagues in Hanoi had quite clearly concluded that the United States could not adhere to its hard-line position in the face of unambiguously changing regional, international, and bilateral circumstances.

In early December 1992, the Vietnamese privately made it clear that half-steps toward the lifting of the embargo would not be helpful. A senior Foreign Ministry official privately stated that it would not suffice for the U.S. to permit businesspeople to agree to contracts that would be executed following the lifting of the embargo and to lift the restrictions in the embargo that prohibit such activities. Hanoi also wanted the U.S. to agree to "work cooperatively with other countries on a program to help Vietnam eliminate its arrears in the IMF." Interestingly, according to the senior Foreign Ministry official, at the same time the Vietnamese Foreign Ministry quietly designated Le Van Bang, the director of the Foreign Ministry's Americas Department, as the ambassador to the United States in anticipation of normalization. Bang was scheduled to travel to New York in early December, where he would serve alongside the incumbent permanent representative to the United Nations, Trinh Xuan Lang, until such time as the U.S. moved into Phase Four. Lang was to return to Hanoi in May 1993 and retire from the foreign service. Beginning in January, Bang was to have the rank of ambassador. Bang rose to an important department-level position following the Seventh National Party Congress, along with a clutch of others, including Nguyen Xuan Phong, who was to take Bang's place as the Americas Department head in January. Bang, who had spent three months in Washington in late 1991 as a guest of the International Center for Development Policy, was close to Le Mai. Lang, on the other hand, was part of the old guard who owed their positions to the former Foreign Minister and represented the more conservative strains in the Vietnamese foreign policy establishment.

In early December 1992, in a clear response to one of Senator Kerry's main points, the VNOSMP issued a communiqué in which it requested that "all those possessing remains or having information about remains believed to be those of U.S. personnel . . . notify or voluntarily hand them into local authorities." In a position intended to respond to recommendations by General Vessey and Senator McCain that the Vietnamese offer a blanket amnesty to bones traders who had obtained and concealed human remains in hopes of extracting a reward for their trouble, in violation of Vietnam's national law, the VNOSMP offered to reimburse "reasonable costs" for those who turned in remains that were found through "scientifically sound experiments" to be the remains of U.S. service personnel.[50] A quiet mid–December follow-up trip by senators Kerry and Smith emphasized to Hanoi the importance of taking some steps to provide reasonable explanations of the disposition of the remains of discrepancy cases, especially those individuals whose remains were clearly in Vietnamese control at the time of their deaths, as evidenced by the photographs.[51] Hanoi anticipated this visit with a ceremony repatriating 20 sets of remains, 3 of which had been turned in by Vietnamese citizens. The 17 other sets of remains were discovered during August and November 1992 by the joint teams working in northern and central Vietnam.

Smith may have extracted a somewhat expanded commitment from Hanoi to conduct live-sighting investigations, to search for information in Vietnamese files relating to pilots downed on the Ho Chi Minh Trail, on Lao territory, and to cooperate more closely with Laos to solve the border cases. Ambiguous statements in Western press reports suggested that the Vietnamese took stock of the progress toward completing the investigations of the 135 discrepancy cases. Finally, Le Duc Anh, Vietnam's president, and General Secretary Muoi reiterated the invitation to family members to come to Vietnam and see for themselves. The Smith-Kerry visit may have resulted in a narrowing of differences that facilitated the writing of one Senate Select Committee report without an explosive minority reclamor. Smith hailed the Vietnamese pledge to "further facilitate" live-sighting investigations as "one of the most significant of the visit." Smith seems to have pressed the Vietnamese to allow U.S. specialists to investigate all reports as they came in, rather than just those in the pipeline or those judged to have merit according to undefined Vietnamese standards of evidence. Hanoi appeared to have moved away from the position the VNOSMP took in late 1991 and early 1992 to the effect that the U.S. should provide the Vietnamese with synopses of candidate live-sighting cases for investigation, a step made easier by the fact that the key backers of the more conservative positions, such as Trinh Xuan Lang, were on their way to retirement.[52]

On 14 December 1992, the White House announced that the U.S. government would begin to permit U.S. firms to sign contracts to be executed when the embargo was lifted. To facilitate this step, the White House announced the U.S. government would begin implementing a further exception to the embargo that would establish a liberal licensing policy to permit U.S. firms to open offices in Vietnam, hire staffs, write and design plans, and carry out preliminary feasibility studies and engineering and technical surveys. The Vietnamese reacted to the White House announcement in a 15 December Foreign Ministry statement which pointed out that though it was positive, this step fell short of "creating favorable conditions" for U.S. companies to engage in business in the Vietnamese market. Vietnamese companies, the spokesperson pointed out, indicated that they would still find it difficult to "have real relations" with American companies under circumstances that mandated deferring the execution of contracts. The Foreign Ministry statement studiously avoided drawing a link between progress on the POW/MIA issue and further steps toward normalization. Departing from the usual formulaic expressions, the Vietnamese emphasized the mutual economic and business advantages of taking further steps that would allow U.S. businesses to "truly engage in business" in Vietnam.[53]

The Vietnamese efforts to cooperate by agreeing to systematic joint research of the holdings of central, regional, and provincial wartime repositories reflected the fact that a new decision-making team was in place in Hanoi and was functioning under new rules and perceptions governing foreign policy decision-making. The new leadership was inclined to be more cooperative, less Byzantine, and less confrontational about U.S. POW/MIA requirements as spelled out in the Roadmap. They had begun to dismantle the policies of the Sixth Party Congress and to reorganize their handling of the POW/MIA issue. Under Foreign Minister Nguyen Manh Cam, the Council of Ministers began to take responsibility for POW/MIA decisions. Deputy foreign ministers played a more active role in Foreign Ministry POW/MIA efforts. The provincial work groups were given a clear and significant high-level chain of command instead of being allowed to exist as ad hoc entities. In early 1992 the leadership of the People's Army became directly involved in decisions concerning access to witnesses and wartime archives. Finally, an important consensus had developed between General Secretary Do Muoi, who was more directly involved in foreign policy than his predecessor, and the new president, Le Duc Anh. Both agreed that the POW/MIA issue could and should be rapidly resolved. Hanoi felt stymied, however, by what it interpreted as U.S. intransigence regarding the embargo.

According to a middle-level Foreign Ministry official, Hanoi's analysis toward the end of the Bush administration was that the U.S. government had made it clear that Washington would move forward only if Vietnam could produce remains. The Vietnamese argued, however, that there were no remains to produce. More than a dozen sets had been repatriated at the end of the 20th or 21st joint field investigations. The official argued that if Hanoi had remains, this would have been an ideal time to produce them. In the end, Bush's promises and his letter to Le Duc Anh merely frustrated the senior Vietnamese leadership, without advancing the process. The Vietnamese Foreign Ministry could never satisfactorily explain to the Politburo why the Americans had veered from the path defined by their own Roadmap, why Phase Two did not begin with the signing of the Paris Agreement on Cambodia, and why the Roadmap did not end with the UNTAC-supervised election in Cambodia. Vietnam had resisted linking progress in bilateral relations with the process of implementing the Paris Peace agreement in Cambodia because Hanoi believed it did not have the ability to influence Hun Sen's government, but once the Roadmap was defined as the U.S. government approach, Hanoi at least expected that Washington would stick with the path it defined.

CHAPTER SIX

POW/MIA Issues and the Trudge Toward Normalization, 1993–1994

Following the 20 January 1993 inauguration of President Bill Clinton, the Vietnamese expressed serious concern over the prospects that the new administration would either launch a prolonged reevaluation of POW/MIA policy and thereby allow a suspension of activities to take place or take a strong position requiring a "full accounting" or a thorough reexamination of each and every case that would lead to the unraveling of cooperation. In response to a 22 January statement by the deputy secretary of state which noted that the new administration would adhere to the same "conditions" for normalizing relations with Vietnam that had guided President Bush's policy, on 25 January the Foreign Ministry reiterated Vietnam's willingness to normalize based on mutual respect, equality, mutual interest, and noninterference and restated the 1987 agreement to cooperate on the "purely humanitarian" POW/MIA issue. Normalization, in the words of the Foreign Ministry spokesperson, would "serve peace and stability in Southeast Asia and the whole world." "No strings" should be attached to normalization.[1]

A 30 January broadcast emphasized the view that Washington was unfairly imposing preconditions for normalization. The broadcast cited the Senate Select Committee report and the words of its chairman to reinforce the message that Hanoi had extended "full cooperation." The broadcast criticized the views of "hardline officials" in the U.S. government who "deliberately refused to accept this fact, and continued to see the POW/MIA issue as a price to be paid, and have set conditions to link it to the normalization of relations with Vietnam." The commentary was caustic and critical of the new president's position on the issue and went beyond the ministry's generally more neutral expressions of commitment to treating the POW/MIA issue in a humanitarian manner. In Hanoi's perception, the additional conditions Washington had set for normalization and the president's decision to delay normalization aroused "indignation" in the United States and the world: "The relatively tough stance adopted by the U.S. government toward U.S.–Vietnamese relations and even in international relations has caused erosion of U.S. public confidence in the Clinton Administration's handling of its foreign policy."[2]

According to a middle-level Foreign Ministry official, Clinton's failure to lift the embargo quickly was a great source of frustration for the Foreign Ministry and the senior-most leadership of Vietnam. The Politburo was concerned because there was no real acknowledgment from the new administration in Washington that the process was working effectively. Finally, the Foreign Ministry and senior leaders were concerned that by early January there had not yet been an authoritative pronouncement on the Soviet document. The Americans, the official argued, knew exactly what it represented: it was a forgery. Failure to say that in a public assessment compounded the frustration in Hanoi.

According to a senior Vietnamese government adviser, through late January Hanoi was confused about initiatives required to convince the new U.S. administration to pick up where things had left off rather than starting anew in a direction that might spoil the momentum. Further, Hanoi's inner policy circle was not certain how to go about convincing the new U.S. government and the American people that Vietnam was interested in taking any and all steps necessary to resolve the POW/MIA issue on terms that complied with the U.S. requirements for the fullest possible accounting. Senior Central Committee advisers had given thought to an appropriate response to the Senate Select Committee report, and by late January they seemed to have accepted the alternative of refraining from reacting to what they viewed as a clear cut U.S. domestic issue. Early in January the Central Committee advisers seemed prepared to recommend that Hanoi take a low-key position that reflected its earnest desire to accomplish the task of cooperating with Washington rather than reverting to standard rhetoric that highlighted Vietnam's humanitarian approach to the issue. Key Vietnamese Politburo officials responsible for the POW/MIA issue understood that the remains issue continued to loom as a potential problem. It appeared to senior Central Committee advisers that the Vietnamese had done all they could on this matter, and they were befuddled about what else they needed to do to comply with Washington's requirements that the Vietnamese make progress in repatriating remains.

In its January 1993 monthly internal review, the General Political Department of the Ministry of Defense noted that according to the view from Washington, Vietnam had still not put forth sufficient effort and had not achieved "tangible results" on the POW/MIA problem. By then, both Bush and Clinton had emphasized the continued importance of actively pursuing the issue on behalf of the families of missing American service personnel. The General Political Department's assessment stated that the senior-most levels of the Vietnamese government had promised cooperation and had committed to fulfilling pledges made to the U.S. The assessment noted that Bush and Clinton both wanted "proof sufficient enough to suggest concentrated efforts to resolve approximately twenty cases which public opinion still doubted in order to reject the opposition of the families of missing Americans." The General Political Department's overview stated that the Vietnamese government, specifically the National Assembly, would continue to treat this issue as a humanitarian one, regardless of the U.S. party in power. Vietnam, the assessment concluded, had informed members of the U.S. Congress that Hanoi would continue to facilitate live-sighting investigations, strengthen the VNOSMP, encourage the search for and repatriation of remains of U.S. personnel, and invite the families of MIAs and American veterans to participate in the resolution of the MIA problem:

> America is now following the trend of abandoning the embargo and normalizing relations with Vietnam. This process is complex and will be lengthy. Relations between the U.S. and Vietnam will produce advantages for both sides. Parallel to this, Vietnam must be prepared for disagreeable aspects, complex problems requiring resolution, and many urgent tasks that must be solved. The Party must be unified regarding its awareness, opinions and actions before the developmental steps that are about to be taken in the relationship between Vietnam and the U.S.

The military, and perhaps veterans groups and others concerned with Vietnam's MIA problem, appeared prepared for a long period of inaction as Washington coped with the domestic dimensions of the normalization issue. Moreover, the Vietnamese military leadership anticipated that knotty bilateral problems would emerge to complicate progress toward normalization.[3]

In February 1993, Hanoi aired its frustration with Washington's approach to the issue, emphasized Vietnam's responsiveness to U.S. government requests for assistance, and stressed the importance of publicizing the results of specific investigations. Once again Hanoi underscored Vietnam's basic humanitarian record on the issue in the face of Washington's politicization of the POW/MIA problem. In early February, Tran Minh Bac, editor in chief of the Vietnam military veteran's journal, told the Fourth American-Vietnamese Dialogue, sponsored by the Aspen Institute, that in spite of the embargo, which hindered Vietnam's efforts to recover from the consequences of the war, and in spite of the lack of concern the U.S. had exhibited for Vietnam's own MIA problem, Hanoi actively searched for information and remains of American service personnel and continued to respond to U.S. proposals related to the MIA issue.[4] In early February the Foreign Ministry spokesperson stated that Hanoi had "repeatedly" asked Washington to reveal publicly the results of the investigation of the 135 priority MIA cases, arguing that the final U.S. assessment had shown that there was "no evidence" that Americans remained alive in Vietnam.[5] On 6 February, Hanoi publicized the results of the 3–4 February technical meeting, which reviewed the 135 priority cases and the live-sighting investigations, and reached agreement to begin the 22d joint field investigations in late February. On 8 February, Hanoi marked the repatriation of 14 sets of remains, bringing the total at that time to 516 sets repatriated on 40 occasions since March 1974, according to Vietnamese statistics. Washington emphasized that fewer than half of the repatriated remains had been identified as belonging to U.S. service personnel. From Washington's perspective, 45 sets of remains had been repatriated since the April 1991 presentation of the Roadmap. Fourteen sets had been returned as the result of unilateral Vietnamese activities and 31 as the result of joint field investigations, but only 3 of the 45 sets of remains had been identified as belonging to U.S. service personnel.[6] Several late–February Vietnamese media pieces urged normalization on the basis of economic opportunities that were being missed by U.S. businesses. An 18 February station commentary quoted French president François Mitterand's characterization of the U.S. embargo as an outmoded policy and Senator Larry Pressler's call for full diplomatic relations and cited recent visits to Vietnam by senior U.S. company representatives scouting for opportunities. A 21 February station commentary summarized Pressler's views, highlighting his call for "a new roadmap" that would chart a course toward full diplomatic relations, beginning with lifting the embargo.[7]

Toward the end of March, the Vietnamese permanent representative to the United Nations, Le Van Bang, and Deputy Foreign Minister Le Mai approached a variety of U.S.–based NGOs with the aim of eliciting their views concerning the U.S. government game plan for Vietnam. Representative to the United Nations Trinh Xuan Lang paid a farewell call on Assistant Secretary of State for East Asia William Clark and stressed Hanoi's intent to move forward.[8] Clearly, the Vietnamese were concerned with the failure of the Clinton administration to take an early and decisive step toward normalization. The Vietnamese side made it amply clear that they felt the U.S. government had ignored the substantial progress and significant cooperation that had led to the conclusion of the discrepancy case investigations, efforts to address the remains issue through an amnesty, and Vietnamese willingness to continue cooperation in the realm of joint field investigations and live-sighting investigations. Bang, Mai, and other senior Vietnamese officials told U.S. NGO officials that they were concerned with the prospects of yet another period of inaction caused by Washington's inability or unwillingness to give credit where credit was due, and with the U.S. government's failure to declare its intentions regarding normalization. Those Vietnamese officials argued that they would be in a weak position if they were to go back to the senior Foreign Ministry leadership with the argument that the Clinton administration would be able to act if Vietnam took several more "confidence building" steps. They feared that the argument that Hanoi needed to do slightly more to earn Washington's trust had dwindling resonance within the ranks of the senior Vietnamese policy-making leadership. The senior officials felt that they would be in a weakened position and would be unable to argue that normalization was near.

Toward the end of March, Hanoi stressed the results of live-sighting investigations conducted during the 22d Joint Field Investigation (22 February–23 March) that yielded "no evidence of living Americans left by the war in Vietnam." The investigations included excavations in the central highlands and continued efforts to locate wartime archives in the military museum in Hanoi which "threw light on the fate of many Americans reported missing in Vietnam," according to Vietnamese media reports. In late March, a special tribunal found two local officials from Quang Tri Province guilty of stealing government funds earmarked for the upgrading of a military cemetery; the officials had faked the graves of soldiers whose remains were to be located, disinterred, and reburied in a new cemetery at Dong Ha. Those two officials were given life sentences, and 44 others, including a commune police chief and the head of the local militia, were given 20-year prison terms.[9] Hanoi also gave prominence to late March statements by senators Claiborne Pell and Richard Lugar, quoting a letter to President Clinton in which the senators argued that a "process has been established for the resolution of the POW/MIA issue with Vietnam that has already produced substantial results and promises to produce even more progress over the coming years."[10]

Hanoi accorded a great deal of significance to the 1 April statement before the Senate Foreign Relations Committee by Winston Lord, assistant secretary of state for East Asia, who noted that the Clinton administration could make a rapid decision on establishing normal relations with Vietnam. Hanoi also paid attention to the early April visit to Vietnam by former secretary of state Edmund Muskie, who led a delegation from the Center for National Policy during 3–8 April which met with General Secretary Do Muoi and Foreign Minister Nguyen Manh Cam. Muskie told his hosts that the Clinton administration was "closely reviewing" the embargo policy. Hanoi's media also highlighted a bill submitted to Congress in early April by Senator Frank Murkowski urging the end to the embargo and an open letter to President Clinton from the U.S.–Vietnam Trade Council supporting the lifting of the embargo. Finally, Hanoi emphasized the extent to which support for the U.S. embargo from Washington's traditional friends and allies was withering away, citing statements by France's President Mitterand and Germany's Foreign Minister Klaus Kinkel. Hanoi took every opportunity to reiterate the importance of "normalization without preconditions" and to emphasize the mutual advantages of ending the embargo, which was, in the words of Foreign Minister Cam, causing American companies to lose ground to their foreign competitors.[11] On 6 April, Prime Minister Vo Van Kiet received the head of the JTFFA and reaffirmed Vietnam's commitment to cooperate in a humanitarian spirit with efforts to resolve the POW/MIA issue quickly. The Vietnamese News Agency summarized the 5–6 April technical session during which the JTFFA and the VNOSMP reviewed the work of the 22d joint field activities, agreed to the repatriation of 16 sets of remains that had been discovered during the field activities, and agreed to conduct the 23d field investigations beginning in late April in Central Vietnam.[12]

In early April 1993, President Clinton asked Presidential Emissary General John Vessey to travel to Vietnam to provide the Vietnamese with an assessment of the work conducted through the early part of 1993 on the discrepancy cases and to provide Hanoi with details of the U.S. government's requirements in four areas: joint investigations, remains repatriations, archival access, and tri-lateral activities regarding the Lao border cases.

In April an Australian academic undertaking research in Moscow archives gained access to a Soviet military intelligence document that contained pur-ported information indicating that in the early 1970s Vietnam held hundreds of more American POWs than U.S. intelligence reporting at the time had con-cluded were in Vietnamese custody. The Soviet military intelligence report was based on a document that was identified as a report to the Vietnamese Com-munist Party's Politburo by General Tran Van Quang. Prior to General Vessey's departure, the president instructed him to raise questions concerning the Soviet document with the Vietnamese.[13]

The Vietnamese were enraged by the public release of the Soviet docu-ment. They reacted by attacking the academic who discovered it and strongly criticizing the basic assertions contained in the text regarding the number of POWs held by Hanoi in late 1972.[14] Hanoi coupled the Soviet document with a string of other fabrications that had come to light in 1972 and concluded that an insidious invisible hand intent on halting progress toward normalization was at work. Vietnam was clearly concerned with the possibility that the revela-tion would derail progress and complicate meetings with General Vessey. In a somewhat more measured tone than that used to castigate its critics in the media, Hanoi officials sought to assure Washington that they were prepared to address the document. During the Foreign Ministry's 15 April routine press conference in Hanoi, the press and information department spokesperson dismissed the document and the accompanying speculation that Hanoi had killed 600 American prisoners as "shameless" fabrications and "an affront to the Vietnamese people who have made and are making great efforts to solve the MIA question in the humanitarian spirit." The spokesperson stated that sober-minded observers could see that the fabrications, including the Soviet document and the three photographs that had surfaced in 1992, were "in-tended to block the progress of Vietnam–U.S. relations." The meeting between General Vessey and Foreign Minister Cam, the spokesperson continued, would enable the emissary to "form objective observations and judgments comfort-able with the real situation."[15]

During 17–19 April, Vessey met with President Le Duc Anh, Foreign Min-ister Nguyen Manh Cam, Deputy Foreign Minister Le Mai, and Deputy Defense Minister Nguyen Thoi Bung in Hanoi. In the plenary session with Foreign Minister Cam, Vessey urged the Vietnamese to agree to further investigations of the remaining 92 discrepancy cases, to provide more information about the individuals on the DIC list received from the Provisional Revolutionary Government in 1973, and to provide information about those MIAs depicted in casualty photographs from Vietnamese archives. Vessey also asked the Vietnamese to help get the Lao to conduct trilateral activities to investigate the Lao border cases along the Ho Chi Minh Trail on Lao territory that was controlled by PAVN during the war. Vessey asked the Vietnamese to grant access to information regarding U.S. MIAs in the files of the General Political Department, Group 875 and Group 559; military region aircraft downing records and the source documents used to compile such references; Military Region Five records; Central Office for South Vietnam (COSVN) records; and sensitive files associated with interrogation, imprisonment, and treatment of U.S. POWs.

Cam gave Vessey six documents: seven separate records of discovery of the graves of American personnel in Quang Nam–Da Nang and sketch maps compiled during April–June 1978 (Phieu Phat Hien Mo Ma Nhan Vien Hoa Ky Va Nguoi Nuoc Ngoai Kem So Do); an undated and handwritten statistical summary of Vietnamese Peoples' Air Force combat engagements during 1965–72 (Thong Ke Chien Dau Cua Khong Quan Tu 1965–72); a roster of dead American forces and of foreign (German) civilians captured in the central region (Danh Sach Tu Binh My Chet Va Danh [Duc] Bi Bat Tai Mien Trung Bo); a report on the death of Frederick J. Burns containing a personal history and a report of causes of death (Bien Ban Ve Ten Tu Binh My Frederick J. Burns Chet, Ngay 02/01/68, So Yeu Ly Lich Va Bao Cao Ve Viec Ten Tu Binh My Frederick J. Burns); a 39-page handwritten ledger of 381 Americans and 5 Southeast Asian allies incarcerated in North Vietnam between 6 August 1964 and 17 February 1973; and a statistical report on American POWs killed in the south following capture. The Vietnamese also agreed to investigate intensively the remaining 92 discrepancy cases by forming a special team to pursue the cases through archival research and witness interviews. The Vietnamese agreed to host the trilateral meeting from 5 to 6 May in Hanoi and to share information extracted from their repositories on the Lao border cases. The Vietnamese formally accepted the work plan for the remainder of 1993.

The Vietnamese made Deputy Defense Minister Tran Van Quang available for a meeting with Vessey. Quang agreed to further meetings with the JTFFA historian and detailed his personal career history and field command responsibilities during the early 1970s. Specifically, in 1972, at the time the Soviet document placed Quang in Hanoi addressing the Politburo, he was commander of the newly created B-4 Front, also known as the Tri-Thien-Hue Military Region. Quang said that he was in the field with his troops through late 1972 when they seized and occupied the provincial capital of Quang Tri. He stated that he entered Hanoi only briefly in December en route to East Germany for medical treatment. The Vietnamese also made Colonel Doan Hanh available for a session with Vessey and an introduction to the JTFFA historian. Hanh, a retired PAVN officer assigned to Group 875 in 1974–75, accepted a proposal for a mid–May meeting with the JTFFA historian and answered an initial set of questions on Group 875.

Cam provided a measure of the success of the amnesty program. During the plenary session, he told Vessey that following public statements carried by the media describing the amnesty program, the Vietnamese people began to respond by turning remains and artifacts in to officials. Cam named 7 cases involving 29 individuals for which information had been obtained as a result of the public appeal.[16] Cam said that the Vietnamese government continued to call upon the people to cooperate via the amnesty program and attributed the success of the 21st and 22d joint field investigations to the support of the people. At the end of the trip, the official U.S. government readout indicated that President Clinton was deeply committed to achieving the fullest possible accounting and that he had emphasized that continued Vietnamese cooperation was a key to future bilateral relations with Vietnam. Clinton made no additional decisions regarding U.S. government relations with Vietnam.

During the course of the meetings in Hanoi, the Vietnamese media denounced the Soviet document as a fabrication and emphasized Vietnam's willingness to be helpful in shedding light on the claims contained in the document. The daily newspaper of the People's Army chose particularly strong words in its 18 April discussion of the document: "This sensational report has prompted a number of right-wingers, newspapers, and television corporations in the United States to extensively fan up and embellish the issue. . . . Apparently, they hoped that this report would receive strong support from U.S. political circles and that those who spread the news would be awarded with big prizes."[17]

In a 21 April station commentary following the visit by the presidential emissary, an editor stated that the visit had prompted the U.S. side to conclude that further analysis of the Soviet document was required, which must have struck Hanoi as a modest but important advantage, especially since Vessey was speaking the view that though the document was an authentic Soviet military intelligence intelligence report, it contained a raft of inaccuracies and anomalies which were not easily explained. Vessey also suggested that having met with General Quang, he had no reason to question his explanation of his role during 1972 and his view of the Soviet military intelligence report.[18] In late April the Vietnamese party's daily newspaper quoted President Clinton as saying that he was optimistic regarding the recent answers from Vietnam on the Soviet document. Clinton was quoted as saying that Hanoi had provided a number of potentially useful documents that could help explain the claims made in the Soviet document and those documents were being evaluated. The Vietnamese newspaper further quoted the president as saying that because of the cooperation from the Vietnamese side regarding the Soviet document, the

U.S. would be able to advance the investigations of some still unresolved cases of missing U.S. personnel.[19] The Vietnamese sustained this level of optimism through the end of the month, expressing confidence in the sentiments Clinton communicated in his letter to President Anh, which advocated speedy normalization and emphasized continued steps toward cooperation.[20] Interestingly, once again Vietnamese claims regarding the difficulty of unearthing archival evidence relevant to U.S. MIAs were followed by a public media transmission of precisely such documentary information.

A 28 April 1993 Hanoi Voice of Vietnam Network broadcast concerning the activities of the 234th Air Defense Regiment in May 1965 mentions the downing of an F-101 in Ha Tay and a 19 May downing of an A-3J aircraft on Le Truc Street in Hanoi. The latter downing resulted in the capture of two pilots who were, according to the broadcast, presented to Ho Chi Minh as a "gift" on the occasion of his birthday in May. The author of the article on which the broadcast was based, Hung Tan, recalled the number of shots it took to down the F-101. According to the late April broadcast, the capture of the pilots of the A-3J was marked by some festivities and a visit to the unit by Ho Chi Minh.[21]

The Vietnamese strained to extract every public relations advantage in May, returning to the practice of characterizing the relative success of joint work and the accomplishments of technical sessions. The Vietnamese media announced that the trilateral discussions held in Hanoi during 6–8 May to define a means of investigating the Lao border cases took place in an "atmosphere of frankness and mutual understanding" and that the participants had "unanimously" agreed that the talks had "brought about positive results."[22] According to Vietnamese media accounts, during the 22–24 May joint field activities the U.S. conducted live-sighting investigations in Quang Ninh, Thanh Hoa, and Ho Chi Minh City, and U.S.–Vietnamese teams undertook crash site excavations. The U.S. side "highly appreciated the close and effective cooperation offered by the local authorities and the people of Vietnam."[23] By mid-1993, however, the Politburo was greatly frustrated by the U.S. government's failure to move forward toward normalization. Senior Vietnamese leaders felt that the U.S. government was out to humiliate Vietnam. Middle-level Foreign Ministry officials argued that Washington was not serious about the POW/MIA issue and merely sought to heap demand upon demand, in a never-ending manner. In part, the more strident Vietnamese tone was the result of increasingly strong criticisms of the Foreign Ministry's management of the POW/MIA issue from National Assembly delegates.

Senator John Kerry visited Hanoi in mid–May to do some advance preparations for a late May visit by a Senate delegation. Kerry delivered a letter from Clinton to Le Duc Anh expressing the desire that humanitarian cooperation be strengthened to create the conditions that would lead to normalization of relations between the U.S. and Vietnam. Kerry urged the Vietnamese to allow

U.S. specialists greater access to wartime documents and to improve the program of interviewing witnesses regarding the details of loss incidents. Kerry also suggested that the Vietnamese open an office in Hanoi "to store all documents related to the POW/MIA issue" and undertake further work that would shed light on the issues raised by the Soviet document. He stressed the importance of improving cooperation in the area of repatriation of remains. Vietnamese broadcasts in May had clearly misjudged the extent to which General Vessey's April visit had stilled the debates generated by the Soviet documents. Radio commentary and newspaper interviews now portrayed Vietnamese cooperation with Kerry and emphasized Vietnam's commitment to be similarly helpful during the scheduled late–May visit by a U.S. Senate delegation in an effort to be directly responsive to the wishes of President Clinton.[24]

Senator Kerry very candidly told his primary interlocutor, Acting Foreign Minister Tran Quang Co, a member of the Central Committee, that domestic political realities in the U.S. exerted real constraints on the kind of actions and decisions that would be taken regarding normalization. In a private session with Co, he gave the Vietnamese his firm assurances that if they complied with his requests, he would be able to enlist the support of influential people to make the case for normalization of relations. In addition to the letter from President Clinton to President Le Duc Anh, Kerry delivered a letter from veterans group leaders which opposed granting access to loans from the international financial institutions unless there was convincing evidence that the Vietnamese had put a process in place that assured the U.S. government of the ability to achieve the fullest possible accounting. Kerry told his Foreign Ministry hosts that if the Vietnamese could deliver on his four items, he would be prepared to return to Hanoi from 31 May to 1 June with Senator McCain and other congressional figures, representatives of the veterans associations, and the media to demonstrate to the American people the extent to which cooperation had increased and had resulted in significant progress toward establishing a mechanism capable of achieving the fullest possible accounting. Kerry also stressed that significant questions remained unanswered on the issues raised by the Soviet document. Whether or not the document was accurate, he averred, further efforts were required to put to rest the assertions it contained. Kerry told the Vietnamese that they should come up with some documentary evidence to demonstrate the "truth" about the document. That might involve releasing portions of the minutes of Politburo meetings, for example, in order to put to rest the argument over the claims contained in the Soviet document. Tran Quang Co promised to brief the government and to present Kerry's recommendation as a "constructive suggestion," but he noted that Hanoi considered this a very sensitive matter involving "sovereignty and dignity." Finally, Kerry told the Vietnamese that they needed to strike on some way to improve responsiveness on the remains issue. He mentioned the Morrison case and said that the Vietnamese either had to do a better job of producing remains or a better job of providing a plausible explanation of why they could not produce remains.

In mid–May, following Kerry's visit, the Vietnamese privately communicated their view of the urgent need for a public statement by the U.S. government providing some evaluation of the veracity of the Soviet document and commenting on the lengths to which Vietnam had gone to assist Washington in clarifying the charges that resulted from the reading of that document. Further, the Vietnamese were apparently waiting for some public acknowledgment of the decision to provide the trove of documents passed to Vessey during his visit to Hanoi. According to a Vietnamese Foreign Ministry official, Hanoi felt it had worked hard to uncover those documents and that a public statement of the utility of the documents in resolving cases would go far toward softening the impact of media attention on the Soviet document which continued to captivate public attention.

In late May 1993, following Kerry's mid–May visit and before the arrival of the Kerry delegation on 31 May, Do Muoi summoned members of the Foreign Ministry and the VNOSMP to a meeting. According to a senior VNOSMP official, Muoi told those present that he would receive the Kerry delegation, but that would be the last delegation he would meet from the U.S. on the POW/MIA issue. Muoi reportedly said that when Vietnam came forward with documents, the U.S. denounced the government for withholding information. This, Muoi argued, was not a helpful approach. According to the VNOSMP official, Muoi stated that Vietnam was prepared to stop looking for information if that approach persisted. Additionally, Muoi told those present that Washington should not believe that Vietnam felt compelled to respond to each and every U.S. request as the result as a means of hastening the lifting of the embargo. The U.S. government, Muoi argued, was mistaken if it believed that Vietnam was in a precarious position and must comply with U.S. requirements on the POW/MIA issue.

During Senator Kerry's 31 May visit to Hanoi, the Vietnamese opened the document center which Kerry had asked them to establish during his mid–May visit. Pham Teo, a longtime deputy on the VNOSMP, was active in efforts to organize the document center. The Vietnamese were unable to respond to some of the specific JTFFA requests for documents, but they did provide a dozen or so potentially useful documents to the Kerry delegation. They did not, however, respond to requests to compile the documents mentioned in a 1988 history of Group 559 written by a group of authors under the auspices of the General Department for Rear Services. They intended to comply and understood the importance of the request, but explained that they could not organize the effort in time for Kerry's visit.

Two of the documents the Vietnamese did produce for Kerry were statistical abstracts. One of those was a 30-page statistical study of Americans captured in North Vietnam. That document contained no names. The other statistical compilation contained 90 names of Americans captured in South Vietnam but released in the north. There were no dates or indications of the originating agency on the texts themselves, but Vietnamese officials privately stated that the General Political Department was the originating agency for all the documents. The Vietnamese also provided the Kerry delegation with a 28 November 1972 letter from the General Staff Department reassigning General Tran Van Quang from the B4 Front to Hanoi well after Quang was said in the Soviet document to have delivered a speech to the Politburo.

Kerry interviewed Tran Van Quang and Doan Hanh, the retired colonel from Group 875 with whom Vessey had spoken during his April visit to Hanoi. Kerry also met with Nguyen Viet Phuong, the head of the committee that wrote the history of Group 559 and the Ho Chi Minh Trail.[25] Quang, Hanh, and Phuong committed themselves to future interviews with JTFFA. The Vietnamese media coverage of the late May–early June Kerry delegation's visit to Vietnam stressed the spirit of mutual cooperation and the delegation's thankfulness for Vietnam's unflagging cooperation and responsiveness. News reports focused on Do Muoi's remarks to Kerry underscoring the humanitarian motivation behind Vietnam's continued efforts to help resolve the MIA issue and Muoi's explanation of Vietnam's foreign policy goals.[26]

Through the middle of the year, the Vietnamese continued to draw a distinction between the imperatives of normalization in an environment of mutual humanitarian cooperation and lifting the economic sanctions which would serve mutual economic interests and benefit other countries as well. In 1992 the Vietnamese leadership had drawn an explicit link between normalization and the end of the embargo and humanitarian cooperation on the POW/MIA issue, arguing that as long as the embargo persisted, it would be difficult to make the case that Washington was seriously concerned with the fate of the Vietnamese people and inclined to share a humanitarian approach to normalization. In 1993, however, the argument evolved in a subtly different manner. The exclusively economic arguments about lifting the embargo were more and more made in contexts distinct from efforts to convey Vietnam's interest in a normal and proper relationship with Washington. The arguments were made in parallel, but the two tracks were more carefully preserved, with discussions of the embargo set in assessments of regional economic developments, U.S. business interests, and global impatience with Washington's position on the trade embargo. At the same time, Hanoi vigorously asserted the seriousness with which it pursued the POW/MIA issue based on strictly humanitarian motivations. For example, a 27 June 1993 article in *Tuoi Tre Chu Nhat*, dateline Ho Chi Minh City, revealed the results of an investigation of a group of organizations based in Saigon's Binh Thanh ward that employed over 3,500 people during 1990 and 1991 in organized efforts to illegally disinter remains from cemeteries to sell them as the remains of U.S. soldiers in order to secure resettlement in the U.S. and financial reward. Five individuals associated with Robert Challiand, a Vietnamese of French descent, the organizer of this "remains-holder program" (dien hai cot), had stored almost 500 remains at various sites in Saigon and surrounding areas during 1990. Other groups investigated had forged files of U.S. servicemen who the group claimed were alive in Vietnam. The group planned to use dog tags and other fabricated information to make money through deals involving remains traffickers such as Challiand. In early 1993, Challiand and ten others were arrested by an unnamed investigative organization. (In May 1994, a court in Ho Chi Minh City convicted Chailland of abusing graves and collecting money from people who brought him remains in return for his promise to assist in their resettlement in the United States. Chailland was sentenced to a 12-year prison term.)[27]

On 2 July, the White House announced the decision to refrain from opposing the efforts of other countries to settle Vietnam's arrears with the International Monetary Funds (IMF). The White House also announced that a high-level delegation would visit Hanoi in July to review progress and to inform the Vietnamese of Washington's decision to cease objecting to settling Hanoi's arrears. The president made it clear that no further steps would be taken toward normalization until the Vietnamese were responsive to U.S. government requests for further action in four areas: the recovery and repatriation of remains; continued joint field investigations of the discrepancy cases and continued live-sighting investigations; trilateral cooperation on Lao border cases; and access to wartime information in Ministry of Defense archival holdings, such as those of Group 875 and Group 559.

The Vietnamese military was less inclined than the Foreign Ministry to see the U.S. government decision to refrain from objecting to the settlement of Vietnam's arrears as a major step forward. The military believed that the U.S. domestic political implications of the POW/MIA issue would prevent the Clinton administration from moving quickly and in an uncomplicated manner toward lifting the embargo, which they saw as the ultimate dividend of Hanoi's policy of cooperation. The military viewed the interim steps, such as those spelled out in Phase Two and Phase Three of the Roadmap, as being of minor importance. They viewed the phased movement toward a normal relationship as cumbersome and not necessarily free of pitfalls for Vietnam. The July 1993 issue of the General Political Department monthly review of key events described the 2 July decision by President Clinton to cease blocking efforts to settle Vietnam's arrears with the IMF as a result of "our correct foreign policy approach and spirited struggle making a stand for our people, with the support of many countries and broad international opinion." The General Political Department report stated that though the U.S. had not lifted the embargo, the step announced by the White House had certain advantages, such as opening the road to IMF, World Bank, and Asian Development Bank loans. The report noted that many forces in the United States vehemently opposed the policy of lifting the embargo and normalizing relations with Vietnam. Consequently, Vietnam's "struggle respecting America to lift the embargo and normalize relations is still difficult and complex." For the third month in a row, the July issue of this 16-page internal document omitted any specific mention of the POW/MIA issue, a matter that had been highlighted regularly in issues from November 1992 through April 1993; this omission manifested the military's utter frustration with the POW/MIA issue. Instead, the General Political Department focused its attention on the importance of serving the interests of demobilized soldiers, retired and chronically ill veterans and war heros, and the families of missing, wounded, and KIA war heros.[28]

The Foreign Ministry was cordial in the public response to Washington's 2 July announcement. The ministry's statement noted that the decision was a "significant step" in line with "the world trend" and one that would be beneficial for the process of normalization. The ministry said that the decision would help build mutual trust and "accelerate resolution of the remaining issues between the two countries." The Vietnamese Foreign Ministry continued to stress the importance of reciprocal respect for humanitarian issues between Washington and Hanoi, thus adhering to the position that Hanoi's cooperation on the POW/MIA issue was dependent upon equal respect for Vietnam's "humanitarian needs."[29]

Privately, though, Foreign Ministry officials with long involvement in the POW/MIA issue were ecstatic. The U.S. government decision represented the culmination of considerable investments by the Foreign Ministry. Many middle and senior Foreign Ministry officials calculated that a negative U.S. government decision would have had a consequential impact on their credibility and their ability to sustain cooperation. To a certain extent, Cam and his ministry labored under the same pressures that ultimately compromised former Foreign Minister Nguyen Co Thach's position: the inability to argue convincingly that responding positively to U.S. government requests for additional cooperation would yield some dividends in the form of significant steps toward ending the embargo for Vietnam. Foreign Ministry officials privately made the case that the U.S. decision to refrain from opposing the settlement of Vietnam's IMF arrears had placed their Ministry in a much better position and had minimized the Foreign Ministry's disadvantage with respect to the Ministry of Interior and Ministry of Defense, both of which were far less confident that increased cooperation might bring forward movement toward normalization that would be helpful to Vietnam. There were, however, limits to the advantage that accrued to the Foreign Ministry. The National Assembly, in session in mid-year, focused on the issue of responding to the social needs of veterans and the needs of the families and dependents of soldiers who died in combat. Key delegates highlighted those issues in their speeches from the floor, and those speeches were given prominence in the media. Foreign Ministry officials were closely questioned by delegates. Middle-level Foreign Ministry officials recognized that the ministry would have to be closely accountable to the National Assembly for any future steps taken in the POW/MIA issue, given the clear interest in resolving domestic humanitarian issues relevant to Vietnam's own veterans and families.[30]

In mid–July 1993, a U.S. presidential delegation headed by Deputy Secretary for Veterans Affairs Hershel Gober and Assistant Secretary of State Winston Lord traveled to Hanoi and met with General Secretary Muoi, Minister of Defense Doan Khue, Minister of Interior Bui Thien Ngo, and Deputy Foreign Minister Le Mai. According to Hanoi's characterization, the delegation held "frank and constructive talks" in which they emphasized the president's 2 July message that stated that the "next steps of development will depend first of all on the concrete results of the settlement of the POW/MIA issue." The delegation turned over to the Vietnamese the first reel in a collection of captured Vietnamese wartime documents as a humanitarian gesture "to help Vietnam account for MIA cases." The U.S. delegation proposed that three State Department officials be dispatched to Hanoi to assist "U.S. POW/MIA families that have been invited by the Vietnamese Government in order to accelerate efforts to account for POWs and MIAs."[31]

The Vietnamese were responsive and positive in their answers to the requests made by the U.S. delegation, but clearly telegraphed the constraints that would limit their ability to respond quickly to the significant shopping list presented by the U.S. delegation. The Vietnamese made the case that joint efforts sometimes led to an ability to identify a general area of gravesites of some U.S. personnel who died in Vietnamese custody, but they expressed no real confidence that they would be able to get much beyond this stage in their investigations. Le Mai noted that further movement would be incremental and not dramatic and whatever future progress took place would be the result of hard work in established channels. The Vietnamese agreed to accelerate work on locating documents relevent to missing U.S. service personnel and to make such documents available to the U.S. side. Muoi and Minister of Interior Ngo informed the U.S. delegation that instructions ordering subordinate units to facilitate this process had been issued. Mai and others indicated that there would probably be marginal returns to the labor involved; documents that would shed light on individual cases would be increasingly difficult to locate. The Vietnamese leadership, however, committed to doing its "level best" (het suc co gang) to locate documents.

Hanoi agreed to pursue aggressively the remaining 92 discrepancy cases, to sustain their cooperation on live-sighting investigations as required, and to continue joint field investigation cooperation. Le Mai stressed that there was little chance of uncovering information of use in explaining what became of the 11 individuals in photographs archived in the Vietnamese Military Museum. He told the U.S. delegation that the photographer who took the photograph of Morrison had died. Mai also stressed that the success of the amnesty program depended upon the motivation of the Vietnamese people to comply with the law and that this was the more difficult part of the matter. He said that Vietnam would cooperate by sustaining the amnesty program and that citizens who turned over remains would not suffer punishment. Minister of Interior Bui Thien Ngo endorsed this same approach.

The Vietnamese agreed to attend a 9 August trilateral meeting on the Lao border cases, endorsed the proposal to do this at a policy level, and stressed the importance of informing the Lao before publicly announcing the meeting. Le Mai was not enthusiastic about interposing with the Lao to get them to agree to attend the session and to understand the importance of trilateral cooperation. The U.S. delegation was privately assured, however, that Foreign Minister Cam, who was in Vientiane, would urge the Lao to cooperate and to join the 9 August meeting.

Hanoi accepted the U.S. proposal to send three U.S. Foreign Service Officers (FSOs) and understood that the motivation behind the request was to free JTFFA personnel from ancillary duties. Additionally, the FSOs would be responsible for supporting American citizens and family members who visited Vietnam and would play a role in U.S. efforts to gain normal consular access to detained and incarcerated Americans, mainly ethnic Vietnamese Americans who were arrested for political activities or violations of Vietnamese laws, and other American citizens who had run afoul of the authorities during visits. Interior Minister Ngo told Lord that he would take into account "the improving relations between our two countries" in handling cases of detained/incarcerated Americans and that he was "willing to go beyond the law" to achieve that goal. At the plenary session, Mai agreed to the U.S. proposal for a dialogue on human rights "on a permanent basis."

The Vietnamese were clearly pleased with the 2 July decision on the IMF arrears issue. In the plenary session and their public statements about the visit, they refrained from pressing the customary points that Washington should lift the embargo to demonstrate that the U.S. took Vietnam's humanitarian needs seriously, that the embargo was the single most potent threat to the livelihood and economic well-being of the Vietnamese population, and that the Vietnamese government found it difficult to motivate popular cooperation while the embargo was still in place. Vietnam's central message was that they would continue to be cooperative in each of the four areas President Clinton enumerated in his 2 July statement and do their best to think of ways to improve cooperation and address the issue of locating and repatriating remains, investigating the 92 discrepancy cases, pursuing trilateral cooperation on the Lao border cases, and providing documents from specific wartime archives.[32] The Vietnamese handling of the presidential delegation demonstrated that in spite of his earlier frustration, Muoi remained engaged in this issue and prepared to take the necessary steps to respond to U.S. government requests. Muoi told the delegation that Hanoi was committed to creating "favorable conditions for the U.S. side to finish resolving" the outstanding issues of American MIAs.[33]

Following the departure of the delegation, a 29 July Vietnamese News Agency broadcast observed that the U.S. and Vietnam had reviewed the results of the 24th joint field investigations at a late July technical meeting, hammered out the details of the next round of field work, discussed means of improving the efficiency of these joint operations, and reviewed the "significant results" of the 24th round of joint investigations during which remains belonging to 18 U.S. MIAs and information "shedding light" on 30 additional cases were uncovered.[34] In the same time frame, the media aired strong views regarding the bipartisan support in the U.S. for the lifting of the embargo and the costs in terms of lost opportunities for U.S. companies caused by the embargo-imposed restrictions.[35]

In early August the Vietnamese publicized plans for a trilateral meeting on the Lao border cases and the agreement to conduct the 25th joint field investigations in Quang Binh, Quang Tri, Thua Thien-Hue, Quang Nam, Quang Ngai, Binh Dinh, Phu Yen, and Khanh Hoa. Hanoi also gave considerable attention to planned visits to Vietnam by U.S. congressional delegations and business groups. On 7 August the VNOSMP released a second communiqué repeating the December 1992 appeal to "all branches of activity concerned and the population in all localities to search for and provide information relating to American MIAs and hand over all the remains in their possession to local authorities, thus contributing to an early settlement of the issue in the humanitarian spirit." The early August communiqué stated that if the remains turned in by Vietnamese citizens were "scientifically" shown to be those of U.S. servicemen, those surrendering the remains would receive a "reasonable reward."[36] From 9 to 11 August, U.S., Lao, and Vietnamese teams conferred in Hawaii on the means of resolving MIA cases along the Lao-Vietnamese border. The three participants agreed to conduct parallel U.S.–Lao and U.S.–Vietnamese field operations in the vicinity of Quang Tri Province in December and to improve exchanges of information and documents in support of such field activities. Hanoi characterized the 9–11 August trilateral meeting as "constructive" and echoed the Lao view that the meeting had produced satisfactory results that would lead to progress on the border cases.[37]

General Secretary Muoi met with Representative Sam Gibbons on 14 August. On 20 August, Senator Charles Robb was received by Prime Minister Vo Van Kiet, Interior Minister Bui Thien Ngo, and Foreign Minister Nguyen Manh Cam, all of whom emphasized fundamental regional changes, the importance of economic cooperation, and especially the importance of quickly resolving the POW/MIA problem. On 27 August, President Le Duc Anh received Representative David McCurdy and affirmed Vietnam's deep sympathy with the concerns of the U.S. Congress and people regarding the MIA issue. On 30 August, Senator Richard Shelby, chairman of the Armed Forces

Subcommittee and a member of the Energy and Banking Committee, was received by Vice President Nguyen Thi Binh, who pledged continued cooperation.[38]

The upbeat tone struck in the media, however, coexisted with a residual pessimism about the prospects of making quick headway toward lifting the embargo. Foreign Minister Cam, for example, returned to the familiar argument that Hanoi's efforts were disproportionate to Washington's humanitarian assistance. "American humanitarian aid," he told reporters on 12 August, "is still small compared with the enormous consequences of the war, and U.S. potential, and with regard to efforts deployed by Vietnam to find American MIAs."[39] By late August, Cam was telling Western reporters that lifting the embargo would "encourage ordinary Vietnamese whose cooperation is essential in the effort to account for [American MIAs]."[40] Although Cam resolved to sustain Vietnam's cooperation, whether or not the embargo was lifted, the edge had returned to the Vietnamese arguments on these matters. The foreign minister was clearly preoccupied with the possibility that the embargo would be extended following the expected mid–September U.S. government review of the Trading with the Enemy Act (TWEA). In this context, a 31 August meeting between the VNOSMP and the Joint Task Force Detachment in Hanoi was not a success. The Vietnamese failed to respond to the U.S. government request for a written assessment of the 84 cases involving remains of U.S. MIAs about which the Vietnamese were most likely to have information, including the sensitive "photograph" cases, the died-in-captivity list cases, cases listed on Vietnamese grave registers for which there had been no accounting, and cases where field investigations had revealed witnesses who indicated that Vietnamese officials recovered remains from wartime burial sites which had not yet been repatriated. Additionally, the Vietnamese failed to turn over documents that Vice Minister Le Mai had said would be made available to the JTFFA at the late–August technical meeting.

Hanoi expressed particular concern with a 1 September statement by Assistant Secretary of State Lord in which he explained that the president's authority to conduct embargos against certain countries would lapse unless he decided to renew that authority following the mid–September review. Lord noted that though Vietnam had been cooperating on the MIA problem, Vietnam's record on human rights, highlighted by the government's refusal to allow Senator Robb to visit an imprisoned dissident, was "discouraging." The Vietnamese Foreign Ministry spokesperson responded cautiously by noting that the ministry had not seen the text of Lord's remarks and did not want to comment, though the spokesperson did state, in words that revealed Hanoi's serious concern, that "if the statement of Mr. Winston Lord includes anything that could compromise the process of normalization between the United States and Vietnam, we will ask for an explanation from the United States."[41]

Vietnam did take several positive steps in early September, however, that were intended to demonstrate the government's commitment to following through on promises even if Washington decided to extend the embargo. On 1 September, Vietnam provided the Joint Task Force with 6 wartime documents, including a 46-page summary of 2,466 aircraft downings claimed by Group 559 during the 1965–75 period; a list of pilots captured by Group 559; and some sketches and thumbnail accounts of air defense actions in which Group 559 participated. On 6 September, Le Mai provided the JTFFA commander with an "updated list" of information concerning remains received from the Vietnamese amnesty program and a document summarizing information on the remains of the 84 Americans who died in Vietnamese custody but whose remains had not been accounted for. Mai also gave the JTFFA commander a letter for Assistant Secretary Lord, Deputy Secretary Gober, and General Michael Ryan that reviewed progress in the four areas—remains repatriation, joint field work, trilateral investigations, and archival information—and informed the U.S. government that the VNOSMP was consulting with the JTFFA to work out a plan to investigate effectively the 84 cases. Additionally, the letter stated that Vietnam had established an MIA task team in Ho Chi Minh City to focus intensively on U.S. personnel in the south in response to a request made following the July visit by the presidential delegation to dedicate more personnel to Vietnamese efforts in the south.

Just days before President Clinton was to review the TWEA, a second document from the Soviet military intelligence archives was revealed and again captured headlines in U.S. papers in a manner that, to Hanoi, threatened to derail progress on the MIA issue. The document, which stated that Vietnam held 735 U.S. aviators as POWs in 1971 instead of the 368 whose names the Vietnamese had publicly released, was said to be a translation of a report to the 20th plenary session of the Central Committee, which according to the document ran from the end of December 1970 to the beginning of 1971. However, the 20th plenary session of the Vietnamese Workers Party Central Committee took place in February 1972, not late 1970 and early 1971. According to the second Soviet document, the report was given by Hoang Anh, secretary of the Vietnamese Workers Party Central Committee. Nothing in Anh's background, career history, or record of party Central Committee work suggests, however, that he was qualified to address the issues discussed in the second Soviet document in a report to the 20th plenary session. During the late 1960s and the early 1970s, Anh was clearly part of the Democratic Republic's agricultural policy apparatus. He was first identified as a member of the party's secretariat in the late 1950s. He did a stint in 1955 as deputy defense minister and operated in central Vietnam during the early 1950s as the chairman of the Interzone Resistance Committee of the Viet Minh. By the late 1950s and early 1960s, Anh was immersed in currency reform, finance, and trade issues. In the mid–1960s, Anh became minister of agriculture; when he relinquished that position in the late 1960s, he retained the chairmanship of the Agricultural

Committee in the Office of the Prime Minister. The second Soviet document claimed that in late 1970 and early 1971, an "opportunist" group argued that a decision to engage in armed combat with the Americans would entail sacrifices and difficulties and threaten the economic construction of the DRV. The speech which the second Soviet document said was given by Hoang Anh to the plenary session sought to argue against that point of view. However, the plenary session itself did not reflect the debate suggested in the second Soviet document. On the contrary, there seemed to be consensus that the "general uprising" had declined in importance, that urban insurrection would not succeed without main force intervention, and that the prospects for a decisive military victory in the rural areas had increased. The debate over the relative merits of proceeding to the stage of armed conflict versus protecting the rear area (i.e., North Vietnam) was carried out in the mid–1960s, not 1970–71. The Third Party Congress balanced the priority of renewed struggle in the south with the effort to preserve and consolidate the DRV. That balance began to unravel during 1965–68 when key leaders, including Vo Nguyen Giap and Truong Chinh, among others, urged a more aggressive "defense," intensified conflict in the south, and an increased role for People's Army of Vietnam regular forces.

The second Soviet document also suggested that the Vietnamese took the position in December 1970 and through at least early 1971 that Hanoi would return U.S. POWs when the U.S. began to withdraw and would complete the repatriation when all U.S. troops were out of Vietnam. From the beginning of the plenary peace talks which convened in Paris in early 1969, however, Hanoi took the position that the complete withdrawal of U.S. troops from Vietnam was the condition for the release of U.S. prisoners. On 31 May 1971, Kissinger expressed willingness to agree on a deadline for the complete withdrawal of U.S. troops in return for the repatriation of U.S. POWs. Between May and October 1971, the U.S. and Hanoi negotiators wrestled with the question of the timing of the release of the prisoners. Washington proposed that the return of POWs begin once the date for the withdrawal of U.S. troops was set. This was rejected by Vietnam. It was not until late June 1971 that Le Duc Tho introduced a nine-point plan to end the war. The second point proposed that "the release of all military men and civilians captured in the war should be carried out in parallel and completed at the same time as the troop withdrawals."

The Vietnamese reacted bitterly to the second Soviet document, denouncing it as an "ill-intentioned fabrication" clearly designed to derail the lifting of the embargo and progress toward the normalization of U.S.–Vietnamese relations. Station commentaries between 10 and 11 September drew links between the disclosure of the first document and the second, quoted U.S. State Department and congressional officials who portrayed the second document as a fabrication, and denounced "ultra-rightist" forces in the U.S. determined to "block or undermine any positive developments in U.S.–Vietnamese relations."[42] The Vietnamese Defense Ministry's daily newspaper, *Quan Doi Nhan*

Dan, underscored the possibility that the second Soviet document was intended to scotch the lifting of the embargo. The 12 September commentary noted that the first Soviet document was released in the midst of President Clinton's review of the U.S. policy of opposing the settling of Vietnam's arrears in the IMF. The commentary cited the story based on claims by Kalugin, a former KGB officer, that the Soviets had interrogated U.S. POWs, reviewed the fabricated photographs which purported to show live American prisoners of war, and suggested that these scams had gone well beyond the insidious schemes of "exiled" overseas Vietnamese to make money. Such scams, which had become "internationalized," could easily become an obstacle to normalization.[43] The Foreign Ministry spokesperson was somewhat less inclined to draw relationships between discrete events or to come to pessimistic conclusions regarding the impact of the document on the normalization process.[44] The criticisms continued beyond the 14 September review of the Trading with the Enemy Act and became even more strident. At a 17 October press briefing, an official spokesperson of the Embassy of the Russian Federation in Hanoi told Western reporters that:

> We have not produced any evidence permitting the confirmation of the accuracy of those facts presented in this document, for instance, the figure of U.S. pilots held captive as prisoners of war in Vietnam during the 1970s.... Our view is that this has created a regrettable situation, that is, the existence of that highly unreliable information has taken place at a time when the process of improving Vietnamese–U.S. relations is drawing to a close.[45]

On 13 September, the White House announced the president's decision to sign a determination renewing his authority under the Trading with the Enemy Act. He thus extended his authority to impose and maintain central control over certain trade assets and funds affecting Vietnam, Cambodia, Cuba, North Korea, and the Baltic nations. In the case of Vietnam, the presidential determination maintained the embargo with an adjustment permitting U.S. firms to bid on projects financed by the International Financial Institutions (IFIs). In explaining the decision, the White House noted that while some progress had been made toward obtaining more remains, resolution of the discrepancy cases, trilateral investigations of the Lao border cases, and access to POW/MIA–related documents, "tangible results" were "not yet sufficient."[46]

The Vietnamese reacted strongly against the decision to keep the embargo in place, but with an eye toward avoiding any possibility of jeopardizing the modest progress toward normalization that had been achieved. The Foreign Ministry spokesperson expressed "regret" that Washington had maintained the embargo, a decision which "ran counter to international and regional development trends and was against the aspiration and interest of Vietnamese and American peoples." At the same time, the Foreign Ministry made it clear that Vietnam would continue to cooperate with the U.S. in the resolution of the

MIA problem.[47] Deputy Foreign Minister Le Mai argued that the decision to extend the embargo ran "counter to the trends of negotiation and cooperation as well as freedom in doing business and trade in the current world situation":

> The Vienna Conference [on human rights] issued a resolution holding that the right to development is one of the fundamental rights of all nations and that all governments must respect the rights of nations to develop. The U.S. representatives at that conference also asserted the U.S. stand on this issue. As a result, I think that the decision to prolong the U.S. embargo has violated the right of development for nations, thus the United States will find it difficult to explain this stance.

Mai also stated that Vietnam would not interrupt progress intended to help resolve the POW/MIA problem. He suggested that Washington and Hanoi should "continue their negotiations and that differences between the two sides should be frankly discussed while efforts should be made to continue cooperation." He stressed the importance of freeing U.S. businesses to compete equally in Vietnam.[48]

Press and radio commentary was less restrained. A 17 September article in *Nhan Dan* denounced the decision as "absurd and out dated":

> In the U.S.–Vietnamese relations, the 13 September decision obviously does not fit in with current reality and is contrary to the U.S. policy statements. The aforementioned decision shows that Washington is not really ready to finish with the past, as the U.S. administration has professed to open a new page in its relation with Vietnam on the basis of equality and mutual respect. In fact, how can the prolongation of the trade embargo help open a new chapter in the Vietnamese–U.S. relationship as declared by the Americans?

U.S. "actions do not match its words," the article continued, terming these actions "absurd" because the "United States itself has many times issued statements praising Vietnam's cooperation in the MIA issue." Moreover, the embargo was seriously out of step with U.S. interests, economic developments, the desires of American businesses, and global trends encouraging the acceleration of trade and economic cooperation with Vietnam. The article declared Vietnam's intention to cooperate with the U.S. to "relieve the pain of the American families whose relatives died in Vietnam."[49] An 18 September Voice of Vietnam network commentary argued that the decision was made by a "person still standing behind the departure line," deprecated Washington's professed interest in turning a new page in U.S.–Vietnamese relations, and cast doubt on Washington's intention to keep the POW/MIA issue a humanitarian one, free of politics and separate from other issues:

> No one fails to realize that the U.S. is the one who started the Vietnam War, causing the Vietnamese people to suffer untold sacrifices and losses. After the

war, the United States should have fulfilled its obligation to help Vietnam restore its war-devastated country. Far from doing so, Washington has imposed an embargo against us—its rival—over the past 18 years. During various contacts with Vietnamese, many responsible U.S. officials have expressed the desire to [close the past and open a new chapter]. Therefore, the 13 September decision to continue the embargo against Vietnam shows that the words of the U.S. do not really match its deeds.[50]

In late September the Vietnamese media paid considerable attention to field cooperation with live-sighting investigations. Broadcasts dissected the minutia of individual cases to demonstrate what Hanoi considered the ludicrous quality of some of the stories of "live captive Americans" that Vietnam was asked to investigate, with the goal of underscoring the far-fetched stories at the core of the live-sighting cases and emphasizing that the government of Vietnam was nevertheless prepared to be helpful to U.S. government efforts to resolve the POW/MIA issue.[51] In late September, Ho Chi Minh City public security forces arrested a Vietnamese who was alleged to have engaged in making a film in August intended to deceive viewers into believing that live U.S. POWs continued to be held in captivity by the Vietnamese government in a hotel within the Ba Son complex in Saigon. The Vietnamese media provided detailed coverage to this episode.[52] The media sustained critical commentary on the embargo decision through the end of the month, quoting congressional leaders, businessmen, and U.S. newspaper editors who castigated Washington's decision as disappointing and inefficient.[53]

Following Washington's decision to allow U.S. businesses to join developmental projects sponsored by the international financial institutions, the Vietnamese made it clear that they were less and less likely to regard the piecemeal approach to lifting the embargo as a serious commitment by Washington to moving toward a normal and proper relationship. Vietnamese officials privately expressed chagrin over the fact that the embargo had not been lifted. Senior Vietnamese officials took exception to still being on the "enemy list." Explanations of the technical complexities of the 1977 statutory provisions which required the U.S. government to keep countries on the TWEA list in order to freeze assets did not assuage the Vietnamese. In late September, the Vietnamese media began to reflect the view that the U.S. government would only grudgingly lift the embargo and had no real interest in the extent to which the embargo inflicted economic hardship on the Vietnamese people. Vietnamese citizens gave freer expression to the view that Washington simply did not want a relationship with Hanoi. The military concluded that many forces in the United States vehemently opposed the policy of lifting the embargo and normalizing relations with Vietnam.

In September, Vietnam took stock of its recent foreign policy successes. Media broadcasts and authoritative articles in party-controlled magazines touted significant steps to implement Vietnam's "open-door" foreign policy and minimized the extent to which Washington's decision to sustain the embargo represented a setback. The media enumerated achievements in efforts to mend relations with China; Vietnam's participation in the 26th ASEAN Foreign Minister's Conference; the sweep through Europe (France, Germany, Britain, Belgium) by Prime Minister Vo Van Kiet and his visit to Japan, Korea, Australia, and New Zealand; official visits to Vietnam by France's President Mitterand and the German foreign minister; and efforts to develop and improve relations with the region, especially Laos and Cambodia. According to the media, all these things were part of Vietnam's "independent, positive and active" foreign policy. The Vietnamese also provided details regarding the unfolding of their relationship with the IFIs. They received the International Monetary Fund director in late September, headlined the creation of the "Friends of Vietnam" group to clear Hanoi's arrears, and noted prominently that the Asian Development Bank was likely to approve its first loan to Vietnam in over two decades in spite of the continuing U.S. trade embargo. An early September 1993 essay broadcast by a Voice of Vietnam Network editor stated that Japan's resumption of Organization Development Agency's assistance to Vietnam was "a significant start for Vietnam to be assimilated into the world economy." The editor went on to say that Vietnam had strengthened its relations with the United States, shown goodwill and active cooperation to resolve the MIA issue, consistently treated the MIA issue as a purely humanitarian one, and done its best to create favorable conditions for the U.S. to carry out activities related to the MIA issue, "despite the fact that the consequences of the war in Vietnam are still immense." The Voice of Vietnam Network editor noted general sympathy for lifting the embargo on the part of "many U.S. delegations," including "administration and American people" who visited Hanoi between July and August, and he went on to assert:

> The U.S. cannot block the development of economic and business cooperation between Vietnam and other countries. Sooner or later, the normalization of ties with the United States will be attained. However, the sooner this can be achieved, the better it will be for the two countries and will meet the aspirations of the Vietnamese and American peoples as well as other peoples of the world.[54]

Basically, Hanoi seemed inclined to argue, as it did in late 1990 following then Foreign Minister Thach's visit to Washington, that Hanoi's integration into the world economy was inexorable, that Washington's efforts to delay recognition by the IFIs would receive decreasing support, and that Vietnam would not allow any of this to deter it from the commitment to resolve the POW/MIA issue in a humanitarian spirit.

In October, the Vietnamese took significant steps toward improving preparations for joint field work and allowed larger U.S. teams to conduct field activities for longer periods. Hanoi agreed to take any steps necessary to insure appropriate preparation for the parallel bilateral operations in Quang Tri in December that involved some Lao border cases. Having cracked open the archives of the General Political Department and Group 559, Hanoi committed itself to searching for more documents by sending out the word to military regions to review repositories yet one more time for potentially useful archival information. In early October a Special Remains Team (SRT) in Military Region 9 obtained information from nine witnesses which assisted in the location of burial sites. The SRT surveyed the sites and recommended three for excavation. In early October the Vietnamese repatriated another 12 sets of remains. Six were uncovered as the result of joint work, and six were uncovered as the result of unilateral efforts, presumably the "amnesty program."

In October, Vietnamese officials associated with the VNOSMP expressed their frustration over the manner in which the U.S. government was, in their perception, floating aimlessly without a clear policy direction or goal. They were not happy with the manner in which "Soviet documents" had interrupted progress, and they were not inclined to be helpful in tracking down further leads pertaining to these documents, which the Vietnamese regarded as provocations fabricated to throw the system off course. In early October, according to Russian radio broadcasts, Foreign Minister Nguyen Manh Cam and Andre Kozyrev, head of the Russian Federation's Foreign Policy Department, met in Moscow and agreed that Moscow would no longer release such documents until there had been time enough to confer with the Vietnamese on any new items unearthed in the archives.[55]

Essentially, the Foreign Ministry had drifted closer to the military view of things: the gradual, piecemeal lifting of the embargo was not satisfactory, did not signal U.S. government seriousness about entering into a relationship, and continued to suggest that Washington was intent on punishing and humiliating Vietnam. In the last quarter of 1992, it was clear that the Vietnamese thought that the POW/MIA issue should be the easiest-to-solve foreign policy problem before them. China had grown demanding and had complicated Hanoi's efforts at rapproachement by taking a hard stand on territorial disputes over the Spratly Islands and adjacent waters. By late 1993, it appeared that the key leaders in Hanoi had come around to the view that the foreign policy problem that was most manageable and would yield important policy dividends for the leadership was the question of Sino-Vietnamese relations, while continued efforts to cooperate with Washington would yield no appreciable foreign policy dividends.

In the last months of 1993, Vietnam remained privately wary of the intentions of the Clinton administration and publicly open to continued humanitarian cooperation, even in the face of unfavorable political decisions regarding the embargo and normalization. Hanoi aired the results of two joint field investigations at the beginning and end of October, stressing the continuity of

the working routines, the freedom U.S. teams were granted to travel throughout the countryside and interview potential witnesses, the cooperation of local
Vietnamese officials, and the deep appreciation expressed by representatives of
the JTFFA detachment in Hanoi for assistance rendered during the investigations.[56] Vietnamese media accounts played up the significance of the 4 October
meeting between Secretary of State Warren Christopher and Deputy Prime
Minister Phan Van Khai in New York during which Khai "affirmed" Vietnam's
commitment to "build a new relationship" between Vietnam and the United
States "conforming to the fundamental and long-term interests of the two
peoples and the trend of history," and restated Vietnamese commitment to
cooperate on a humanitarian basis to resolve the POW/MIA issue.[57] The Vietnamese media stated that the meeting "marked a new step of development in
the relations between the two countries," while noting that "at present, not
everything is settled" in the bilateral relationship.[58]

Vietnamese concerns that the achievements of cooperation would be
undermined and that progress toward the lifting of the embargo would be
compromised were accentuated in the last quarter of 1993. In early October,
Hanoi reacted to stories carried in the U.S. press that Vietnamese government
officials had bribed Commerce Secretary Ron Brown to lift the economic embargo. The Foreign Ministry spokesperson denied the accusations, stated that
Vietnamese officials had never had contact with Brown, and emphasized that
government-to-government discussions with numerous official Washington
delegations afforded Hanoi the "best forum" to discuss bilateral relations.
Privately, Vietnamese officials expressed the fear that the episode would derail
progress toward normalization.[59]

In early November the Vietnamese were extremely concerned about the
report the U.S. government had requested regarding unilateral investigations
conducted by the Vietnamese into the so-called 84 cases which represented the
most compelling instances in which the U.S. government had information indicating that the Vietnamese had control over the remains of a U.S. serviceman
at the time of his death. The Vietnamese privately expressed the view that
Washington was placing too much stock in this report and that it would have
an adverse impact on any possibility of a decision before the end of the year
to move ahead toward lifting the embargo. The Vietnamese discreetly sought
the advice and guidance of nongovernmental organizations regarding how
Hanoi might proceed, indicating that there was much confusion within the
VNOSMP on how to approach this report. VNOSMP officials appeared to be
preoccupied with the political consequences of compiling a report that indicated Hanoi had not really done very much to track the 84 cases. While there
was general agreement that something must be done to comply with this U.S.
government request, there was no consensus on the timing for providing such
a report to Washington. The issue may have transcended the normal scope
of POW/MIA interagency consultations; senior government advisers seem to

have become involved in determining the likely impact of the report on the process of normalization. The Vietnamese believed that they had complied with the U.S. government request for information on the 84 cases by forming the Special Remains Teams; indeed, JTFFA may have reinforced that perception. The National Security Council was insistent, however, on having a separate, detailed, and written account of Vietnamese efforts in this area, to the point that it had become a litmus test of Vietnamese cooperation and figured prominently in efforts to assess Vietnamese cooperation in the months following the president's 2 July statement.

While the Vietnamese had not sought assurances that the report would result in positive forward movement toward lifting the embargo, they felt themselves caught in a double bind situation. They appeared to believe that if they turned in a report aimed at demonstrating that the Vietnamese had made real efforts but could not account for the remains, that report would guarantee that the conservative forces in the U.S. would mobilize to get the decision to lift the embargo delayed additional painful months. If they handed in a report that was short on details and replicated information they had already provided, or no report at all, they ran the risk of affording the conservatives in the U.S. the opportunity to argue that Hanoi was still in a "cover up" mode and would not be forthcoming about the remains issue. The Vietnamese appeared to believe that the intensive work undertaken by the Special Remains Teams, agreed to in mid-year, had yielded no real political dividends and had clearly not hastened progress toward normalization.

Beginning in late November and early December, the Vietnamese granted the JTFFA archivist access to personal memoirs of senior People's Army officers and archival copies of provincial newspapers in the Ministry of Defense library. Although the case-specific information uncovered by research in this trove did not speak to the issue of the fate of U.S. pilots, it confirmed JTFFA detachment views that useful information on U.S. losses might be contained in provincial and municipal newspapers which reflected local military committee reporting about wartime incidents. The Vietnamese were also cooperative in preparing and carrying out the December trilateral operations involving Lao–U.S. and Vietnamese–U.S. teams operating on their respective sides of the Vietnamese-Lao border in the vicinity of Quang Tri province and contributed positively to the efforts of the Special Remains Teams to investigate the 84 cases for which the U.S. government had information indicating that the Vietnamese had control over the remains of a U.S. serviceman at the time of his death.

Assistant Secretary Lord visited Hanoi during 13 to 15 December 1993 to restate the importance of tangible progress in the four areas specified by President Clinton in his July 1993 statement. Lord met with Prime Minister Vo Van Kiet, Foreign Minister Cam, and Deputy Foreign Minister Nguyen Duy Nien. He told his interlocutors that the U.S. expected concrete results from Vietnamese government efforts to recover American remains, continued resolution of the remaining discrepancy cases and live–sighting reports, further assistance in implementing trilateral investigations with the Lao, and accelerated efforts to provide the U.S. with wartime archival documents that would assist in shedding light on the fate of the MIAs.

Lord visited the site of the first U.S.–Vietnamese-Lao trilateral field work in Quang Tri province and participated in a repatriation ceremony in Hanoi. He presented the Vietnamese with the full set of the Combined Document Exploitation Center microfilm collection of wartime documents captured by U.S. forces as part of the U.S. commitment to respond to Vietnam's humanitarian needs and to assist Vietnam's efforts to account for its own missing. Lord also told the Vietnamese that the State Department planned to announce that the U.S. government would provide up to $2 million in additional funds for reintegration assistance to help asylum seekers who voluntarily returned to Vietnam and that the U.S. would provide $25,000 in Office of Federal Disaster Assistance relief funds to sites in southern and central Vietnam affected by recent flooding. For their part, the Vietnamese provided the Lord delegation with over 18 documents, including summaries of unilateral and bilateral efforts to investigate the 84 cases involving U.S. personnel who died in Vietnamese custody but whose remains had not been accounted for, as well as reports of unilateral investigations and remains collection efforts carried out in 1988. The Vietnamese also provided the U.S. side with a 1978 document compiled by Group 875's successor, the Military Justice Department, listing remains judged to be unrecoverable.

The Vietnamese media stated that the meetings took place in a "frank and constructive" atmosphere. Kiet acknowledged the "contribution to the promotion of mutual understanding" made by the visit, reaffirmed Vietnam's commitment to continue cooperation, and noted the "positive developments" in U.S.–Vietnam relations that it was hoped would lead to normalization of relations.[60] According to Vietnamese media accounts, Kiet told Lord that Vietnam sympathized with the U.S. "on its internal difficulties, which have resulted in a setback in the normalization process and have not met the aspirations of the two peoples," a clear indication that the senior-most Vietnamese leadership believed that the question of normalization remained a hostage to Washington's reluctance to incur the wrath of veterans organizations and POW/MIA family and activist groups by lifting the embargo against Vietnam. Kiet told Lord that "we should not leave the impression that the MIA issue blocks normalization of relations."[61] Echoing that sentiment, in December middle-level Vietnamese officials pointed out that National Assembly delegates and the senior leadership of the Vietnamese Communist Party, which was preparing for a mid-term Central Committee conference that would assess foreign and domestic policies, were debating Hanoi's policies toward the U.S., which had become the target of strong domestic criticism. The Vietnamese sought to telegraph the view that continued equivocation by the U.S. government on the decision to lift the embargo represented a problem that could result in a scaling back of the vastly improved Vietnamese POW/MIA cooperation.

In January 1994, the Vietnamese turned a spotlight on U.S. companies that were investigating investment opportunities in infrastructure rehabilitation and real estate development and reiterated Vietnam's interest in normalizing relations. For example, Deputy Prime Minister Phan Van Khai received a delegation of major American companies in mid–January and told the visitors that Vietnam would continue to pursue an "open" foreign policy and that Hanoi hoped Washington would normalize relations in the interest of peace and progress.[62] The Vietnamese also gave prominent and positive coverage to a steady stream of congressional delegations. On 9 January, General Secretary Muoi received a delegation led by the chairman of the Senate Committee on Energy and Natural Resources, signaling Vietnam's recognition of the importance of congressional support to White House strategists attempting to manage the decision to lift the embargo.[63] Vietnamese newspapers highlighted the strongest statements of support for the lifting of the embargo spoken by Senator Bennett Johnston, the delegation's leader, and by Senator Mark Hatfield. The media recounted in detail the meeting with Muoi during which Johnston pledged to urge President Clinton to lift the embargo as soon as possible and Muoi promised to sustain Vietnam's humanitarian policy of cooperation in the interest of achieving a resolution to the problem of American MIAs.[64] On 10 and 11 January, senators Daniel Inouye and Ted Stevens, the chair and the vice chair of the Defense Subcommittee of the Senate Appropriations Committee, were received by the National Assembly's vice chair, Dang Quan Thuy, and senior Foreign Ministry and economic officials. The Vietnamese media carried their expressions of support for "[closing] the sorrowful page of the past in U.S.–Vietnamese relations in order to build a better future" for the American and the Vietnamese people and for the congressional delegation's statement of appreciation for Vietnam's cooperation in the POW/MIA issue.[65] On 15 January, Prime Minister Vo Van Kiet met with Senator John Kerry, who strongly supported lifting the embargo and stressed that Hanoi had worked closely with the U.S. to establish a mechanism for cooperation on the POW/MIA issue. Kerry made the case that in order to prod Washington to go beyond the domestic political problems surrounding the issue, Vietnam must sustain its cooperation. Returning to the idea that the POW/MIA issue loomed as an obstacle to the lifting of the embargo, Kiet told Kerry that many countries had domestic problems and special interests, but in trying to overcome such internal difficulties those countries did not generally seek to exert influence over other nations. Vietnam, Kiet continued, conducted its foreign policy on the basis of respect for sovereignty and hoped that the U.S. would do the same in order to contribute to the process of U.S.–Vietnamese normalization.[66]

During 17 and 18 January, Admiral Charles Larson, commander in chief of the Pacific Command (CINCPAC), the highest-ranking U.S. military officer to visit Vietnam since 1975, paid a call on President Le Duc Anh, was received by the deputy defense minister and the foreign minister, and visited the site of a joint excavation in central Vietnam. Authorized Vietnamese media reports prominently mentioned Larson's expression of appreciation for Vietnam's "effective cooperation" and his wish that "in the coming time, with the efforts and cooperation of both sides, further progress would be made . . . so that the two countries would soon open a new chapter in their relations." According to Vietnamese news accounts, Anh told Larson that during his visit he would receive "direct and realistic" first-hand information on the resolution of the MIA problem and the "efforts of Vietnam in that area during the period in which Vietnam still had many difficulties stemming from the war." Anh reaffirmed Vietnam's pledge to continue cooperating to settle the MIA issue and, repeating the formulaic expression, noted his country's readiness to "close the past and look to the future in relations with the U.S." for the benefit of "the two countries and for peace, stability and development in the region and the world."[67]

The Vietnamese understood the importance of the momentum that had been built up by the congressional delegations and the visit by Admiral Larson. Hanoi also recognized the influence that positive remarks regarding Vietnam's cooperation spoken by Secretary of State Warren Christopher and recommendations from U.S. businesses supportive of lifting the embargo, plus endorsements from senators McCain and Kerry, could have on the White House. Hanoi was by no means confident, however, that such support would be convincing enough to the National Security Council and sufficient to nudge the process toward a decision. Publicly, the Vietnamese were critical of the "outdated attitude" of the U.S. government that had prevented the embargo from being lifted earlier, but were prepared to stay the course. A mid–January radio commentary concluded: "It would be much better if the U.S. lifts the embargo. Nevertheless, if the U.S. still keeps its outdated attitude, Vietnam will continue to develop its cooperative relations with other countries. Now the ball is in the American court."[68] Privately, Vietnamese officials responsible for the issue lamented that Hanoi seemed to have run out of ways to influence Washington and that confidence-building steps elicited only marginal returns to labor. The Vietnamese media was closely attentive to the content of a late January Senate debate on the trade embargo and a majority resolution which called for the lifting of the embargo to help resolve the fate of missing Americans. The Foreign Ministry called the resolution a "positive gesture" but made clear its understanding that the matter was still a "domestic American affair" essentially beyond Hanoi's ability to influence. Vietnam's senior foreign policy leadership had drawn the conclusion that the facts of Vietnam's cooperation were not sufficient to coax Washington beyond the threshold level of confidence necessary to convince the White House that unbearable consequences would not befall the administration once the president announced the lifting of the embargo.[69]

In early February, just prior to the decision by the U.S. to lift the embargo, Vietnamese radio reports quoted U.S. media predictions based on comments by "senior U.S. officials" that President Clinton would end the 30-year long economic sanctions against Vietnam. The Vietnamese were cautiously positive. At the regularly scheduled news conference, the Foreign Ministry spokesperson stated that Vietnam would welcome a presidential decision to lift the embargo because it would "suit the actual situation and the aspirations of the two peoples and the world community."[70] The military was unambiguous, however, about its pessimistic assessment of the likelihood of shifting U.S.-Vietnamese relations to a normal footing. At roughly the same time, Minister of Defense Doan Khue honored the 30th anniversary of the Red Star (Sao Vang) Air Force Regiment. In a letter of greeting broadcast on 2 February, Khue complimented the regiment for "having invented many wise and audacious combat tactics and for having defeated the enemy right from the first battle, shooting down many of their modern airplanes and scoring countless outstanding combat exploits during aerial battles, thus contributing daily to the causes of national liberation and unification and of building a socialist Vietnamese fatherland."[71]

On 3 February 1994, President Clinton announced the decision to remove the provisions of the TWEA that prohibited Americans from doing business in Vietnam and to expand the official U.S. presence in Vietnam to the level of a liaison office. The president stated that he had made the decision that "the best way to ensure cooperation from Vietnam and to continue getting the information Americans want on POWs and MIAs is to end the trade embargo." The establishment of a liaison office would enable the U.S. to "provide services for Americans" in Vietnam and facilitate U.S. efforts to "pursue a human rights dialogue with the Vietnamese government." President Clinton stated: "These actions do not constitute a normalization of our relationship. Before that happens, we must have more progress, more cooperation, and more answers."[72]

On 4 February, the Vietnamese foreign minister issued a Foreign Ministry statement which characterized the presidential decision to lift the embargo as a "positive and significant decision which contributes to opening a new page in the U.S.–Vietnam relationship which will be to the advantage of the people of both countries." Vietnam, the statement proceeded, "reaffirms its policy of always attaching much importance to the relationship with the United States and hopes to have a normal relationship between the two countries based on respect for independence, sovereignty, non-interference in one another's internal affairs, equality and mutual benefit." The statement noted Vietnam's agreement to the exchange of liaison offices as a transitional step in advancing toward full diplomatic relations. The statement reiterated Vietnamese government policy of "always viewing Americans missing in the war as a humanitarian problem not linked to any political problem." Consonant with its humanitarian tradition and policies, "the government and the people of Vietnam have, are and will continue to cooperate in a constructive spirit with the government and the people of America in order to resolve this problem to the fullest extent possible."[73]

The Vietnamese spoke of the 3 February decision to lift the embargo as a "step forward," but in restrained tones using measured words, clearly recognizing that the practical economic impact would be minor for Vietnam until Vietnamese access to U.S. markets was granted in the form of Most Favored Nation trading status, a step that Washington had made clear would take place as part of a future agenda, following efforts to resolve more fully the POW/ MIA problem and deal with claims and consular matters as well as human rights issues.[74]

Vietnamese officials quickly sought to establish the parameters for this new relationship. Hanoi reiterated that if the U.S. wanted the benefits of a normal relationship with Vietnam, "it must treat Vietnam equally, with respect for independence and sovereignty, and then the prospects for a U.S.-Vietnamese relationship would develop." Additionally, Hanoi precluded the possibility that U.S. firms would be accorded a priority or unfair advantage over firms from other countries in bids to engage in business of any sort in Vietnam. The Vietnamese acknowledged that this first transitional step was important to them and that they understood considerable work on the modalities of a future relationship would have to be tackled, beginning with frozen assets questions and human rights discussions. For the moment, however, a critical hurdle had been overcome and, as the media put it, America and Vietnam could begin to regard one another as friends.[75]

CHAPTER SEVEN

Conclusion: Vietnam's Approach to the POW/MIA Issue — Concepts, Negotiating Style, and Decision-Making

Basic Definitions

The Vietnamese defined the POW/MIA issue in a manner that differed significantly from Washington's view of the problem, in part as a result of the way ideology and nationalism shaped Hanoi's perspective on the world, in part as an artifact of wartime antipathy toward the U.S., and in part as a product of how Hanoi viewed its long-term goals in the bilateral relationship with Washington. Those starting points shaped Hanoi's approach to the practical aspects of searching for missing U.S. personnel.

Vietnam was drawn into a discussion of the POW/MIA issue in the early 1970s as part of the process of negotiating a peace agreement. The POW/MIA issue had little resonance to Vietnam, but Hanoi quickly calculated the political advantages of sustaining a dialogue with Washington on this issue. To Hanoi, the issue was a bargaining chip that could be used to pry concessions from Washington. The POW/MIA issue was not a separate and distinct matter, walled off from the other political issues of the war. For Vietnam, the issue was inextricably linked to a range of other political issues, including the nature of postwar bilateral relations with the U.S.; delinking the POW/MIA issue was not a practical or political possibility.

Vietnam and the U.S. had distinctly different understandings of the humanitarian character of the issue and what that meant in terms of the manner in which discussions about missing Americans would be conducted, how agreements would be reached, and how other issues would be affected by U.S.-Vietnamese POW/MIA talks. From the start, Vietnam's view of the humanitarian dimensions of the issue had less to do with the practical aspects of engaging in formal, official discussions with the U.S. than with the symbolism and nomenclature that would surround the issue. For Vietnam, the issue could be described as humanitarian, but the talks had to encompass a wider range of political issues with bilateral and regional implications. Vietnam was content to describe as humanitarian its agreement to discuss the issue, its decision to repatriate prisoners at Operation Homecoming, and the return of U.S. remains, but it never completely subscribed to the U.S. terms of reference and ground rules for conducting purely humanitarian talks. For example, during the early and mid–1980s, Vietnamese cooperation on the issue was turned on and off in a manner intended to communicate very deliberate political messages. Remains repatriations increased in response to Washington overtures and decisions judged favorably by Hanoi and decreased when Hanoi wanted to telegraph its unhappiness over a particular turn in the policy. Technical meetings were delayed or cancelled by Hanoi in order to drive home critical points about America's handling of particular aspects of the bilateral relationship and sometimes to signal Vietnam's displeasure over regional and even extraregional issues and U.S. policies of concern to Hanoi.

From the beginning, Vietnam subscribed to a significantly different understanding of the issue than did the United States. For Vietnam, at the outset of discussions with Washington and through at least 1992, the issue did not include the "live prisoner" question. Hanoi steadfastly maintained that it had repatriated all living American prisoners in 1973. From 1987 to 1992, Hanoi was a reluctant partner to discussions led by the presidential emissary on the subject of discrepancy cases, insofar as those cases suggested that the U.S. POWs involved may have been alive at the end of the war or may have survived in captivity beyond Operation Homecoming. Although the U.S. viewed cases in which there was no satisfactory explanation of the disposition of the remains as unresolved, the Vietnamese took the position that cases in which the fate of the individual was known, but no remains had been recovered, should nevertheless be considered resolved. Throughout the years of dialogue with the presidential emissary, the Vietnamese argued that two categories of cases were sufficient: killed in action (KIA), or missing in action/body not recovered (MIA/BNR).

The kinds of public interests and organizations that shaped the issue in the United States did not exist in Vietnam until perhaps the late 1980s and the early 1990s, when they emerged in a weak and tentative way that did not impose a real burden on policymakers. The Vietnamese government, at least at the outset, could define and control the parameters and character of the issue for the Vietnamese public in a manner that limited Hanoi's obligations to account for Vietnamese missing and focused public attention on what Hanoi described as the manipulative, demanding, and heavy-handed American approach to the issue and its impact on national sovereignty. The issue became one of defending national pride, protecting Vietnam's rights and interests, and resisting the blandishments and demands of the U.S.

For Vietnam, the strongest linkage existed between the POW/MIA issue and U.S.–Vietnamese normalization. Hanoi consistently dismissed U.S. government statements to the contrary as disingenuous and viewed the efforts of Washington to define the terms according to which the POW/MIA issue would be resolved, en route to a normal relationship, as unhelpful, dissembling, and insulting. Ten years worth of U.S. government statements stipulating that the "pace and scope" of progress toward normalization would be conditioned by progress toward the "fullest possible accounting" did not convince Hanoi that Washington was fair-minded and reasonable about this issue. The Roadmap, presented by the U.S. government to Hanoi in April 1991, outlined how normalization could proceed following the signing of the Paris Agreement on Cambodia. The Roadmap heavily emphasized rapid progress toward the resolution of the POW/MIA issue through early Vietnamese agreement to a two-year plan of action to investigate jointly as many cases as possible, quick action to resolve the remaining last-known-alive cases, establishment of a means of investigating the live-sighting reports, and the unilateral repatriation of the remains of missing Americans. Hanoi refused to acknowledge the Roadmap as a negotiating document and considered it a unilateral demand that violated the terms according to which the MIA issue would be settled in a humanitarian spirit. The Roadmap, from Hanoi's perspective, locked Vietnam into a position of responsibility for the success of the implementation of the Paris Agreement on Cambodia, and made resolution of the MIA issue the single greatest obstacle to normalization.

From the Vietnamese perspective, the domestic situation in the U.S. exerted a powerful influence on the relationship and determined the manner in which the POW/MIA issue was used as a precondition to normalization. From the late 1970s Hanoi perceived that organized opposition to normalization used the MIA issue as a means of galvanizing public opinion against progress toward a normal bilateral relationship. Hanoi believed that the constituency that sought resolution of the POW/MIA issue was politically less significant than the forces they viewed as anti–Vietnamese interests. Hanoi also believed that important elements of the U.S. government did not earnestly want to make real progress toward resolving the POW/MIA issue, but wanted instead to derail the possibility of a rapprochement. In Hanoi's opinion, these elements utilized the POW/MIA issue as a means of preventing forward movement toward normalization.

For Vietnam, economic calculations were often at the core of decisions to improve cooperation with the U.S. in efforts to account for missing Americans. In the early and mid–1970s, in 1985, 1987, and 1990–92, Hanoi deliberately sought ways of being more responsive to the U.S. efforts to resolve the POW/MIA issue. Those periods of flexibility and enhanced cooperation coincided with efforts to solidify relations with the West and with the U.S. with the goal of rescuing Vietnam's economy, expanding the pool of potential trade partners and aid donors, and garnering support and sympathy for international financial assistance through the World Bank and International Monetary Fund.

Vietnam's negotiating approach to the POW/MIA issue emerged from these starting points.

Talking and Fighting: Negotiating with Hanoi

In Hanoi's negotiating approach, every moment of discussion at the technical and policy level was highly politicized and often highly theatrical. Negotiations had a certain dimension of choreography and ritual to them that was intended to maximize the impact of Hanoi's political message. Hanoi viewed discussions concerning the POW/MIA issue as a means of achieving specific tactical advantages and strengthening its standing and image.

Hanoi often pursued extremes of reciprocity in negotiating both practical and principled aspects of this issue and seemed less inclined to worry about the meaning of the point at the heart of a particular bargain than about the idea of achieving a matching benefit for concessions which it conferred. In the mid-1980s, Hanoi pressed Washington to discuss the utility of opening a U.S. office in Hanoi that would manage the daily casualty resolution process. Washington was unenthusiastic. In arguing the case for a reciprocal right to open an office in Washington that would represent Hanoi's interests regarding this issue, the Vietnamese allowed themselves to be put in the position of having to face a U.S. counterargument premised on the view that Hanoi did not need a representative section in Washington because the U.S. did not hold any Vietnamese prisoners. To Hanoi, the more important point was that Vietnam deserved and required a reciprocal advantage for every agreement it struck with Washington. The Vietnamese side was less concerned with retaining balance in its approach or with narrowing Washington's maneuverability than with being able to lay claim to having extracted an equal concession from the U.S. for nearly every point it granted.

For example, during the 1991–92 period, Vietnam's willingness to agree to enhanced access to wartime archival information bearing on cases of U.S. MIAs was to an extent made conditional on a Vietnamese request for equivalent access to U.S. wartime archives. In October 1990, then Foreign Minister Thach and General Vessey reached an agreement that included a Vietnamese commitment to provide U.S. technical experts with greater access to information in Vietnamese wartime archives bearing on missing Americans. In January and March 1991, the Department of Defense dispatched an information research team to Hanoi to discuss the modalities of this agreement. During the course of these discussions and again during several high-level policy discussions in 1991 and 1992, the Vietnamese stated that the process of information research and information sharing must be a "two way street." In November 1991, during talks with Assistant Secretary Solomon, Deputy Foreign Minister Le Mai said that the Vietnamese required access to U.S. government information on wartime air missions with the same kind of urgency that prompted the U.S. to argue that access to Vietnamese archival information would help resolve cases of missing Americans. Mai strongly implied that this information was a necessary "quid" for the Vietnamese Ministry of Defense and would make it easier to obtain access to Vietnamese documents. In early March, Vietnam's ambassador to the United Nations, Trinh Xuan Lang, echoed the view that Hanoi would like the U.S. to provide access to its military documents because the effort must come from both sides.

The Vietnamese may have been looking for nothing more than a symbolic act that would underscore U.S. government willingness to "trade" information. The Vietnamese Ministry of National Defense and the Ministry of Interior had separately expressed some reservations concerning the agreement struck by Thach and had thrown up obstacles to U.S. efforts to gain access to historical records. The Foreign Ministry, it appeared, was expressing the view that in order to get full agreement to the U.S. request for access to wartime documents, the U.S. had to be willing to provide Hanoi with Washington's own wartime reports on incidents in which U.S. pilots became missing in action and mission action reports of units that operated in the same areas where U.S. pilots were shot down or crashed and remained unaccounted for. Hanoi's elliptical fashion of raising this issue and its inability to be specific about the nature of the reports requested put Washington in the position of having to spend an inordinate amount of time attempting to discern just how serious Vietnam was about the request, whether it represented another temporizing tactic, or whether they had in mind a specific research approach intended to compliment other information research efforts. In order to respond to the Vietnamese request for listings of every sortie flown on a given day in the area in which a loss incident involving an American occurred, the Naval Historical Center provided declassified U.S. Navy summaries of the 7th Fleet Monthly Operations and monthly summaries from the Naval Forces Vietnam records, and the Center for Air Force History provided declassified unit histories. It did not matter that Hanoi had regularly received information from the U.S. in the form of case narratives presented at technical sessions. What mattered to Hanoi was the impact of insisting on reciprocity before granting access to documents and witnesses.

While insisting on extremes of reciprocity was of intrinsic importance to Hanoi, it also offered a means of achieving tactical advantages. When Hanoi needed to play for time, to delay proceedings, or to complicate discussions in a manner that would exert a drag effect on negotiations, the Vietnamese side simply made clear that it could not proceed until Washington met Vietnam's concerns for equivalent concessions. Often, the concessions were irrelevant to Hanoi, but being able to exert a choke hold on proceedings was advantage enough, especially when Washington became preoccupied with concocting inventive means of meeting such demands and anticipating Vietnamese requests for reciprocity. For example, periodically during 1989–91, Hanoi pointed to their own MIAs in order to demonstrate how difficult it was to convince the Vietnamese people who were struggling with their own missing to support their government's efforts to respond to U.S. demands to find U.S. missing. During those years it was not clear whether the Vietnamese were serious about the issue or considered it a means of turning U.S. positions aside, demonstrating the extent to which they were selflessly addressing Washington's concerns while their own domestic issues festered, and blunting U.S. efforts to stress the magnitude of the POW issue for Washington.

In the context of POW/MIA negotiations, Hanoi sought to make use of a variety of American private voluntary organizations and nongovernmental channels to communicate its views, test Washington's temperature, develop sympathy via "people-to-people" diplomacy, and in some contexts compromise and discredit the U.S. government policy regarding the POW/MIA issue. To a considerable extent during the late 1970s and early 1980s, Hanoi relied on friendly private voluntary organizations as a source of information on U.S. attitudes toward Hanoi and for readings of how Vietnam's policies and positions played in the U.S. In the early 1980s, Vietnam expressed dissatisfaction with Washington's views on the POW/MIA issue by very ceremoniously providing remains to a visiting U.S. veterans group, ignoring the primacy Washington had placed on developing a "government-to-government" channel. In the mid- and late 1980s Hanoi relied on such American organizations as an important window onto U.S. government policy. In the 1988–92 period, Hanoi approached selected nongovernmental organizations and individuals to help clarify Vietnam's desire to move quickly toward normalization and to resolve the POW/MIA impasse that threatened to scuttle progress toward that goal.[1]

The extent to which Hanoi relied on these nongovernmental organizations and individuals varied directly with the leadership's confidence that its approach to the issue had yielded dividends and negotiating advantages, that it retained control over the course of events, and that the U.S. was seriously disarmed by Vietnamese actions and initiatives, stymied by internal disagreements over the next practical steps, or besieged by critical public opinion. In many ways Nguyen Co Thach in particular believed that by utilizing nongovernmental channels, especially those that were not friendly toward Washington or predisposed to accept the U.S. policy toward Indochina in general, he seriously confused and disoriented U.S. policymakers, distracted them from pressing Vietnam on this difficult issue, and discredited the U.S. government by communicating the message that Washington was clumsy and ineffective whereas the nongovernmental organizations, many of which were sympathetic to Vietnam, were capable of accomplishing infinitely more than the U.S. government. Curiously, though, in his pursuit of people-to-people diplomacy, Thach often selected odd bedfellows, frequently miscalculated the reaction of the concerned American public, and rarely caused Washington to pause for more than a quick reassessment of tactics. Generally, Washington's patient response was to remind the Vietnamese of the importance of relying exclusively on government-to-government channels and to make it clear that Hanoi would simply get no credit for resolving the issue via other channels.

For example, Ross Perot, the Texas billionaire businessman who in 1992 mounted a bid for the presidency, visited Vietnam in April 1987 after years of activism on behalf of the POW/MIA issue that frequently pitted him against government policy. Perot returned from his visit to promote the establishment of a Vietnamese economic representative in a third country embassy, the opening of a reciprocal American business office in Hanoi, and other gestures aimed at building Hanoi's confidence and moving Vietnam toward agreement to release America POWs. According to media accounts, in a report written in early April 1987 for President Ronald Reagan, Perot claimed that the Vietnamese, who were interested in direct assistance from the private sector, were primarily interested in Perot himself and had studied Perot in detail. Thach, who met with Perot, had clearly sought to play on Perot's long years as a critic of U.S. policy and his impatient interest in instigating a breakthrough where he thought Washington was deficient, slow, and unable to seize the initiative. As is evident in Perot's letter to President Reagan, Thach had convinced Perot that Washington had adopted a flawed negotiating approach that was missing a crucial element of reciprocity that would make cooperation more attractive for Hanoi. Thach complained of the manner in which the U.S. treated the issue and apparently persuaded Perot that the level of U.S. government representation had to be enhanced and that the U.S. teams that dealt with the issue consisted of "minor figures" with whom the Vietnamese did not want to deal.[2]

Perot was persuaded that economic incentives would yield the most effective response from Hanoi and therefore urged Reagan to do precisely what U.S. policymakers had cautioned against doing—reward Hanoi with concessions without requiring Vietnam to come across with remains, information on missing service personnel, access to witnesses, and enhanced cooperation in planning and executing joint field investigations. According to Western newspaper reports, in June 1990 Thach designated Perot and his company as a business agent of Hanoi to "help attract U.S. investment once trade and diplomatic ties were normalized." Perot claimed to have rejected Thach's 1990 letter in which the foreign minister proposed this arrangement with Perot. Nevertheless, Thach retained the interest of Perot, whose associate traveled to Hanoi and met with Thach in August 1991. According to Le Van Bang, then director of the Foreign Ministry's Americas Department, Perot and his colleague promised money, medicine, and other unspecified humanitarian assistance and assistance in the area of electronics, computers, oil and gas, transportation, and property development. Perot denied these claims. Nevertheless, it appears that Thach, at a particularly difficult moment in his efforts to manage the POW/MIA issue, had sought to revive connections with Perot and to enlist his inclination to urge opening economic lines at a time when Hanoi was pushing hard to discredit U.S. government efforts to use the embargo as leverage to pressure Hanoi to take quicker steps toward accounting for missing U.S. service personnel.[3]

Hanoi worked hard, with often uneven results, to read congressional viewpoints and frequently sought to utilize what it viewed as differences between the Hill and the administration to its advantage. For example, during December 1990, in advance of the end-of-year National Assembly session, Hanoi made clear in editorials and newspaper articles, as well as speeches by luminaries including Vo Van Kiet, that in its calculations, congressional impatience with Washington's policy toward Indochina was likely to damage the administration's position on the POW/MIA issue. In the Vietnamese view, attention would shift from (1) Vietnamese cooperation as the determining factor of the pace and scope of progress toward normalization to (2) business and commercial interests engendered by Japanese, Southeast Asian and European economic activism in Vietnam. The Vietnamese concluded that there was a shrinking base of support within Congress for the administration's policies toward Vietnam and Cambodia. They noted that their bilateral relations with the World Bank and the Asian Development Bank had improved in spite of the continuing embargo, and they implied that it would become more difficult to rationalize and defend the embargo. The Vietnamese calculated that there was considerable likelihood that Congress would place increased pressure on the administration and therefore Hanoi should focus on being cooperative without going to any great lengths to comply with Washington's requests for agreements to expand POW/MIA activities.

By late 1990, the Vietnamese calculated that pressure was growing on Washington from business quarters and congressional interests to loosen some of the economic embargo, such as restrictions on group travel and commerce in humanitarian items. Hanoi believed that such pressure would make it easier for Vietnam to achieve the goal of forcing the end of the embargo without having to strain so much to comply with the political conditions for normalization. Hanoi seemed to have reached the conclusion that congressional pressure would work to Vietnam's advantage, given the long-standing impatience of important senators and representatives with the administration's policy on Cambodia. Through early 1991, the Vietnamese continued to take the position that they had done all they could be expected to do and had still not pleased the U.S. government, in part as an appeal to what they viewed as sympathetic elements in Congress. In March 1991, the Vietnamese looked forward to a visit from senators McCain and Kerry and scheduled that event just one week prior to a trip planned by the presidential emissary with the intention of extracting some leverage from an advance session with congressmen who they assumed would be predisposed to recognizing Vietnam's positive contribution to the POW/MIA issue.

The Vietnamese were tenacious, skilled negotiators with infinite patience, a sense of theater, a flair for the dramatic, and an unrelenting manner. While the Vietnamese had a strong sense of reciprocity, the efforts to pick up on Vietnamese hints to the effect that some tit-for-tat step was required in order to move discussions forward did not often yield appreciable progress toward a goal. In January 1992, for example, Hanoi officials were very explicit regarding the need to respond to their requests for additional efforts to meet Vietnam's humanitarian needs. Their message was that Hanoi would not go any further until the U.S. government made good on what Vietnam interpreted as promises to assess and respond to those needs. Washington's perception was that responding to the Vietnamese request would have a direct impact on progress toward the fullest possible accounting in specific and measurable ways.

In fact, the Vietnamese were seeking a level negotiating field and were not suggesting that the U.S. government could achieve a quantum leap in cooperation by complying with Vietnam's requests for additional humanitarian assistance. The U.S. government repeatedly assumed a cause and effect relationship between negotiating initiatives and Vietnamese responses: if the U.S. government took a step toward meeting Hanoi's expectations, then Hanoi would respond in kind with a compromise or accommodation that would net the U.S. what it required to proceed with POW/MIA work. In some ways, the Vietnamese approached such situations very differently, regarding the process as a delicately staged minuet in which one partner must get the other to follow his lead, without necessarily enhancing the dance itself. However, instead of sweeping steps, only minor changes in posture resulted from that kind of give-and-take.

There were no dividends for a well-scripted set of points. The Vietnamese worked with little paper in front of them. They made their views known succinctly through the voice of the delegation leader. The U.S. government side was always encumbered by a lengthy set of points, bulkily packaged, laboriously read. The Vietnamese understood that to mean that the negotiating team from Washington had little leeway and a totally unflexible mandate, and that made the Vietnamese less inclined to discuss alternatives or probe for inventive solutions. Indeed, the formal, scripted approach to negotiations necessitated the "private meeting," in which the delegation heads took one another's exact measurements in a way that was not possible in the formal context of the plenary meeting.

There was real value to a balance between protocol-consciousness and the willingness to be flexible, friendly, and unstarched in discussions with Hanoi's negotiators. The Vietnamese observed the rules of diplomatic intercourse. They were well versed in conducting formal, diplomatic discussions. At the same time, they preferred a bit of familiarity and informality, though not necessarily friendliness, as another stage on which they could easily, in less labored terms, express the strength of their views, the seriousness of their position, and the problems associated with a particular proposal. Representational dinners were more relaxed atmospheres in which the Vietnamese could restate their positions in a setting with rules but not necessarily with the same rigidity associated with a negotiating table. Discussions on the margins of meetings were not necessarily only opportunities for the Vietnamese to prod their negotiating partners beyond their mandates or to feel around for weak points and gather impressions regarding the next steps. They were also opportunities for the Vietnamese to informally add substance and personal insights into the particular course chosen by the Vietnamese side and to reinforce their official views in a personal manner. Department-level officials were adept at relating the manner in which the MIA issue affected their families, and assuring U.S. counterparts that they personally understood the need to keep looking for answers. Some underscored the extent to which that personal experience convinced them that searching for remains prolonged the pain and deferred the process of healing. There were real limits, however, to the extent to which the Vietnamese allowed negotiating counterparts to become privy to their thoughts. The apt metaphor in this instance is the Vietnamese home with its various concentric circles in which progressively more intimate life transpires toward the center. Negotiators were welcomed at points relatively removed from the center, where guests were received, and were only gradually allowed to move beyond the first entry point, into an anteroom that was still distant from the heart of the living space.

The Other MIAs: Vietnam and Its Unaccounted For Soldiers

In response to Hanoi's argument that Vietnam had its own massive MIA problem, during his August 1987 visit to Hanoi, General Vessey carried with him a book of maps and reports about PAVN grave sites at large military actions during the war for presentation to his interlocutors. During a mid–1990 technical meeting, the U.S. government again provided the Vietnamese side with declassified documents on gravesites of Vietnamese soldiers. The Vietnamese took the occasion of such initiatives by the U.S. side to make the strong point that the U.S. government did not have accurate enough information to help in accounting for Vietnamese MIAs and the U.S. should not expect Hanoi to possess such records. In October 1990, Foreign Minister Thach and General Vessey reached an agreement that included a Vietnamese commitment to provide U.S. technical experts with greater access to information in Vietnamese wartime archives bearing on missing Americans. In January and March 1991, as noted above, the Department of Defense dispatched an information research team to Hanoi to discuss the modalities of this agreement. At that time Hanoi made it clear that Vietnam's willingness to agree to enhanced access to wartime archival information bearing on cases of U.S. MIAs was conditioned on equivalent access to U.S. wartime archives. The Vietnamese took the position that the process of information research and information sharing must be a "two way street."

Importantly, during the January 1991 military meetings to review the draft documents for discussion at the Seventh National Party Congress, participants in a local military party committee session made the point that one of the tasks before the PAVN was to "strive to resolve" the consequences of war, including the search for persons missing as a result of the hostilities. Thereafter, the Vietnamese spoke of 300,000 MIAs in order to demonstrate exactly how much of a domestic problem they had and how difficult it was for Vietnamese struggling with their own missing to support their government's efforts to respond to U.S. demands to find U.S. missing. According to a middle-level Foreign Ministry official, of the 842,405 Vietnamese troops killed in action, the remains of 496,409 individuals were recovered. The remains of over 200,000 individuals had not been recovered by August 1993, and there was no information on 82,405 individuals. Additionally, 484,324 soldiers were wounded during the course of the war.

The subject of the status of survivor benefits, veterans retirement policies, and the MIA issue became increasingly pressing issues for the Vietnamese leadership after the mid–1991 Seventh National Party Congress. Beginning in early 1991, veterans groups and party organizations within the military, in commenting on the draft platform for the National Party Congress, made it clear that Vietnam's 300,000 MIAs represented a groundswell issue to which the leadership had to respond, not a manufactured issue used as a negotiating ploy. In mid–1992, a middle-level bureaucrat with access to senior Vietnamese Foreign Ministry and VNOSMP officials argued that a U.S. government decision to provide a little information on this matter, perhaps by soliciting the names of Vietnamese MIAs or POWs from American servicemen, would go a long way toward helping and would truly move the Vietnamese people. The official made the point that the people in the provinces who expressed concern with the way Hanoi had neglected accounting for Vietnamese missing were not aware of the politics of this issue. They just expressed their personal belief that more should be done, especially since the government was spending so much time helping the Americans to account for their missing.

In early April 1992, a remains repatriation group operating under the authority of the Nghe An Province military command pledged to continue to search for the remains of fallen Vietnamese soldiers in the former mountainous war zone adjacent to Nghe Tinh Province in Laos. Between 1984 and 1992, the repatriation group reportedly undertook "thousands" of trips to the mountainous areas in Laos and returned the bodies of approximately 8,000 Vietnamese combatants that had been interred in various cemeteries in Khammouane, Bolikhamsai, and Xieng Khoang provinces to a military cemetery in Nghe Tinh's Anh Son District. (On 9 April 1994 the Vietnamese minister of labor, war veterans and social welfare and the Lao minister of labor and social welfare signed a memorandum of understanding on completing the excavation and repatriation of the bodies of Vietnamese combatants from Lao wartime cemeteries in Oudomsai, Attopeu, and Xieng Khoang provinces in 1994. The memorandum referred to a mutual commitment to building a monument in Laos to fallen soldiers.[4])

By 1993, the variety of interests groups that emerged during the process of planning for the Seventh National Party Congress, including veterans organizations, felt relatively free to make points about their constituencies' interests during General Secretary Nguyen Van Linh's tenure. Vietnamese efforts to place on the agenda requests concerning their missing could no longer be considered to be merely delaying tactics in POW/MIA negotiations. Rather, they reflected the views of legitimate organizations and interests in a position to lobby in support of their views and to attract public opinion in a modestly more free press. In a 12 August 1993 interview, Foreign Minister Cam appealed to the U.S. government to "concretely pursue cooperation" with Vietnam's efforts to find its own 300,000 MIAs.[5]

On 1 June 1993, Foreign Minister Cam told Senator John Kerry that the American side should assist Vietnam in efforts to resolve the problem of missing Vietnamese. His aim was not to introduce obstacles, but to illustrate the serious concerns of the Vietnamese people regarding disabled veterans, separated families, and Vietnamese families affected by the MIA issue. At an early June technical session with the Joint Task Force–Full Accounting, the Vietnamese asked that the U.S. side work to unearth information about Vietnamese military prisoners who had died in captivity while in the custody of the Republic of Vietnam or the U.S. side. In his 17 June speech to the National Assembly, Deputy Prime Minister Phan Van Khai stated that the U.S. had a responsibility to help resolve the problem of Vietnamese MIAs. In mid–June, the new Vietnamese ambassador to Thailand, Le Cong Phung, raised the importance of U.S. government assistance to Vietnam's efforts to provide an accounting for its missing soldiers. Prime Minister Vo Van Kiet spoke to this same issue in his discussions with Asian counterparts, stressing the need to get Washington to provide information that might help Hanoi account for its missing. By mid–1993 various provinces had initiated surveys of the number of wounded and missing, as well as surveys of the needs of veterans who survived and the families of war heros.[6]

Press articles in the Vietnamese Communist Party's authoritative daily newspaper in early 1993 suggested that the highest levels of the Vietnamese leadership were focused on the issue of responding to the social needs of veterans and the needs of the families and dependents of soldiers who died in combat. Moreover, some articles suggested that groups hitherto uninvolved in the POW/MIA issue and unconcerned with the shape of U.S.–Vietnamese relations, were prepared to take firm stands regarding the importance of Vietnam's efforts to seek answers to questions from its own MIA families. One article represented a professorial opinion on Vietnam's "human rights" policies in the 14 May issue of the party's daily newspaper and argued that it was a human right and the government's humanitarian duty to provide answers to the families of fallen heros whose bodies had not been recovered. The article noted that out of an altruism born of historical practice, the Vietnamese would continue to work hard to return the remains of foreign soldiers, just as they did during the reigns of Le Loi and Nguyen Trai after fighting with "foreign aggressors."[7]

In mid–1993, the U.S. government Interagency Working Group agreed to provide the Vietnamese with a copy of the Combined Document Exploitation Center (CDEC) collection, a massive collection of unindexed microfilmed documents that were collected in the field by the U.S. military. The majority of the documents were collected in battlefield conditions from PAVN casualties. The bulk of the material was in the form of diaries, letters, identification media, Vietnamese political tracts and other propaganda, and captured messages and instructions. In the early 1980s, the Vietnamese had approached JCRC members during visits to Hanoi and raised the possibility of obtaining the CDEC collection. The mid–1993 decision was intended to signal U.S. understanding of Vietnam's MIA issue and to demonstrate Washington's willingness to respond to Hanoi's requests for assistance. The delegation that traveled to Hanoi in July 1993 delivered the first microfilm reel to the Joint Document Center. VNOSMP officials indicated that the Foreign Ministry saw this as a significant symbolic act of considerable importance that would enable them to make the case that Hanoi's humanitarian concerns were not being neglected by the U.S.

Decision-Making Leadership

The Vietnamese approach to the POW/MIA issue was shaped by the myriad of leaders involved in its management of the issue. At the outset, Le Duc Tho retained central control over the issue as key interlocutor with the U.S. during the Paris peace talks. A range of ambassadors and central government officials played supporting roles, but no real single group of POW/MIA issue managers emerged until the 1975–78 period. During those years Politburo members, including Pham Van Dong, and key foreign policy officials, including Deputy Foreign Minister Phan Hien and senior Foreign Ministry official Vu Hoang, were required to meet with American delegations and explain Vietnamese policy to congressional visitors. Beginning in the mid–1980s a range of senior Foreign Ministry personnel, including Hoang Bich Son, Ha Van Lau, Tran Quang Co, Nguyen Duy Nien, Trinh Xuan Lang, and Le Mai, developed roles as defenders of Hanoi's policy or as facilitators of initial communications with the U.S. The central role was played, however, by Nguyen Co Thach, who dominated the issue for the decade during which he served as foreign minister (1980–91).

Thach cut his teeth in the diplomatic corps in the 1950s. He was appointed to a vice-ministerial position in the Foreign Ministry in the mid–1960s. As Foreign Minister Nguyen Duy Trinh's first deputy in the 1970s, Thach held major responsibilities for regional relations with Southeast Asia and played a role in defining Vietnam's China policy. He became a Central Committee member in 1976 at the Fourth Party Congress and was appointed Foreign Minister in February 1980. Thach was elevated to alternate Politburo status at the Fifth Congress of the Vietnamese Communist Party in 1982. Thach orchestrated the foreign policy of the newborn Socialist Republic and figured prominently in defining postwar Indochina unity and asserting Vietnam's political imperatives in the Sino-Vietnamese conflict. He was appointed vice chairman of the Council of Ministers in February 1987.

Thach's policy toward the POW/MIA issue crystallized as a response to Washington's 1987 appointment of a presidential emissary, which elevated the issue, and to the U.S. government's agreement to address certain of Vietnam's humanitarian concerns. Thach approached the issue in the context of Vietnam's own perception of the need to diversify its foreign relations, rebuild credibility in the West, and lay the groundwork for rapprochement with Washington in order to attract investment and repair the economy. Under Thach, the Vietnamese turned over more material evidence and remains, permitted the beginning of joint field investigations of crash and grave sites, and engaged in fairly regular technical discussions to plan investigative activities.

Thach was a tough negotiating partner, theatrical in the extreme, tactical and crafty, polished and urbane in his presentation, and thoroughly calculating in his approach to issues. In tight negotiating corners, Thach did not hesitate to throw back his chair, jump from his seat, and state his inability to proceed in circumstances in which his word and personal integrity were being questioned. He was not above summarily halting dialogue to make political points and angle for negotiating advantage. Thach's guidance concerning the POW/MIA issue came from Politburo member Le Duc Tho, who involved himself in the details of the issue as a result of his concern with U.S.–Vietnamese normalization. Essentially, in the early 1980s, Tho urged a cautious approach to the normalization, warning of the consequences of a blind rush toward the embrace of Washington. Thach benefited from Tho's tenure. Tho's support enabled Thach to stack the Foreign Ministry with strong allies, including Tran Quang Co, Dinh Nho Liem, and Le Mai. Additionally, Tho probably had a hand in both the elevation of Thach to full Politburo membership and the foreign minister's promotion to the concurrent position of vice chairman of the Council of Ministers.

Tho retired from his active party positions in March 1986 at the Sixth National Party Congress, along with two other senior leaders, Truong Chinh and Pham Van Dong. The three were named "advisers" to the Central Committee. Tho was widely assumed to have retained significant behind-the-scenes influence by virtue of a complex system of alliances that evolved from his sponsorship of the careers of many significant Politburo and Central Committee figures, including Thach. Tho's retirement was clearly the result of a well-choreographed agreement between members of the inner circle in the interest of a smooth leadership transition. The influence he exercised in his retirement was not unlimited, but he retained relationships to leaders whose careers he had sponsored. However, perhaps as a result of his failing health, he did not play nearly as public a role as an adviser as did Pham Van Dong and Truong Chinh, who were, for example, regularly called upon to lend their prestige to certain public events.

Tho was often cited as the mainstay of the conservative wing of the Politburo. It is important, however, to understand that as early as 1986 Tho clearly stated his views on the importance of internal party reforms and offered his support to the initial reformist program articulated by General Secretary Nguyen Van Linh. Tho had a long track record of support for reformist positions concerning party organization. By the Fifth Congress, Tho had become the spokesman for reforms calling for the separation of party and state functions through redefining the division of party-state labor in precise terms and through prohibiting the arrogation of multiple party and state roles by party officials, a common practice at the time. Tho also advocated retraining party secretaries, the everyday workhorses of the organization, in order to equip them with modern managerial abilities and technical administrative knowledge. Tho supported the injection of younger and formally trained cadres into an aging party organization and the revitalization of subprovincial organizations through a program of rotational training periods aimed at assigning provincial cadre to district party structures. These were important themes which became part of the litany of reform plans for the party organization in subsequent years.

Tho focused on every aspect of the POW/MIA issue and was especially sensitive to matters bearing directly on the question of the pace and scope of normalization. For example, in August 1988, Assistant Secretary of State Gaston Sigur told Congress that the U.S. government did not support the establishment of an interest section or any other form of office in Hanoi. Although his testimony on this matter did not go beyond the long-standing U.S. government position, the Vietnamese were offended by the manner in which the point was made. The Foreign Ministry dispatched a message to its embassy in Bangkok directing that the U.S. Embassy be informed that the Vietnamese government took exception to Sigur's words. On the Sunday following the

congressional hearing, department-level officials were summoned to the Foreign Ministry and instructed by Thach to draft a letter to General Vessey saying
that Vietnam was prepared to halt cooperation as a result of the views expressed
by Sigur. North American Department personnel recommended that the
minister not send such a letter because Vietnam's concerns had already been
communicated in a routine and effective manner. Thach informed his staff that
Le Duc Tho had himself voiced the need to send a strongly worded letter to
Vessey and the Foreign Ministry would follow this recommendation.

From 1987 to 1988, General Secretary Nguyen Van Linh granted Thach
considerable independence in formulating and implementing foreign policy.
Linh allowed Thach to form a supportive, devoted policy team and was himself
predisposed to a policy that would move deliberately toward U.S.–Vietnamese
normalization without sacrificing other foreign policy equities. However, by
mid–1988 Linh had endured some slippage in his political standing as a result
of the inadequacies of, and reversals suffered by, the economic reform program
and as a consequence of increasing internal party opposition to aspects of Linh's
efforts to renovate the party. By mid–1988 the leverage that Linh was able to
bring to bear through extra-party structures, an unleashed media, and newly
enfranchised political interests had been diminished by the reaction of more
cautious influences inclined to reassert party dominance. This impacted on
Linh's ability to protect Thach from criticism. Importantly, Thach is said to
have been upbraided at the December 1986 Party Congress for his haste in pursuing a route toward normalization of relations with the United States. He was
able to exercise a fairly free hand for most of 1987 and some of 1988, but by
late 1989, when the "peace dividends" from the withdrawal of Vietnamese
forces from Cambodia did not materialize, Thach found his ability to maneu-
ver more and more constrained and encountered increasing opposition to his
approaches to foreign policy issues.

Thach confronted a series of foreign policy crises in 1990 that ultimately
contributed to his isolation in the Politburo. Thach defended a position on
Cambodia in late 1989 and in early 1990 that was premised on a modest role
for the United Nations and early elections according to the Namibia and
Nicaraguan experiences. He thought that the Permanent Five Agreement
would guarantee Beijing continuing influence in Indochina and compel Vietnam to abandon the Phnom Penh regime. This prompted Thach to urge holding out for better terms and resulted in a policy decision that seemed to roll
back the early flexibility that Thach had demonstrated about the Permanent
Five Agreement and cast Vietnam as the spoiler of what had in early 1990
seemed like an acceptable and workable means of ending the conflict in Cambodia. In 1990 Vietnam had to contend with massive cuts in material assistance
when the Council for Economic Mutual Assistance (CEMA) was suddenly rendered moribund by rapid changes of regimes in the Soviet bloc and by a severely
curtailed Soviet ability to underwrite Hanoi's military and economic develop-

ment. Thach and other supporters were put on the defensive by the turmoil in Eastern Europe.

In September, Nguyen Van Linh, Do Muoi, and Pham Van Dong traveled to Chengdu, China, for secret discussions with their Chinese counterparts that presumably touched on Cambodia, the state of bilateral relations, and economic assistance from Beijing. Hanoi, miffed at leaks that the meeting had occurred, denied that any understandings on the settlement of the Cambodian conflict had been reached. Thach was put in an awkward position by press rumors that a high-level meeting had taken place without his participation and by reports that the Chinese had made it clear that they would not meet with any party that included the foreign minister. Following Hanoi's denial that a separate peace had been sought during the Chengdu meeting, Thach was rumored to have labored hard to quash any minor success that might have resulted from the secret meeting. Finally, by 1990, after four years of policy-level discussions with the U.S. presidential emissary and numerous technical meetings in Hanoi, Thach had not managed to move the POW/MIA issue one step closer to resolution. Thach, a proponent of improved U.S.–Vietnamese relations, was criticized for his inability to show any progress toward closure on the POW/MIA issue.

Thach's view of normalization had all along been that it would be good for Vietnam if only because it would end the embargo on World Bank loans. He also seemed to believe that it could be achieved without sacrificing major policy equities, especially in light of the fundamental policy decision to withdraw from Cambodia. In short, Thach wanted to normalize but at a minimal cost to Vietnam's regional interests and self-respect. Thach argued that Hanoi had withdrawn its combat troops from Cambodia, though they had clearly left an elaborate advisory structure in place. Hanoi had been responsive to Washington's requirements regarding cooperation on the POW/MIA issue. Vietnam had made witnesses accessible to U.S. specialists, devoted more time and resources to preparing for field investigations, mobilized provincial committees to cooperate with U.S. investigative teams, formed an information team and committed itself to searching for wartime documents which could contribute to resolving individual cases. However, Hanoi's inability to get beyond this issue with Washington compelled Thach to seek some quick victories to show that he had been tough and unrelenting in his dealings with the Americans. Thach paid a price for miscalculating the ease with which the POW/MIA issue could be resolved. He became steadily more isolated within the Politburo and was criticized for going as far as he did toward satisfying Washington's requests for increased access to witnesses, longer and larger field operations, and responsiveness on the issue of access to information in wartime documents. According to a senior Foreign Ministry official, by late 1990 Thach was derisively called "Mr. America" and was accused of defending U.S. government policy positions.

Thach's successor, Nguyen Manh Cam, former ambassador to the Soviet Union, did not duplicate the status and influence of his predecessor. He did not hold a position commensurate with Thach's vice chairmanship of the Council of Ministers and was not elevated to Politburo status until January 1994. Cam was a quietly competent though colorless diplomat who emerged as foreign minister in an environment in which regional and global changes had vigorously intruded on Vietnam's world view and at a time when the balance of power within the Vietnamese system was in flux.

Decision-Making Organization

In February 1973, Prime Minister Pham Van Dong signed a decree establishing the VNOSMP (Co Quan Viet Nam Tim Kiem Tin Tuc Nguoi Mat Tich Trong Chien Tranh Viet Nam), which was composed of "permanent representatives" from the Foreign Ministry, Ministry of Defense, Ministry of Public Security, and the Health Ministry. The office functioned in an essentially ad hoc manner during the 1970s and was overshadowed by Nguyen Co Thach during his decade as foreign minister. From 1975 to 1978, a small group of senior Vietnamese Politburo members and top foreign policy managers shaped decisions and determined tactical approaches to the POW/MIA issue. In March 1977 Phan Hien, deputy foreign minister, met with President Carter's designated emissary, Ambassador Leonard Woodcock, to discuss the question of missing American service personnel. Woodcock's delegation also met with Foreign Minister Nguyen Duy Trinh and called on Pham Van Dong. A month later Richard Holbrook met with Phan Hien in Paris. During 1975–78, the strong influence of senior economic planners, including Le Thanh Nghi, had an impact on Hanoi's decision to argue for a link between cooperation on resolving the POW/MIA issue, normalization, and reparations.

During his 1977 discussions with Woodcock, Phan Hien announced the establishment of a special office to seek information on MIAs and recover remains. In 1979, Vietnamese officials told visiting U.S. congressmen that the organization, which had been established in March 1974 with 60 personnel, had a formal structure of organization, a chief and a staff director, an elaborate network below the central apparatus, an insufficient budget, and a small cadre of technical specialists assigned on a permanent basis. According to a middle-level Vietnamese Foreign Ministry official, however, the office was little more than a shoestring operation involving a handful of individuals with no clear mandate to handle the issue and no formal organizational structure tied to existing ministries. In 1982, when Richard Armitage visited Hanoi, the senior Vietnamese officials with whom he met were supported by an assortment of middle-level Foreign and Defense Ministry officials who had been brought together in 1980–81 to form an invigorated core for the VNOSMP that was tied closely to the Foreign Ministry's North American Department and overseen by senior department-level officials with close ties to Foreign Minister Thach. By the time General Vessey traveled to Hanoi in August 1987, the Vietnamese had begun to assign working-level personnel from the Ministry of Defense and active duty military officers to the VNOSMP. That structure served the diplomatic and political goals of Foreign Minister Thach until he relinquished his Politburo seat and cabinet position in 1991.

The military's role in the POW/MIA issue varied over time. During the war the Defense Ministry's General Political Department was responsible for managing prison facilities, caring for prisoners, exploiting the American POWs for propaganda value, and retaining records regarding the fates of U.S. casualties and the disposition of U.S. prisoners. Subordinate elements of the General Political Department played central roles in the process, including the Enemy Proselyting Department, which was responsible for interrogation of prisoners, and the Military Justice Department, which managed the prison system in cooperation with the General Rear Services Department and the Public Security Service of the Ministry of Interior. In the late 1960s, enemy proselyting sections subordinate to military regions administered POW camps, processed U.S. and ARVN prisoners, and oversaw proselyting activities and interrogations involving U.S. and ARVN prisoners. During the late 1960s, the Central Office, South Vietnam (COSVN), which was the headquarters of the Vietnam Worker's Party in the south, determined policies concerning the treatment of prisoners in the south. COSVN organized policy sections which inspected prison camps, made decisions concerning prison populations, and received reports on U.S. prisoners from subordinate offices and field units. Group 875 was a subordinate entity of the Defense Ministry's General Political Department which was established in late 1972 to implement efforts to recover and preserve the remains of U.S. service personnel and to administer PAVN's POW camps for U.S. personnel.

PAVN's role in the issue after 1974 lessened significantly. Group 875 was disbanded in 1974. Personnel were reassigned to the Enemy Proselyting Department and the Military Justice Department, which were given responsibilities for the administration of the reeducation camp system for former ARVN officers. Elements in the Military Justice Department were placed in charge of programs to recover and preserve remains of U.S. service personnel during the period following the disbandment of Group 875. In the late 1970s, PAVN seems to have detailed officers who had been associated with Group 875 to the VNOSMP. The Defense Ministry apparently had a continuing interest in the security implications of joint field activities during the late 1980s and the question of U.S. access to wartime archival information and prison facilities, matters which Washington raised with Hanoi with increasing vigor beginning with General Vessey's first visit to Hanoi in August 1987.[8]

Under Nguyen Co Thach's successor, Nguyen Manh Cam, certain things changed about the manner in which the Vietnamese administered the POW/MIA issue. There were signs in late 1991 and early 1992 that the level of leadership of the VNOSMP had been slightly elevated and set more firmly in the context of the Foreign Ministry's chain of command. The Foreign Ministry began to coordinate more systematically the management of the POW/MIA issue with ministerial counterparts in Defense and Interior and with senior government and party officials.

Within the Politburo, the locus of power shifted and remained fluid as a result of the leadership changes of the Seventh National Party Congress. The Foreign Ministry was obviously playing in a very different institutional circumstance in which the "National Security" bloc could easily outvote the Foreign Ministry. The Foreign Ministry itself was without a Politburo-level vote following Nguyen Co Thach's "retirement" from that body, until January 1994 when Cam was given a seat on the Politburo. Additionally, the balance of power in the Vietnamese foreign policy establishment shifted away from the foreign service professionals to the politicos who populated the party's Foreign Relations Department of the Central Committee. That, coupled with the party general secretary's interest in overturning foreign policy decisions that had the imprimatur of Nguyen Co Thach yielded a situation in which the normally collegial Vietnamese decision-making apparat had begun to play according to more competitive rules, based on the distinct interests of different bureaucracies in a political system beset by diminishing resources.

During the preparations for the mid–1991 Seventh Congress of the Vietnamese Communist Party, Western journalists spoke of the emergence of a structure resembling the National Security Council that would marry Ministry of Interior and Ministry of National Defense resources and focus on security-related priorities such as internal and external threats perceived by these ministries, whose equities were often compromised by the manner in which the Foreign Ministry under Thach defined policy goals and managed relationships with foreign countries. While such an NSC-like structure did not emerge in any formal sense and had certainly not been provided for in the reorganization of the government discussed at the January 1992 National Assembly session, a condominium of Defense and Interior Ministry interests developed, if only by virtue of increasingly similar viewpoints and perspectives on security issues. The Foreign Ministry became the minor partner by mid–1991, a role to which Cam, the technician and foreign policy manager, adapted admirably in a way that Thach, the foreign policy maestro, could never have done.

Foreign Minister Cam became part of a well-orchestrated system of redistributed power that evolved rather quickly following Thach's retirement. Under Thach, the Foreign Ministry had at times been clearly competitive with the Defense Ministry and had been capable of standing up to it. After the Seventh National Party Congress, and until Cam's promotion to the Politburo in 1994, the system began to resemble a troika in which the Foreign Ministry was without representation at the highest levels of the ruling party, and the two other sides of the triangle, the Ministries of Defense and Interior, had seats on the inner circle and a mandate to function more in concert with one another.

Cam functioned smoothly and effectively in this context, taking the maximum position in negotiations and clearly deferring to senior government leaders to set the stage for a resolution of issues. He played his role according to cues provided by the senior leadership. Whereas in the past Thach reserved this central dramatic moment for himself, Cam was primed to have senior government officials shape the moment of decision. For example, during Vessey's January 1992 visit to Hanoi, Cam made his maximum position clear in plenary session discussions. He was clearly authorized to reward the U.S. interlocutor with some agreements on live-sighting investigations, access to information and trilateral cooperation. He backed away, however, from opportunities to define compromises and reach accommodations and allowed his seniors in the Ministry of Defense to trigger the accommodation and to signal acceptance of Vessey's position. Cam's job was to supervise Foreign Ministry efforts to hammer out the details of the agreement.

By early 1992 the Vietnamese seemed to have modified their policy-making chain of command responsible for POW/MIA decisions or were at least prepared to advertise changes in the decision-making mandate of various levels of the government in order to suggest that a higher level was involved. A senior department-level Foreign Ministry official stated that the top level of government concerned with this issue was the chairman of the Council of Ministers, who made decisions and issued directives guiding the MIA mechanism. That mechanism was responsible for obtaining authorizations from the chairman of the Council of Ministers. This was a distinctly more involved posture for the Council of Ministers and its chairman. The senior official also described the provincial work groups as being simultaneously under the authority of the VNOSMP and the chairman of the Council of Ministers and suggested that these structures had been stiffened and rationalized and given a clear and significant high-level chain of command instead of being allowed to exist as ad hoc entities activated only in the context of joint field activities with the U.S. Finally, the senior official described the Vietnamese "MIA mechanism" as being organized according to principles that guided the work of other mass organizations and grassroots systems, and he indicated that the POW/MIA apparat was to operate according to standards against which other organizations were judged in performing their public missions and interacting with other organizations.

The VNOSMP operated independently of the senior policy-making officials under Nguyen Co Thach, who was prepared to make agreements in principle and act on them in a marginal, lethargic manner or not at all. Cam was impatient with this, especially since he had to live with the policy consequences of such an approach. The responsibility for technical-level affairs had by early

1992 moved up a notch. Nguyen Xuan Phong, deputy director of the Foreign Ministry's Americas Department, assumed responsibility for coordinating the daily affairs of the VNOSMP. In the past, the VNOSMP muddled along under the supervision of department-level officials, with a senior directorate-level official attached to the Office of the Foreign Minister assuming the responsibilities for meeting U.S. government counterparts. Beginning in early 1992, a senior Foreign Ministry official played a more direct role in the daily business of the VNOSMP and was the chief interlocutor for the Joint Task Force leadership. This left the VNOSMP director without the leverage and responsibilities he held from the late 1980s to 1991. Moreover, Le Mai, deputy foreign minister, had become engaged on a continuing basis in the POW/MIA issue. Previously, Thach had directed deputy foreign ministers to walk on stage as conditions required an assistant secretary–level representative. Under Cam, deputy ministers played a more formal role and were more directly involved in the Foreign Ministry's management of the POW/MIA issue.

General Secretary Do Muoi played a stronger role than his predecessor did in the foreign policy realm. He accepted the proposition that Vietnam must do what it could to gain access to quick economic assistance and made this the starting point for his decision to move toward quick normalization with China and to improve cooperation with Washington. Muoi also seemed, however, to have decided to take issue with the manner in which Thach handled the "Roadmap" question. Muoi probably shared Le Duc Anh's view that Chinese normalization should be the first priority. Muoi also shared Anh's long-standing gripe that Thach was able to gain nothing at all for the withdrawal of PAVN troops from Cambodia in September 1990, in spite of the promised foreign policy windfall advantages that were supposed to be reaped from Thach's policy of disengagement. Finally, Muoi seems to have shared Anh's view of Thach's mishandling of the U.S.–Vietnamese relationship. Anh very actively accused Thach of squandering Vietnamese resources in an effort to comply with Washington's urgings to be cooperative on the POW/MIA issue. At a meeting before the Seventh National Party Congress, Anh reportedly denounced Thach for failing to deliver the promised normalization with the U.S. through cooperation on humanitarian issues.

At the same time, though, Muoi seriously wanted to do what was required to resolve the POW/MIA issue by complying with Washington's requirements for accounting for missing service members, repatriating remains, and investigating live sightings. The POW/MIA issue must have seemed to be the easiest to solve of Hanoi's foreign policy problems. Hanoi had to face the possibility of being held accountable for the difficulties encountered in implementing the peace plan in Cambodia. By mid-1992, rapprochement with China had bogged down in territorial disputes involving the Spratly Islands. Therefore, Muoi drew the conclusion that it would be sensible to mute criticism of the Roadmap and assume a more accommodating posture. Hanoi needed to clear the underbrush of its foreign relations and simplify its approaches to issues in the face of its disadvantages in an extremely fluid situation. Muoi's decision to pledge his support for resolving this issue to the Senate Select Committee was the result of the desire to cut through the entangled thicket of positions and approaches to the POW/MIA issue that had developed during the past decade, which had begun to encumber policy in a fast-moving world.

NOTES

Chapter One

1. Hearings before the Select Committee on POW/MIA Missing or Prisoner in Southeast Asia, DoD Accounting Process, 24 June 1992; testimony by Chuck Trowbridge, deputy director, Defense Intelligence Agency Special Office, POW/MIA Affairs, p. 121; testimony by Admiral Moorer, former chief of the Joint Chiefs of Staff, p. 171. See Project Contemporary Historical Examination of Current Operations (CHECO) Southeast Asia report, *Joint Personnel Recovery in Southeast Asia*, 1 September 1976, p. 7. The Joint Personnel Recovery Center (JPRC), activated in September 1966, served as the coordinating agency for the recovery of U.S. military and civilian personnel in Indochina. Also see memorandum of conversation between Henry Kissinger and Nguyen Van Thieu, Saigon, 17 August 1972 (declassified). On the Paris peace talks and the POW/MIA issue, see Alan Goodman, *The Lost Peace: America's Search for a Negotiated Settlement of the Vietnam War* (Stanford, Calif.: Hoover Institution Press, 1978); Gareth Porter, *A Peace Denied: The United States, Vietnam and the Paris Agreement* (Bloomington: Indiana University Press, 1975); Marvin and Bernard Kalb, *Kissinger* (New York: Little, Brown, 1974); Walter Issacson, *Kissinger: A Biography* (New York: Simon and Schuster, 1992); Bo Quoc Phong, *Cuoc Chien Tranh Xam Luoc Thuc Dan Moi Cua De Quoc My O Viet Nam* (Hanoi: Vien Lich Su Quan Su, 1991); Luu Van Loi and Nguyen Oanh Vu, *Tiep Xuc Bi Mat Viet Nam Hoa Ky Truoc Hoi Nghi Pa-Ri* (Hanoi: Vien Quan He Quoc Te, 1990); Mai Van Bo, *Tan Cong Ngoai Giao Va Tiep Xuc Bi Mat* (Ho Chi Minh City: Nha Xuat Ban Thanh Pho Ho Chi Minh, 1985).

2. Steve Holmes, "Perot Goes Heavy on Drama, Light on Details," *New York Times*, 27 April 1992, p. A14; "Background: Paris Peace Accords," Senate Select Committee on POW/MIA Affairs, circulated in August 1992, undated; Robert F. Turner, *Vietnamese Communism: Its Origins and Development* (Stanford: Hoover Institution Press, 1975), pp. 268–73; statement of Henry A. Kissinger before the Senate Select Committee on POW/MIA Affairs, 22 September 1992; Paul Mather, "The MIA Story in Southeast Asia," manuscript, 1990, Chapter 1. I have drawn heavily from Paul Mather's fine account. Mather was the chief of the Joint Casualty Resolution Center (JCRC) Liaison Office in Bangkok, Thailand, from 1973 to 1988. Also see memorandum of conversation between Henry Kissinger and Le Duc Tho, Essonne, France, 26 September 1972 (declassified); memorandum of conversation between Henry Kissinger and Xuan Thuy, Paris, France, 16 August 1971 (declassified); and memorandum to General Haig from Henry Kissinger, 27 September 1972 (declassified).

3. *Hai Nam Thi Hanh Hiep Dinh Paris, Ngay 27-01-1973* (Saigon: Viet Nam Cong Hoa Bo Ngoai Giao, 1975), pp. 99.

4. Walter Scott Dillard, *Sixty Days to Peace: Implementing the Paris Peace Accords, Vietnam 1973* (Washington, D.C.: National Defense University, 1982), pp. 99,

169; *POW-MIA Fact Book*, Department of Defense, July 1989, p. 3; *Joint Personnel Recovery in Southeast Asia*, 1 September 1976, pp. 13–17; testimony of Roger Shields, former deputy assistant secretary of defense, hearings before the Select Committee on POW/MIA Affairs, U.S. Senate Hearing on Americans Missing or Prisoner in Southeast Asia, DoD Accounting Process, 25 June 1992, p. 17; testimony of Admiral Moorer, former chairman of the Joint Chiefs of Staff, hearings before the Select Committee on POW/MIA Affairs, U.S. Senate Hearing on Americans Missing or Prisoner in Southeast Asia, DoD Accounting Process, 24 June 1992, pp. 159–62. Also see memorandum for General Haig from Colonel Guay, Paris, France, 14 December 1972 (declassified); Washington Special Actions Group, subject: Vietnam Planning Summary of Conclusions, 8 November 1972 (declassified); memorandum for the assistant to the president for national security affairs from the secretary of defense, subject: Essential Negotiating Points, 10 November 1972 (declassified); Kalb and Kalb, *Kissinger*, pp. 395–422; and Douglas Clarke, *The Missing Man: Politics and the MIA* (Washington, D.C.: National Defense University, 1979), pp. 53–55.

5. Hearings before the Select Committee on POW/MIA Affairs, U.S. Senate Hearing on Americans Missing or Prisoner in Southeast Asia, DoD Accounting Process, 25 June 1992, pp. 13–14. Also see Washington Special Actions Group, subject: Vietnam Planning Summary of Conclusions, 29 January 1973 (declassified); cable from Henry Kissinger to Ambassador Bunker, DTG: 112000Z January 1973 (declassified); memorandum of conversation between General Haig and President Thieu, 2 October 1972 (declassified); Dillard, *Sixty Days to Peace*, Chapter 4.

6. A 1990 Hanoi International Service transmission stated that Pham Van Dong had signed the decree in question in 1972. See Hanoi International Service in English, 1000 GMT, 13 May 1990, *Foreign Broadcast Information Service — East Asia*, 90–093, 13 May 1990, p. 54. Each ministry issued an implementing directive. See Vu Thong Tin Bao Chi, Bo Ngoai Giao Cong Hoa Xa Hoi Chu Nghia Viet Nam, *Ve Van De Nguoi My Mat Tich Trong Chien Tranh O Viet Nam* (Hanoi, 1980), pp. 27–28. Also see Hanoi International Service in English, 1000 GMT, 13 May 1990, *Foreign Broadcast Information Service — East Asia*, 90–093, 13 May 1990, p. 54.

7. Memorandum for the assistant to the president for national security affairs, subject: U.S. POW/MIA personnel in Laos, from secretary of defense, 28 March 1973. Also see memorandum for the secretary of defense from Acting Assistant Secretary Lawrence Eagleburger, subject: U.S. POW/MIA personnel in Laos, I-35174-73, 28 March 1973; memorandum for the secretary of defense from Acting Assistant Secretary Eagleburger, subject: Status Report on Return of POWs/Accounting for MIAs, I-3548/73, 19 March 1973; memorandum for the assistant to the president for national security affairs from secretary of defense, subject: U.S. POW/MIA personnel in Laos, I-35174/73, 28 March 1973; National Security Council memorandum for Henry Kissinger, subject: Minutes of the Washington Special Actions Group Meeting of 13 March 1973, 16 March 1973 (declassified); memorandum for the president from Henry Kissinger, subject: Response to Continued North Vietnamese Infiltration and Logistics Activity in the South, 14 March 1973 (declassified); wire from Brent Scowcroft to Colonel Guay, 20 March 1973 (declassified); cable from Colonel Guay to General Scowcroft, DTG: 021118Z 2 February 1973 (declassified); cable from Colonel Guay to General Scowcroft, 1 February 1973 (declassified); cable from General Scowcroft to Colonel Guay, DTG: 311630Z, 31 January 1973 (declassified).

8. Statement of Henry A. Kissinger before the Senate Select Committee on POW/MIA Affairs, 22 September 1992, p. 12; Kalb and Kalb, *Kissinger*, p. 433; testimony

of George H. Aldrich, legal adviser to the State Department, before the Senate Select Committee on POW/MIA Affairs, 21 September 1992, hearings before the Select Committee on POW/MIA Affairs, 21 September 1992. Also see Washington Special Actions Group, subject: Steps for Implementation of a Southeast Asia Agreement, 30 October 1972 (declassified); memorandum of conversation between Henry Kissinger and Le Duc Tho, St. Nom La Breteche, France, 23 May 1973 (declassified); cable from General Haig to Colonel Guay in Paris, 20 October 1972; message in the name of the prime minister of the government of the DRV in reply to the message of the president of the United States, dated 20 October 1972, 21 October 1972; Dillard, *Sixty Days to Peace*, p. 149.

9. Mather, "The MIA Story," 1:13; *Ve Van De Nguoi My Mat Tich Trong Chien Tranh, O Viet Nam*, p. 3.

10. CHECO, *Joint Personnel Recovery in Southeast Asia*, 1 September 1976, p. 34.

11. *Ve Van De Nguoi My Mat Tich Trong Chien Tranh O Viet Nam*, p. 3.

12. George R. Dunham and David A. Quinlan, *U.S. Marines in Vietnam — The Bitter End, 1973–1975*, (Washington, D.C.: History and Museum Division, Headquarters, United States Marine Corps), pp. 6–7.

13. CHECO, *Joint Personnel Recovery in Southeast Asia*, 1 September 1976, pp. 32–33.

14. Ibid., pp. 31–32.

15. Ibid., p. 46.

16. "General Summary," undated U.S. government chronology, pp. 1–3; CHECO, *Joint Personnel Recovery in Southeast Asia*, 1 September 1976, pp. 35–36.

17. Douglas Pike, ed., *The Bunker Papers: Reports to the President from Vietnam 1967–73*, vol. 3, (Berkeley, Calif.: Institute of East Asian Studies, University of California at Berkeley, Indochina Research Monograph Number Five), pp. 854–55; hearings before the Select Committee on POW/MIA Affairs, U.S. Senate Hearing on Americans Missing or Prisoner in Southeast Asia, DoD Accounting Process, 25 June 1992, p. 112.

18. U.S. FPJMT, *Conditions in PRG Areas Permit Search for MIA Information*, Section G.

19. *History of the U.S. Delegation, Four Party Joint Military Team, 31 March 73–30 April 75*, pp. 7–12; Republic of Vietnam, *One Year After the Paris Agreement: Statement of the RVN Military Delegation to the Central Two-Party JMC at the Meeting on 15 January 1974*, pp. 21–22.

20. "General Summary," p. 15.

Chapter Two

1. Joseph Zasloff and MacAlister Brown, *Communist Indochina and U.S. Foreign Policy* (Boulder, Colo.: Westview Press, 1978), p.12.

2. Vu Thong Tin Bao Chi, Bo Ngoai Giao Long Hoa Xa Hoi Chu Nghia Viet Nam, *Ve Van De Nguoi My Mat Tich Trong Chien Tranh O Viet Nam* (Hanoi, 1980), p. 4.

3. "General Summary," undated U.S. government chronology, p. 39; Fred Brown, *Second Chance: The United States and Indochina in the 1990's* (New York: Council on Foreign Relations Press, 1989), pp. 20–21; *Recent Reports of U.S. PWs and Collaborators in Southeast Asia*, DDI-2430-9-77, 1 April 1977, prepared by Resources and Installations Division, Directorate for Intelligence Research, Defense Intelligence

Agency, p. 69. Also see Douglas Clarke, *The Missing Man: Politics and the MIA* (Washington, D.C.: National Defense University, 1979), pp. 53–55.

4. Paul Mather, "The MIA Story in Southeast Asia," manuscript, 1990, 1:37, 40.

5. Clarke, *The Missing Man*, p. 83. Also see "General Summary," p. 16. Also see Zasloff and Brown, *Communist Indochina and U.S. Foreign Policy*, pp. 10–11.

6. U.S. Congress, Senate Committee on Foreign Relations, *Vietnam 1976: A Report to the Committee on Foreign Relations by George McGovern*, Washington, D.C., U.S. Government Printing Office, 1976; Clarke, *The Missing Man*, pp. 85–86.

7. "General Summary," p. 18; Clarke, *The Missing Man*, pp. 85–86.

8. Zasloff and Brown, *Communist Indochina and U.S. Foreign Policy*, p. 18.

9. Ibid.

10. *Policy Related Events, Decisions, Comments from 1973 Onward Concerning Unaccounted for American POWs and MIAs in Southeast Asia*, prepared by the Office of the Vice Chairman of the Senate Select Committee on POW/MIA Affairs, 21 September 1992; Nguyen Duy Trinh, *Mat Tran Ngoai Giao Thoi Ky Chong My Cuu Nuoc, 1965–1975* (Hanoi: Nha Xuat Ban Su That, 1979), pp. 255–82; Nayan Chanda, "Puzzling Blast from Hanoi," *Far Eastern Economic Review*, 26 November 1976, p. 16; Clarke, *The Missing Man*, pp. 91–93.

11. *The Presidential Commission on Americans Missing and Unaccounted for in Southeast Asia: Report on Trip to Vietnam and Laos, 16–20 March 1977*, pp. 6–9; "Services to Resume Status Reviews on U.S. Servicemen Unaccounted for in Southeast Asia," Office of the Assistant Secretary of Defense, Public Affairs, 16 August 1977, pp. 2–4; Mather, *The MIA Story*, 2:34; Clarke, *The Missing Man*, p. 105.

12. Zasloff and Brown, *Communist Indochina and U.S. Foreign Policy*, p. 11; Brown, *Second Chance*, pp. 26–27.

13. Brown, *Second Chance*, p. 29.

14. Brown, *Second Chance*, pp. 29–31; Nayan Chanda, *Brother Enemy: The War After the War—A History of Indochina Since the Fall of Saigon* (New York: Harcourt Brace Jovanovich, 1986), pp. 268–96; Mather, "The MIA Story," 2:26; "General Summary," p. 41.

15. "General Summary," p. 27.

16. Department of Press and Information, Ministry of Foreign Affairs, *On the Question of Americans Missing in the Vietnam War*, 1980, p. 11. The Vietnamese language text describes Garwood as "an American soldier who of his own will went over to the Liberation Army in 1965, and after the war was concluded of his own will asked permission to earn his living, and was repatriated to America in order to resume a normal life with his family." *Ve Van De Nguoi My Mat Tich Trong Chien Tranh O Viet Nam*, p. 10.

17. General Summary," p. 28; Mather, *The MIA Story*, 3:24.

18. *Ve Van De Nguoi My Mat Tich Trong Chien Tranh O Viet Nam*, p. 12.

19. *POW-MIA Factbook*, Department of Defense, July 1988, p. 21, and July 1991, p. 5; *POW/MIAs in Indochina and Korea*, hearing before the East Asia Subcommittee of the House Foreign Affairs Committee, House of Representatives, 101st Cong., 28 June 1990, p. 39.

20. *On the Question of Americans Missing in the Vietnam War*, p. 24.

21. Ibid., p. 27.

Chapter Three

1. *POW-MIA Factbook*, Department of Defense, June 1984, pp. 4–5; testimony of Richard Childress, former staff member, National Security Council, before the Senate Select Committee on POW/MIA Affairs, 12 August 1992, pp. 2–3.

2. *POW-MIA Factbook*, June 1984, pp. 4–5; "POW/MIA Agreements Between the U.S. and SRV, February 1982–Present," National League of Families, June 1992, p. 1.

3. "POW/MIA Agreements," National League of Families, p. 2; Paul Mather, *The MIA Story in Southeast Asia*, 1990, 3:32; Chanda, *Brother Enemy*, p. 403.

4. *Final Interagency Report* of the Reagan administration on the POW/MIA issue in Southeast Asia, Washington, D.C., 19 January 1989, p. 7; testimony of Richard Childress, p. 3.

5. "POW/MIA Agreements," National League of Families, p. 2.

6. Ibid., p. 3.

7. "POW/MIA Agreements," National League of Families, p. 3.

8. *Final Interagency Report*, p. 7; "POW/MIA Agreements," National League of Families, June 1992, p. 4.

9. Hanoi Domestic Service in Vietnamese, 1000 GMT, 12 June 1985, *Foreign Broadcast Information Service* (hereafter *FBIS*), 14 June 1985, p. K1.

10. *Final Interagency Report*, p. 7.

11. Nayan Chanda, "No More Bones to Pick," *Far Eastern Economic Review*, 19 September 1985, pp. 42–43.

12. "POW/MIA Agreements," National League of Families, p. 4.

13. *Final Interagency Report*, p. 7; "POW/MIA Agreements," National League of Families, p. 4.

14. Robert Sutter, "Vietnam–U.S. Relations: The Missing in Action (MIAs) and the Impasse Over Cambodia," Congressional Research Service, 20 May 1988, pp. 4–5; Mather, *The MIA Story*, 5:9–13.

15. "POW/MIA Agreements," National League of Families, p. 5.

16. *Nhan Dan*, 1 March 1986.

17. Mather, *The MIA Story*, 5:8.

18. "POW/MIA Agreements," National League of Families, p. 6. Schwab was repatriated in August 1986.

19. *Final Interagency Report*, p. 7; *Defense Issues*, 1, no. 55 (1986): 4–5; "POW/MIA Agreements," National League of Families, p. 6.

20. Hanoi Vietnamese News Agency in English, 1446 GMT, 7 May 1987, *FBIS*, 8 May 1987, p. K1.

21. Hong Kong AFP in English, 0822 GMT, 26 May 1987, *FBIS*, 26 May 1987, p. K1; Hong Kong AFP in English, 1412 GMT, 27 April 1987, *FBIS*, 29 April 1987, p. K1.

22. Hong Kong AFP in English, 0809 GMT, 28 May 1987, *FBIS*, 29 May 1987, p. K1. Hanoi Vietnamese News Agency in English, 0719 GMT, 28 May 1987, *FBIS*, 29 May 1987, p. K1.

23. Tokyo Kyoda in English, 1057 GMT, 22 July 1987, *FBIS*, 22 July 1987, p. N1.

24. Hong Kong AFP in English, 1115 GMT, 21 July 1987, *FBIS*, 22 July 1987, p. N2; Hong Kong AFP in English, 1201 GMT, 23 July 1987, *FBIS*, 23 July 1987, p. N1.

25. Hong Kong AFP in English, 1430 GMT, 27 July 1987, *FBIS*, 28 July 1987, p. N1.

26. Hong Kong AFP in English, 0943 GMT, 1 August 1987, *FBIS*, 3 August 1987, p. N1; testimony of Richard Childress, p. 6.

27. Hong Kong AFP in English, 1333 GMT, 1 August 1987, *FBIS*, 3 August 1987, p. N1.

28. "POW/MIA Agreements," National League of Families, p. 7.

29. U.S. humanitarian aid to Vietnam was later expanded to encompass child survival assistance. "POW/MIA Agreements," National League of Families, pp. 7–8; "POW/MIA Significant Events," Office of the Assistant Secretary of Defense for Public Affairs, 7 August 1991, p. 1; "De Cuong Phat Bieu Tai Cuoc Gap Doan Tro Ly Thuong-Ha Vien My Sang Tim Hieu Tinh Hinh Giai Quyet Van De Nguoi My Mat Tich O Viet Nam," 21 July 1991, pp. 3–4.

30. Hanoi International Service in English, 1000 GMT, 3 August 1987, *FBIS*, 3 August 1987, p. N3.

31. Hong Kong AFP in English, 1012 GMT, 25 August 1987, *FBIS*, 87-164, 25 August 1987, p. 35; Hanoi Vietnamese News Agency in English, 1520 GMT, 28 August 1987, *FBIS*, 87-168, 31 August 1987, p. 39; Hanoi Vietnamese News Agency in English, 1452 GMT, 12 November 1987, *FBIS*, 87-219, 13 November 1987, pp. 43–44; "POW/MIA Agreements," National League of Families, p. 8.

32. Hong Kong AFP in English, 0259 GMT, 30 March 1988, *FBIS — East Asia*, 88-061, 30 March 1988, p. 50; Hong Kong AFP in English, 1227 GMT, 18 May 1988, *FBIS — East Asia*, 88-096, 18 May 1988, pp. 44–45.

33. *POW-MIA Fact Book*, Department of Defense, July 1989, pp. 12–13.

34. "POW/MIA Agreements," National League of Families, p. 8.

35. Ibid.

36. "POW/MIA Significant Events," p. 2; Ronald Cima, ed., *Vietnam: A Country Study* (Washington, D.C.: U.S. Government Printing Office, 1989), p. 228; OASD/ISA, "Progress on the POW/MIA Issue," October 1987; *POW-MIA Factbook*, July 1989, pp. 2–8; Hanoi Vietnamese News Agency in English, 1532 GMT, 6 April 1988, *Foreign Broadcast Information Service — East Asian Service* (hereafter *FBIS-EAS*), 88-067, 7 April 1988, p. 48; Hanoi Vietnamese News Agency in English, 0709 GMT, 15 April 1988, *FBIS-EAS*, 88-067, 7 April 1988, pp. 50–51; *Final Interagency Report*, p. 10; Hong Kong AFP in English, 1406 GMT, 12 July 1988, *FBIS-EAS*, 88-061, 13 July 1988, pp. 57–58.

37. Hanoi Vietnamese News Agency in English, 1555 GMT, 28 July 1988, *FBIS-EAS*, 88-146, 29 July 1988, p. 54.

38. Hanoi Domestic Service in Vietnamese, 1100 GMT, 3 August 1988, *FBIS-EAS*, 88-149, 3 August 1988, p. 6; "Mot Quan Diem Di Nguoc Lao Chien Huong Du Luan Va Nguyen Vong Cua Nhan Dan My," *Nhan Dan*, 31 July 1991, p. 4; Hanoi Domestic Service in Vietnamese, 0500 GMT, 31 July 1988, *FBIS-EAS*, 88-147, 1 August 1988, pp. 59–60; Hanoi Domestic Service in Vietnamese, 2300 GMT, 30 July 1988, *FBIS-EAS*, 88-147, 1 August 1988, p. 60; Hanoi International Service in English, 1000 GMT, 1 August 1988, *FBIS-EAS*, 88-147, 1 August 1988, p. 60.

39. "The U.S. Side Must Bear Full Responsibility for Impediments in the Pace of Solving the MIA and Other Humanitarian Issues," Hanoi, 12 August 1988.

40. "Bo Truong Ngoai Giao Nguyen Co Thach Gui Thu Cho Dac Phai Vien Tong Thong My-Tuong Gion Vet Xi," *Nhan Dan*, 31 August 1988, pp. 1, 4.

41. *Final Interagency Report*, p. 10.

42. *POW-MIA Fact Book*, July 1989, p. 14; "POW/MIA Agreements," National League of Families, p. 9. Gaston Sigur attended this meeting.

43. "Thong Bao Cua Van Phong Co Quan Viet Nam Tim Kiem Nguoi Mat Tich," *Nhan Dan*, 6 January 1989, p. 4.

44. *POW-MIA Fact Book*, July 1989, pp. 16–17.

45. "POW/MIA Significant Events," 2 July 1990, p. 5.

46. *Cong An Thanh Pho Ho Chi Minh*, 22 November 1989, translated in *Joint Publication Research Service—Southeast Asia* 90-001-L, 17 January 1989, p. 14.

47. Testimony of Carl Ford, principal deputy assistant secretary of defense for international security affairs, before the Subcommittee on East Asia and the Pacific, House Foreign Affairs Committee, 28 June 1990, pp. 21–24; "POW/MIA Agreements," National League of Families, p. 9.

48. "Oa Sinh Ton Phe Phan Hanh Dong Khien Khich Cua Mot So Tu Nhan My Chong Cac Nuoc Dong Duong," *Nhan Dan*, 18 February 1989, p. 4.

49. *Final Interagency Report*, p. 21.

50. "Ket Luan Cua Nha Trang: Khong Co Bang Chung Nao Cho Thay Tu Binh My Con Song O Viet Nam," *Nhan Dan*, 22 January 1989, p. 4.

51. "Dai Su Trinh Xuan Lang Tiep Dai Dien To Chuc Giai Phau Dem Lai Nu Cuoi Cho Cac Em," *Nhan Dan*, 13 February 1989, p. 4.

52. "Thong Bao Cua Van Phong Co Quan Viet Nam Tim Kiem Nguoi Mat Tich," *Nhan Dan*, 6 January 1989, p. 4. Also see *The Future of U.S.–Indochina Relations: An International Symposium* (New York: Asia Society, 1989), pp. 58–61; and *U.S. Policy Toward Indochina*, hearing Before the Subcommittee on East Asian and Pacific Affairs of the Committee on Foreign Relations, U.S. Senate, 101st Cong., 1st sess., 2 October 1989 (Washington, D.C.: U.S. Government Printing Office, 1990).

Chapter Four

1. Hanoi International Service in English, 1000 GMT, 6 December 1990, *FBIS-EAS*, 90-236, 7 December 1990, p. 50; Hanoi Domestic Service in Vietnamese, 1430 GMT, 31 January 1991, *FBIS-EAS*, 90-024, 5 February 1991, pp. 66–67; Hanoi International Service in English, 1000 GMT, 9 November 1990, *FBIS-EAS*, 90-219, 13 November 1990, p. 74.

2. "POW/MIA Agreements Between the U.S. and SRV, February 1982–Present," National League of Families, June 1992, p. 6; "POW/MIA Significant Activities," Office of the Assistant Secretary of Defense/Public Affairs, 7 July 1990, p. 7.

3. Hanoi International Service in English, 1000 GMT, 21 May 1990, *FBIS-EAS*, 90-009, 22 May 1990, p. 66. The May technical session was postponed and finally took place in early July.

4. *POW/MIAs in Indochina and Korea*, hearing before the East Asia Subcommittee of the House Foreign Affairs Committee, House of Representatives, 101st Cong., 28 June 1990, pp. 13, 39.

5. Hanoi Vietnamese News Agency in English, 1609 GMT, 30 June 1990, *FBIS-EAS*, 006, 2 July 1990; *POW/MIAs in Indochina and Korea*, pp. 23–25, 47–48.

6. Hanoi Domestic Service in Vietnamese, 1430 GMT, 21 September 1990, *FBIS-EAS*, 90-185, 24 September 1990, pp. 63–64.

7. Frederick Brown, *Second Chance: The United States and Indochina in the 1990's* (New York: Council on Foreign Relations Press, 1989), p. 33.

8. Hanoi Vietnamese News Agency in English, 0720 GMT, 11 November 1990, *FBIS-EAS*, 90-219, 13 November 1990.

9. U.S. Department of State, "Vietnam Vice Premier Thach's Visit to Washington," 15 October 1990; "POW/MIA Agreements," National League of Families, p. 10.

10. Hanoi International Service in English, 1100 GMT, 5 November 1990, *FBIS-EAS*, 90-215, 6 November 1990, p. 69.

11. Hanoi International Service in English, 1000 GMT, 6 December 1990, *FBIS-EAS*, 90-236, 7 December 1990, p. 50.

12. Hanoi Domestic Service in Vietnamese, 1430 GMT, 9 November 1990, *FBIS-EAS*, 90-219, 13 November 1990, p. 74.

13. Susan Katz Keating, "Pentagon Fears Another MIA Hoax in Vietnam," *Washington Times*, 9 November 1991, p. 3.

14. William Branigan, "Vietnamese Find Profit in POW-MIA Hoaxes," *Washington Post*, 2 October 1991, p. 29; *FBIS-EAS*, 91-016, 21 January 1991, p. 56.

15. Phan Doan Nam, "Van De Phoi Hop Giua An Ninh, Quoc Phong va Ngoai Giao Trong Giai Doan Cach Mang Moi," *Tap Chi Cong San* (March 1991): 31.

16. *FBIS-EAS*, 91-016, 24 January 1991, p. 56.

17. Hanoi Vietnamese News Agency in English, 0629 GMT, 25 December 1991, *FBIS-EAS*, 92-001, 3 January 1992, p. 73; Robert Karniol, "Vietnam Forgets Its Missing POWs," *Jane's Defense Weekly*, 2 May 1992, p. 742.

18. Monika Jensen-Stevenson and William Stevenson, *Kiss the Boys Good Bye* (New York: Dutton, 1990); David Evans, "POW Issue Is off the Back Burner," *Chicago Tribune*, 4 November 1990, p. 3; "VFW Commander Reviewing POW/MIA Report," VFW news release, Washington, D.C., 1 November 1990; Tommy Denton, "Book Exposes U.S. Coverup on POW," *Star Tribune*, 12 October 1990, p. 198; Monika Jensen-Stevenson and William Stevenson, "Legacy of Covert War—The Boys We Left Behind," *Washington Post*, 28 October 1990, p. C1; "Bring the Boys Home," *Washington Times*, 2 October 1990, p. G2; Karen Tumulty, "POWs May Still Be Held in Southeast Asia, Ex-Pentagon Official Says," *Los Angeles Times*, 31 May 1991, p. A8; Susan Katz Keating, "Puppet Masters," *Soldier of Fortune* (August 1991): 102–19, 123. *Soldier of Fortune* published the "Request for Relief" memorandum from Colonel Peck to DIA senior officials. Also see statement by Tracy E. Usry, special investigator, Senate Foreign Relations Committee Minority Staff, before the Minnesota State Senate Veterans Affairs Committee, 6 February 1991; *Veterans of Foreign Wars* (September 1991): 22; and *Congressional Record*, 19 March 1991.

19. Al Kamien, "U.S. Officials Say Vietnam May Cooperate Fully on MIAs," *Washington Post*, 14 January 1991, p. 14.

20. General John Vessey, "Opening Statement to the House Foreign Affairs Subcommittee on Asian and Pacific Affairs," 17 July 1991.

21. Hanoi Vietnamese News Agency in English, 1503 GMT, 27 January 1991, *FBIS-EAS*, 11 January 1991. Hanoi Vietnamese News Agency in English, 1457 GMT, 16 January 1991, *FBIS-EAS*, 91-001, 16 January 1991, pp. 53–54.

22. Hanoi Vietnamese News Agency in English, 1455 GMT, 7 February 1991, *FBIS-EAS*, 91-027, 8 February 1991, p. 62.

23. General John Vessey, "Opening Statement"; *Quan Doi Nhan Dan*, 28 April 1991, p. 2.

24. Hong Kong, AFP in English, 1043 GMT, 19 April 1991, *FBIS-EAS*, 91-076, 19 April 1991, pp. 66–67.

25. Hanoi International Service in English, 1000 GMT, 11 April 1991, *FBIS-EAS*,

91-071, 12 April 1991, p. 59; Richard Solomon, "Cambodia and Vietnam: Time for Peace and Normalization," testimony before the House Foreign Affairs Committee Subcommittee on East Asian and Pacific Affairs, 10 April 1991; Richard Solomon, "Vietnam: The Road Ahead," testimony before the Senate Foreign Relations Committee Subcommittee on East Asian and Pacific Affairs, 25 April 1991.

26. "U.S. to Open an MIA Office in Hanoi," *New York Times*, 21 April 1991, p. 3; Hong Kong, AFP in English, 1043 GMT, 19 April 1991, *FBIS-EAS*, 91-076, 19 April 1991, p. 66; Hanoi International Service in English, 1000 GMT, 19 April 1991, *FBIS-EAS*, 91-076, 19 April 1991, p. 67.

27. Hanoi Domestic Service in Vietnamese, 1430 GMT, 20 April 1991, *FBIS-EAS*, 91-077, 22 April 1991, p. 51.

28. Hanoi International Service in English, 1000 GMT, 23 April 1991, *FBIS-EAS*, 91-078, 23 April 1991, pp. 60–61.

29. Hanoi Voice of Vietnam Network in Vietnamese, 2300 GMT, 19 May 1991, *FBIS-EAS*, 91-100, 23 May 1991, pp. 56–57; Hong Kong AFP in English, 1201 GMT, 4 July 1991, *FBIS-EAS*, 91-129, 5 July 1991, p. 45.

30. Hanoi Voice of Vietnam Network in Vietnamese, 1400 GMT, 23 June 1991, *FBIS-EAS*, 91-123-S, 26 June 1991, p. 6; Hanoi Vietnamese News Agency in English, 1514 GMT, 27 June 1991, *FBIS-EAS*, 91-027-S, 2 July 1991, p. 19; Murray Hiebert, "More of the Same," *Far Eastern Economic Review*, 11 July 1991, p. 11. Also see Lewis M. Stern, *Renovating the Vietnamese Communist Party: Nguyen Van Linh and the Programme for Organizational Reform, 1987–1991* (Singapore: Institute of Southeast Asian Studies, 1993), Chapter 5.

31. Testimony of the secretary of defense before the Senate Select Committee, reprinted in *Defense '92*, January/February 1992, p. 11–12; "Note of the Ministry of Foreign Affairs of the SRV to the U.S. Department of State, the Department of Defense and the U.S. Special Presidential Emissary General John W. Vessey, Jr.," Hanoi, 19 July 1991; Hong Kong AFP in English, 1042 GMT, *FBIS-EAS*, 91-144, 26 July 1991, p. 66; Hanoi Vietnamese News Agency in English, 1429 GMT, 20 July 1991, *FBIS-EAS*, 91-140, 22 July 1991, p. 67.

32. Hanoi Voice of Vietnam in English, 1000 GMT, 20 July 1991, *FBIS-EAS*, 91-140, 22 July 1991, p. 67.

33. Hong Kong AFP in English, 0642 GMT, 20 July 1990, *FBIS-EAS*, 91-140, 22 July 1991, p. 67; Hanoi Voice of Vietnam Network in Vietnamese, 1100 GMT, 20 July 1991, *FBIS-EAS*, 91-140, 22 July 1991, p. 68; Hanoi Vietnamese News Agency in English, 1326 GMT, 27 July 1991, *FBIS-EAS*, 91-145, 29 July 1991, p. 62; Hong Kong AFP in English, 1213 GMT, 19 July 1991, *FBIS-EAS*, 91-144, 26 July 1991, p. 66.

34. Hanoi Voice of Vietnam Network in Vietnamese, 1000 GMT, 6 August 1991, *FBIS-EAS*, 91-151, 7 August 1991, p. 36.

35. Hanoi Vietnamese News Agency in English, 0705 GMT, 10 September 1991, *FBIS-EAS*, 91-175, 10 September 1991, p. 81; Hanoi Voice of Vietnam Network in Vietnamese, 0015 GMT, 10 September 1991, *FBIS-EAS*, 91-175, 10 September 1991, p. 81; Hanoi Vietnamese News Agency in English, 1439 GMT, 19 August 1991, *FBIS-EAS*, 91-163, 22 August 1991, pp. 63–64; "POW/MIA Agreements," National League of Families, p. 10.

36. Hanoi Vietnamese News Agency in English, 1319 GMT, 15 August 1991, *FBIS-EAS*, 91-159, 16 August 1991, p. 51.

37. General John Vessey, "Opening Statement to the Senate Foreign Relations Committee POW/MIA Subcommittee," 5 November 1991.

38. Hanoi Voice of Vietnam Network in Vietnamese, 0015 GMT, 4 October 1991, *FBIS-EAS*, 91-193, 4 October 1991, p. 56.

39. Hanoi Voice of Vietnam Network in Vietnamese, 1430 GMT, 2 October 1991, *FBIS-EAS*, 91-192, 3 October 1991, p. 53.

40. Hanoi Voice of Vietnam Network in Vietnamese, 1430 GMT, 2 October 1991, *FBIS-EAS*, 91-192, 3 October 1991, p. 53; Hanoi Voice of Vietnam Network in Vietnamese, 0015 GMT, 4 October 1991, *FBIS-EAS*, 91-193, 4 October 1991, p. 56.

41. Hong Kong AFP in English, 1043 GMT, 8 October 1991, *FBIS-EAS*, 91-196, 9 October 1991, p. 40.

42. U.S. Department of State Office of the Assistant Secretary of State Spokesman, "U.S.–Vietnam Talks," 21 November 1991; Hanoi Voice of Vietnam in English, 1100 GMT, 23 November 1991, *FBIS-EAS*, 91-227, 25 November 1991, p. 65.

43. Hanoi Voice of Vietnam in English, 1430 GMT, 15 November 1991, *FBIS-EAS*, 91-221, 15 November 1991, p. 51. Also see Hanoi Voice of Vietnam Network in Vietnamese, 0015 GMT, 12 November 1991, *FBIS-EAS*, 91-219, 13 November 1991, pp. 64–65.

44. Hanoi Voice of Vietnam Network in Vietnamese, 0015 GMT, 12 November 1991, *FBIS-EAS*, 91-219, 13 November 1991, pp. 64–65.

45. Hong Kong AFP in English, 0237 GMT, 6 December 1991, *FBIS-EAS*, 91-235, 6 December 1991, pp. 52–53.

46. "De Cuong Phat Bieu Tai Cuoc Gap Doan Tro Ly Thuong-Ha Vien My Sang Tim Hieu Tinh Hinh Giai Quyet Van De Nguoi My Mat Tich O Viet Nam," 21 July 1991, pp. 3–4; Hanoi Vietnamese News Agency in English, 1523 GMT, 9 December 1991, *FBIS-EAS*, 91-237, 10 December 1991, p. 46.

47. Hanoi Vietnamese News Agency in English, 1506 GMT, 9 December 1991, *FBIS-EAS*, 91-237, 10 December 1991, p. 46.

48. Hanoi Vietnamese News Agency in English, 1519 GMT, 16 December 1991, *FBIS-EAS*, 91-242, 17 December 1991, p. 52; Hanoi Vietnamese News Agency in English, 0600 GMT, 13 December 1991, *FBIS-EAS*, 91-240, 13 December 1991, p. 55.

49. Hanoi Voice of Vietnam Network in Vietnamese, 0015 GMT, 8 December 1991, *FBIS-EAS*, 91-236, 8 December 1991, pp. 65–66.

50. Douglas Pike, *Report from Vietnam: 1991* (Berkeley, Calif.: Indochina Studies Project, 1991), pp. 47–55.

51. The Aspen Institute, *The American-Vietnamese Dialogue, Conference Report*, 11-14 February 1991, pp. 4–5.

Chapter Five

1. Hanoi Vietnamese News Agency in English, 1437 GMT, 9 January 1992, *FBIS-EAS*, 92-007, 10 January 1992, p. 64; "Press Release: Kalugin's Statement Denied," SRV Permanent Mission to the United Nations, 01/BC, 4 January 1992.

2. Hanoi Vietnam Television Network in Vietnamese, 1200 GMT, 5 January 1992, *FBIS-EAS*, 92-009, 14 January 1992, pp. 67–68.

3. Hanoi Voice of Vietnam Network in Vietnamese, 0015 GMT, 12 January 1992, *FBIS-EAS*, 91-009, 14 January 1992, p. 68.

4. Hanoi Voice of Vietnam in English, 1000 GMT, 15 January 1992, *FBIS-EAS*, 91-010, 15 January 1992, p. 38.

5. "Note of the VNOSMP to the U.S. MIA Office In Hanoi," 20 January 1992.

6. *Nhan Dan*, 20 January 1992, p. 3.

7. Joint Statement, 1 February 1992; Hanoi Voice of Vietnam in English, 1000 GMT, 7 February 1992, *FBIS-EAS*, 91-026, 7 February 1992, p. 52; "Toi Hy Vong Ca Hai Phia Se Cung Buoc Nhay Vot," *Quan He Quoc Te*, February 1992, pp. 8–9.

8. Hanoi Voice of Vietnam in English, 1000 GMT, 7 February 1992, *FBIS-EAS*, 91-026, 7 February 1992, p. 52.

9. Hong Kong AFP in English, 0724 GMT, 11 February 1992, *FBIS-EAS*, 92-028, 11 February 1992, p. 52.

10. *The Nation* (Bangkok, Thailand), 29 February 1992, p. A3.

11. Hanoi Vietnamese News Agency in English, 1459 GMT, 20 February 1992, *FBIS-EAS*, 92-035, 21 February 1992, p. 52. Also see Vu Thong Tin Bao Chi, Bo Ngoai Giao Cong Hoa Xa Hoi Chu Nghia Viet Nam, *Ve Van De Nguoi My Mat Tich Trong Chien Tranh O Viet Nam* (Hanoi, 1980), pp. 9–10.

12. Hanoi Voice of Vietnam in English, 0015 GMT, 21 February 1992, *FBIS-EAS*, 92-035, 21 February 1992, pp. 52–53.

13. "Prepared Statement of Richard H. Solomon," *Update on U.S. Indochina Policy and Other Matters*, hearing before the Committee on Foreign Relations, U.S. Senate, 102nd Sess., 31 March 1992, pp. 6–7.

14. Michael Zielenziger, "Embargo Is the Final Siege," *San Jose Mercury News*, 24 May 1992, p. 1; Department of State, "Statement: Vietnam—Humanitarian Exceptions to the Embargo," Office of the Assistant Secretary, 29 April 1992.

15. Hanoi Voice of Vietnam in English, 0015 GMT, 5 March 1992, *FBIS-EAS*, 92-044, 5 March 1992, p. 37; Hong Kong AFP in English, 0653 GMT, 5 March 1992, *FBIS-EAS*, 92-044, 5 March 1992, p. 37.

16. Hanoi Voice of Vietnam Network in Vietnamese, 1000 GMT, 6 March 1992, *FBIS-EAS*, 92-045, 5 March 1992, pp. 37–38; Hanoi Voice of Vietnam Network in Vietnamese, 1100 GMT, 4 March 1992, *FBIS-EAS*, 92-044, 5 March 1992, p. 38.

17. Hanoi Vietnamese News Agency in English, 0628 GMT, 6 March 1992, *FBIS-EAS*, 92-045, 6 March 1992, p. 38.

18. Hanoi Voice of Vietnam Network in Vietnamese, 1430 GMT, 10 March 1992, *FBIS-EAS*, 92-048, 11 March 1992, p. 65.

19. Hanoi Vietnamese News Agency in English, 1527 GMT, 31 March 1992, *FBIS-EAS*, 92-064, 2 April 1992, p. 38.

20. Hanoi Vietnamese News Agency in English, 0630 GMT, 23 March 1992, *FBIS-EAS*, 92-056, 23 March 1992, p. 53; Hanoi Vietnamese News Agency in English, 1406 GMT, 27 March 1992, *FBIS-EAS*, 92-061, 30 March 1992, p. 48; Hanoi Voice of Vietnam Network in Vietnamese, 1000 GMT, 26 March 1992, *FBIS-EAS*, 92-059, 26 March 1992, p. 38.

21. Hanoi Voice of Vietnam Network in Vietnamese, 1430 GMT, 7 April 1992, *FBIS-EAS*, 92-069, 9 April 1992, pp. 52–53.

22. Hanoi Voice of Vietnam Network in Vietnamese, 1400 GMT, 6 April 1992, *FBIS-EAS*.

23. Department of State, "Statement: Vietnam—Lifting Telecommunications Ban," Office of the Assistant Secretary, 13 April 1992; Department of State, "Statement: Vietnam—Humanitarian Exceptions to the Embargo."

24. Hong Kong AFP in English, 0550 GMT, 30 April 1992, *FBIS-EAS*, 92-084, 30 April 1992, p. 41.

25. Hanoi Voice of Vietnam Network in Vietnamese, 1430 GMT, 22 April 1992, *FBIS-EAS*, 92-079, 23 April 1992, pp. 28–29.

26. "News Conference by Five Members of the Senate Select Committee on POW/MIA Affairs," *Reuters Transcript Report*, 28 April 1992, p. 2.

27. *Congressional Record*, vol. 138, no. 56, 29 April 1992.

28. Hanoi Voice of Vietnam Network in Vietnamese, 1430 GMT, 22 April 1992, *FBIS-EAS*, 92-079, 23 April 1992, pp. 28–29; Hanoi Vietnamese News Agency in English, 0604 GMT, 23 April 1992, *FBIS-EAS*, 92-079, 23 April 1992, p. 29; Victor Mallet, "Hanoi Offers All Help in Hunt for Missing GIs," *London Financial Times*, 23 April 1992, p. 4; Hanoi Vietnamese News Agency in English, 1000 GMT, 11 May 1992, *FBIS-EAS*, 92-092, 12 May 1992, p. 50.

29. Kathleen Callo, "U.S. Team Finds Remains, Reports MIA Deaths," *Washington Times*, 12 May 1992, p. 9.

30. Hanoi Vietnamese News Agency in English, 1536 GMT, 6 May 1992, *FBIS-EAS*, 92-098, 7 May 1992, p. 38.

31. Tran Quang Co, "The Future of Vietnam's Relations with Countries of the Asia-Pacific Region and Implications for Vietnam's Economic Development," presented to George Mason University–East/West Center Conference, Arlington, Virginia, 22 May 1992.

32. Hanoi Vietnamese News Agency in English, 0629 GMT, 28 May 1992, *FBIS-EAS*, 92-103, 28 May 1992, p. 50; Hanoi Voice of Vietnam Network in Vietnamese, 1430 GMT, 27 May 1992, *FBIS-EAS*, 92-106, 2 June 1992, p. 54.

33. Hanoi Voice of Vietnam Network in Vietnamese, 1000 GMT, 29 May 1992, *FBIS-EAS*, 92-105, 1 June 1992, p. 53.

34. Barbara Crossette, "Hanoi Official Sees MIA Searches as Spying," *New York Times*, 9 August 1992, p. 17.

35. Hanoi Voice of Vietnam Network in Vietnamese, 0015 GMT, 25 September 1972, *FBIS-EAS*, 92-200, 15 October 1992, pp. 67–68.

36. Hanoi Voice of Vietnam Network in Vietnamese, 1430 GMT, 16 September 1992, *FBIS-EAS*, 92-196, 8 October 1992, p. 38.

37. Hanoi Voice of Vietnam Network in Vietnamese, 2330 GMT, 16 September 1972, *FBIS-EAS*, 92-201, 16 October 1992, p. 61.

38. "Summary of DIA Photo Analysis," 28 October 1992.

39. Thomas W. Lippman, "U.S. Ex-Operative in Hanoi Obtained MIA Photos," *Washington Post*, 22 October 1992, p. A6; Barbara Crossette, "Central Link in Release of Hanoi MIA Photos: A U.S. Researcher," *New York Times*, 25 October 1992, p. 10; Susumu Awanohara and Jonathan Friedland, "Back to the World: Progress on MIAs Boosts Chance of Vietnam Ties," *Far Eastern Economic Review*, 5 November 1992, pp. 9–10; "Bao Tang Quan Doi Viet Nam," *Cac Bao Tang Quoc Gia Viet Nam* (Hanoi: Viet Kinh Te Thong Tin, 1990), pp. 65–76.

40. Hanoi Voice of Vietnam in English, 1000 GMT, 7 October 1992, *FBIS-EAS*, 92-195, 7 October 1992, p. 52; Hanoi Vietnam News Agency in English, 1433 GMT, 10 October 1992, *FBIS-EAS*, 92-199, 14 October 1992, p. 39; Hanoi Vietnam News Agency in English, 1447 GMT, 10 October 1992, *FBIS-EAS*, 92-199, 14 October 1992, p. 39.

41. Hanoi Voice of Vietnam Network in Vietnamese, 1430 GMT, 19 October 1992, *FBIS-EAS*, 92-202, 19 October 1992, p. 56; Hanoi Voice of Vietnam in English, 1000 GMT, 20 October 1992, *FBIS-EAS*, 92-204, 21 October 1992, p. 54.

42. Barbara Crossette, "Bush Says Photos Are Major Break," *New York Times*, 23 October 1992; Barbara Crossette, "Hanoi Said to Vow to Give MIA Data," *New York Times*, 24 October 1992, pp. 1, 2. On the same day as the president's Rose Garden

statement, the Vietnamese News Agency noted that Hoa Lo Central Prison, the one-hundred-year-old French jail facility which was used to incarcerate U.S. POWs during the war, would be torn down and replaced by a hotel supermarket complex to be named the Hanoi Tower Center. Hanoi Vietnamese News Agency in English, 1336 GMT, 24 October 1992, *FBIS-EAS*, 92-210, 29 October 1992, p. 55.

43. Hanoi Voice of Vietnam in English, 1000 GMT, 29 October 1992, *FBIS-EAS*, 92-211, 30 October 1992, p. 54.

44. Hong Kong AFP in English, 1109 GMT, 5 November 1992, *FBIS-EAS*, 92-215, 5 November 1992, pp. 52–53.

45. Statement by Robert Destatte, senior historian, JTFFA, before the Senate Select Committee on POW/MIA Affairs, 4 December 1992; statement by Admiral Charles Larson, commander in chief, U.S. Pacific Command, before the Senate Select Committee on POW/MIA Affairs, 4 December 1992.

46. Philip Shenon, "U.S. Team in Hanoi Studies the Relics of the Missing," *New York Times*, 15 November 1992, p. 1; Mary Kay Magistad, "Vietnamese See Positive U.S. Policy Shift," *Boston Globe*, 25 October 1992, p. 14.

47. Philip Shenon, "For Vietnam, Settling the Past Could Be Good Business," *New York Times*, 22 November 1992, p. E5; statement by Theodore Schweitzer, Department of Defense contract researcher, before the Senate Select Committee on POW/MIA Affairs, 4 December 1992.

48. "MIA Disclosures," *Washington Post* editorial, 24 November 1992, p. 20; Don Oberdorfer, "Senators Urge U.S. Gesture to Vietnam," *Washington Post*, 24 November 1992, p. 4; statement of PDASD/ISA Carl Ford before the Senate Select Committee on POW/MIA Affairs, 4 December 1992; closing remarks by Senate Select Committee chair, Senator John Kerry, 4 December 1992.

49. Hanoi Vietnamese News Agency in English, 1423 GMT, 18 November 1992, *FBIS-EAS*, 92-223, 18 November 1992, pp. 37–38; Hanoi Voice of Vietnam in English, 1000 GMT, 19 November 1992, *FBIS-EAS*, 92-224, 19 November 1992, p. 37; Hanoi Voice of Vietnam Network in Vietnamese, 1430 GMT, 20 November 1992, *FBIS-EAS*, 92-226, 23 November 1992, pp. 51–52; Hanoi Voice of Vietnam in English, 1000 GMT, 23 November 1992, *FBIS-EAS*, 92-228, 25 November 1992, pp. 37–38; Hanoi Voice of Vietnam in English, 1000 GMT, 25 November 1992, *FBIS-EAS*, 92-229, 25 November 1992, pp. 47–48. On 23 November, Hanoi radio carried an account of the 20th joint field investigations, conducted from 22 October to 18 November at 12 sites across Vietnam, and live-sighting investigations conducted in conjunction with the field work in Hanoi, Ho Chi Minh City, Quang Nam-Da Nang, Quang Tri, Thanh Hoa, and the Mekong Delta. See Hanoi Vietnamese News Agency in English, 1505 GMT, 23 November 1992, *FBIS-EAS*, 92-227, 24 November 1992, p. 47. For the communiqué of the VNOSMP, see Hanoi Voice of Vietnam Network in Vietnamese, 0500 GMT, 5 December 1992, *FBIS-EAS*, 92-235, 7 December 1992, p. 50.

50. "Thong Cao Cua Co Quan Viet Nam Tim Kiem Nguoi Mat Tich," 5 December 1992; Hanoi Voice of Vietnam Network in Vietnamese, 5 December 1992, *FBIS-EAS*, 92-235, 7 December 1992, p. 50.

51. Hong Kong AFP in English, 1212 GMT 18 December 1992, *FBIS-EAS*, 92-244, 18 December 1992, p. 35.

52. Hong Kong AFP in English, 1010 GMT, 15 December 1992, *FBIS-EAS*, 92-241, 15 December 1992, pp. 80–81.

53. Hanoi Voice of Vietnam Network in Vietnamese, 1430 GMT, 15 December 1992, *FBIS-EAS*, 92-242, 16 December 1992, p. 55.

Chapter Six

1. Hanoi Vietnamese News Agency in English, 1430 GMT, *FBIS-EAS*, 25 January 1993, p. 71; Hanoi Voice of Vietnam in English, 1000 GMT, 26 January 1993, *FBIS-EAS*, 93-016, 27 January 1992, pp. 53–54.

2. Hanoi Voice of Vietnam Network in Vietnamese, 0015 GMT, 30 January 1993, *FBIS-EAS*, 93-019, 1 February 1993, pp. 66–67.

3. Quan Doi Nhan Dan Viet Nam, Tong Cuc Chinh Tri, Cuc Tu Tuong Van Hoa (Thong Bao Noi Bo), "Tinh Hinh The Gioi, Trong Nuoc Va Luc Luong Vu Trang, Thang 1-1993," pp. 1–2.

4. Tran Minh Bac, "The U.S.–Vietnam Normalized Diplomatic Relations Meets the Practical Requirements of the Situation," paper presented to the Vietnamese-American Dialogue sponsored by the Aspen Institute, Hawaii, 8–11 February 1993.

5. Hanoi Voice of Vietnam in English, 1000 GMT, 5 February 1993, *FBIS-EAS*, 93-023, 5 February 1993, p. 52.

6. Hanoi Vietnamese News Agency in English, 1442 GMT, 6 February 1993, *FBIS-EAS*, 93-024, 8 February 1993, pp. 44–45; Hanoi Vietnamese News Agency in English, 1319 GMT, 8 February 1993, *FBIS-EAS*, 93-024, 8 February 1993, p. 45; Hanoi Voice of Vietnam in English, 1000 GMT, 5 February 1993, *FBIS-EAS*, 93-023, 5 February 1993, p. 52; "Remains Repatriated from Vietnam Since 1991 Roadmap Presentation," 18 February 1993.

7. Hanoi Voice of Vietnam in English, 1000 GMT, 18 February 1993, *FBIS-EAS*, 93-035, 24 February 1993, p. 55; Hanoi Voice of Vietnam in English, 1000 GMT, 21 February 1993, *FBIS-EAS*, 93-034, 23 February 1993, p. 68.

8. Hanoi Voice of Vietnam Network in Vietnamese, 1100 GMT, 20 March 1993, *FBIS-EAS*, 93-053, 22 March 1993, pp. 55–56.

9. Hanoi Vietnamese News Agency in English, 1420 GMT, 23 March 1993, *FBIS-EAS*, 93-055, 24 March 1993, p. 38; Murray Hiebert, "Merchants of Death," *Far Eastern Economic Review*, 22 April 1993, p. 25.

10. Hanoi Vietnamese News Agency in English, 1331 GMT, 22 March 1993, *FBIS-EAS*, 93-054, 23 March 1993, p. 64.

11. "Tong Bi Thu Do Muoi Tiep Thuong Si Et Mon Mot-xki," *Nhan Dan*, 6 April 1993, pp. 1, 4; "Ve Quan He My-Viet Nam," *Nhan Dan*, 3 April 1993, p. 4; Hong Kong AFP in English, 1232 GMT, 3 April 1993, *FBIS-EAS*, 93-063, 5 April 1992, pp. 32–33; Hanoi Voice of Vietnam in English, 1000 GMT, 6 April 1993, *FBIS-EAS*, 93-064, 6 April 1993, pp. 61–62; Hanoi Voice of Vietnam in English, 1000 GMT, 5 April 1993, *FBIS-EAS*, 93-065, 7 April 1993, pp. 56–57; Hanoi Voice of Vietnam Network in Vietnamese, 1100 GMT, 20 March 1993, *FBIS-EAS*, 93-053, 22 March 1993, p. 54.

12. Hanoi Vietnamese News Agency in English, 1438 GMT, 7 April 1993, *FBIS-EAS*, 93-066, 8 April 1993, p. 69; Hanoi Vietnamese News Agency in English, 1414 GMT, 8 April 1993, *FBIS-EAS*, 93-067, 9 April 1993, pp. 53–54.

13. Stephen J. Morris, "The '1205' Document: A Story of American Prisoners, Vietnamese Agents, Soviet Archives, Washington Bureaucrats, and the Media," *The National Interest* (Fall 1993): 28–42.

14. Hanoi Vietnamese News Agency in English, 1408 GMT, 13 April 1993, *FBIS-EAS*, 93-070, 14 April 1993, pp. 54–55; Hong Kong AFP in English, 0730 GMT, 14 April 1993, *FBIS-EAS*, 93-070, 14 April 1993, pp. 55–56; Hanoi Vietnamese News Agency in English, 1000 GMT, 14 April 1993, *FBIS-EAS*, 93-070, 14 April 1993, p. 56; Hong Kong AFP in English, 0652 GMT, 13 April 1993, *FBIS-EAS*, 93-069, 13 April

1993, pp. 61–62; press release, Socialist Republic of Vietnam Permanent Mission to the United Nations, 13 April 1993, No. 11/BC; 12 April 1993, No. 10/BC; 21 April 1993, No. 14/BC.

15. Hanoi Vietnamese News Agency in English, 1448 GMT, 15 April 1993, *FBIS-EAS*, 93-072, 16 April 1993, p. 38.

16. Press release, Socialist Republic of Vietnam Permanent Mission to the United Nations, 20 April 1993, No. 13/BC; Hanoi Voice of Vietnam Network in Vietnamese, 1430 GMT, 19 April 1993, *FBIS-EAS*, 93-074, 20 April 1993, pp. 55–56.

17. *Quan Doi Nhan Dan*, 18 April 1993; Hanoi Voice of Vietnam Network in Vietnamese, 1430 GMT, 18 April 1993, *FBIS-EAS*, 93-073, 19 April 1993, pp. 55–56. Also see Hong Kong AFP in English, 0525 GMT, 18 April 1993, *FBIS-EAS*, 93-073, 19 April 1993, pp. 67–68; Hong Kong AFP in English, 0444 GMT, 19 April 1993, *FBIS-EAS*, 93-073, 19 April 1993, p. 68; Hong Kong AFP in English, 0537 GMT, 19 April 1993, *FBIS-EAS*, 93-073, 19 April 1993, p. 68; Hanoi Voice of Vietnam in English, 1000 GMT, 19 April 1993, *FBIS-EAS*, 93-073, 19 April 1993, p. 69.

18. Hanoi Voice of Vietnam in English, 1000 GMT, 21 April 1993, *FBIS-EAS*, 93-075, 21 April 1993, p. 53.

19. "Tong Thong My B. Clinton: Chinh Phu Viet Nam Thanh Thuc Hoc Tac Trong Van De POW/MIA," *Nhan Dan*, 26 April 1993, p. 4.

20. Nguyen Manh Cam, "Tren Duong Trien Khai Chinh Sach Doi Ngoai Theo Dinh Huong Moi," *Quan He Quoc Te*, April 1993, pp. 2–3; *Bangkok Post*, 27 April 1993, p. 7.

21. Hanoi Voice of Vietnam Network in Vietnamese, 2330 GMT, 28 April 1993, *FBIS-EAS*, 93-086, 6 May 1993, p. 51.

22. Hanoi Vietnamese News Agency in English, 1508 GMT, 8 May 1993, *FBIS-EAS*, 93-088, 10 May 1993, p. 55; Hanoi Voice of Vietnam in English, 1000 GMT, 4 May 1993, *FBIS-EAS*, 93-087, 10 May 1993, p. 41.

23. Hanoi Voice of Vietnam Network in Vietnamese, 2300 GMT, 21 May 1993, *FBIS-EAS*, 93-098, 24 May 1993, p. 66.

24. Hanoi Voice of Vietnam Network in Vietnamese, 1000 GMT, 20 May 1993, *FBIS-EAS*, 93-096, 21 May 1993, p. 49; Hanoi Voice of Vietnam in English, 1000 GMT, 19 May 1993, *FBIS-EAS*, 93-096, 20 May 1993, p. 55; "Chu Tich Le Duc Anh Tiep Thung Nghi Si Gion Ke-ry," *Nhan Dan*, 17 May 1993, pp. 1, 4.

25. Nguyen Viet Phuong, *Van Tai Quan Su Chien Luoc Tren Duong Ho Chi Minh Trong Khang Chien Chong My* (Hanoi: Tong Cuc Hau Can, Bo Quoc Phong, 1988).

26. "Tong Bi Thu Do Muoi Tiep Doan Nghi Si Va Cuu Binh My," *Nhan Dan*, 2 June 1993, pp. 1, 4; Hanoi Vietnamese News Agency in English, 1429 GMT, 1 June 1993, *FBIS-EAS*, 93-103, 1 June 1993, p. 51; Hanoi Voice of Vietnam Network in Vietnamese, 1430 GMT, 1 June 1993, *FBIS-EAS*, 93-104, 2 June 1993, p. 51; Hanoi Voice of Vietnam in English, 1000 GMT, 8 June 1993, *FBIS-EAS*, 93-108, 8 June 1993, p. 54.

27. Hoang Linh, "Lua Dao Tren Nhung Bo Khung Nguoi," *Tuoi Tre Chu Nhat*, 27 June 1993, p. 13. Also see *Far Eastern Economic Review*, 2 June 1994, p. 13, on Chailland's sentencing. Also see Hanoi Voice of Vietnam in English, 1000 GMT, 4 June 1993, *FBIS-EAS*, 93-107, 7 June 1993, p. 51; Hanoi Voice of Vietnam in English, 1000 GMT, 14 May 1993, *FBIS-EAS*, 93-093, 17 May 1993, p. 62. On 8 June, Hanoi announced the repatriation of 26 sets of remains "collected" during the 23rd joint investigations. See Hanoi Vietnamese News Agency in English, 1350 GMT, 8 June 1993, *FBIS-EAS*, 93-109, 9 June 1993, p. 55. A 17 June broadcast provided details about the Joint

Documents Center. See Hanoi Voice of Vietnam in English, 1000 GMT, 17 June 1993, *FBIS-EAS*, 93-116, 18 June 1993, p. 53.

28. Quan Doi Nhan Dan Viet Nam, Tong Cuc Chinh Tri (Thong Bao Noi Bo), "Tinh Hinh The Gioi, Trong Nuoc Va Luc Luong Vu Trang," July 1993, pp. 1–3; also see April, May and June 1993; Vu Oanh, "Trach Nhiem Va Tinh Nghia Sau Nang Voi Nhung Nguoi Con Trung Hieu Cua Dat Nuoc," *Nhan Dan*, 31 March 1993, p. 3; Phan Van Son, "Cuoc Song Moi Cua Nguoi Linh Cu," *Nhan Dan*, 30 April 1993, p. 3.

29. Hanoi Voice of Vietnam Network in Vietnamese, 0500 GMT, 3 July 1993, *FBIS-EAS*, 93-128, 7 July 1993, pp. 66–67; press release, Socialist Republic of Vietnam Permanent Mission to the United Nations, 5 July 1993, No. 20/BC; Hanoi Voice of Vietnam Network in Vietnamese, 1100 GMT, 3 July 1993, *FBIS-EAS*, 93-127, 6 July 1993, p. 65.

30. Hanoi Voice of Vietnam Network in Vietnamese, 0800 GMT, 1 July 1993, *FBIS-EAS*, 93-131, 12 July 1993, p. 70.

31. Hanoi Voice of Vietnam Network in Vietnamese, 1430 GMT, 17 July 1993, *FBIS-EAS*, 93-136, 19 July 1993, pp. 53–54.

32. Hanoi Vietnamese News Agency in English, 1510 GMT, 16 July 1993, *FBIS-EAS*, 93-136, 19 July 1993, pp. 51–52; Hanoi Vietnamese News Agency in English, 1521 GMT, 17 July 1993, *FBIS-EAS*, 93-133, 19 July 1993, pp. 52–53; Hanoi Voice of Vietnam Network in Vietnamese, 1430 GMT, 17 July 1993, *FBIS-EAS*, 93-136, 19 July 1993, pp. 53–55.

33. Hanoi Voice of Vietnam Network in Vietnamese, 1430 GMT, 17 July 1993, *FBIS-EAS*, 93-136, 19 July 1993, pp. 53–54.

34. Hanoi Vietnamese News Agency in English, 1532 GMT, 29 July 1993, *FBIS-EAS*, 93-145, 30 July 1993, p. 52; Hanoi Vietnamese News Agency in English, 1334 GMT, 20 July 1993, *FBIS-EAS*, 93-138, 21 July 1993, pp. 55–56.

35. Hanoi Voice of Vietnam in English, 1000 GMT, 20 July 1993, *FBIS-EAS*, 93-137, 20 July 1993, p. 57.

36. "Thong Bao Cua Co Quan Viet Nam Tim Kiem Nguoi Mat Tich," *Lao Dong*, 12 August 1993, p. 1.

37. Hanoi Vietnamese News Agency in English, 1507 GMT, 14 August 1993, *FBIS-EAS*, 93-156, 16 August 1993, p. 38; Vientiane Hengsat Radio Network in Lao, 0000 GMT, 17 August 1993, *FBIS-EAS*, 93-158, 18 August 1993, pp. 38–39.

38. Hanoi Voice of Vietnam in English, 1000 GMT, 6 August 1993, *FBIS-EAS*, 93-150, 6 August 1993, p. 39; Hanoi Voice of Vietnam Network in Vietnamese, 0015 GMT, 4 August 1993, *FBIS-EAS*, 93-150, 6 August 1993, pp. 39–40; "Hoat Dong Doi Ngoai," *Quan He Quoc Te*, August 1993, p. 3; "Hoat Dong Doi Ngoai," *Quan He Quoc Te*, September 1993, p. 2; Hanoi Voice of Vietnam in English, 1000 GMT, 10 August 1993, *FBIS-EAS*, 93-153, 11 August 1993, p. 54; Hanoi Voice of Vietnam in English, 1000 GMT, 12 August 1993, *FBIS-EAS*, 93-155, 13 August 1993, p. 53; Hanoi Vietnamese News Agency in English, 1507 GMT, 14 August 1993, *FBIS-EAS*, 93-156, 16 August 1993, p. 39; Hanoi Vietnamese News Agency in English, 1431 GMT, 27 August 1993, *FBIS-EAS*, 93-165, 27 August 1993, p. 28; Hanoi Vietnamese Television Network in Vietnamese, 1100 GMT, 9 August 1993, *FBIS-EAS*, 93-152, 10 August 1993, p. 55; Hanoi Vietnamese News Agency in English, 1442 GMT, 9 August 1993, *FBIS-EAS*, 93-152, 10 August 1993, pp. 55–56.

39. Hong Kong AFP in English, 0531 GMT, 12 August 1993, *FBIS-EAS*, 93-154, 12 August 1993, p. 39.

40. Hong Kong AFP in English, 0806 GMT, 26 August 1993, *FBIS-EAS*, 93-164, 26 August 1993, p. 39.

41. Hong Kong AFP in English, 1023 GMT, 1 September 1993, *FBIS-EAS*, 93-169, 2 September 1993, p. 38.

42. Hanoi Voice of Vietnam Network in Vietnamese, 1100 GMT, 9 September 1993, *FBIS-EAS*, 93-174, 10 September 1993, p. 52; Hong Kong AFP in English, 0636 GMT, 9 September 1993, *FBIS-EAS*, 93-174, 10 September 1993, p. 52; Hanoi Voice of Vietnam Network in Vietnamese, 0015 GMT, 11 September 1993, *FBIS-EAS*, 93-175, 13 September 1993, pp. 54–55; Hanoi Voice of Vietnam in English, 1000 GMT, 10 September 1993, *FBIS-EAS*, 93-175, 13 September 1993, p. 54.

43. Quang Loi, "Mot Kien Kinh Doanh Tren Noi Dau Nguoi Khac," *Quan Doi Nhan Dan*, 12 September 1993, p. 4.

44. Hanoi Voice of Vietnam Network in Vietnamese, 1100 GMT, 9 September 1993, *FBIS-EAS*, 93-174, 10 September 1993, p. 52.

45. Hanoi Voice of Vietnam Network in Vietnamese, 1100 GMT, 22 September 1993, *FBIS-EAS*, 93-182, 22 September 1993, p. 41; Hanoi Voice of Vietnam Network in Vietnamese, 1400 GMT, 20 September 1993, *FBIS-EAS*, 93-182, 22 September 1993, pp. 42–43.

46. Office of the White House Press Secretary, "Renewal of the Trading with the Enemy Act and U.S. Policy Toward the Embargo Against Vietnam," 13 September 1993.

47. Hanoi Voice of Vietnam in English, 1000 GMT, 14 September 1993, *FBIS-EAS*, 93-176, 14 September 1993, p. 53.

48. Hanoi Voice of Vietnam Network in Vietnamese, 1100 GMT, 14 September 1993, *FBIS-EAS*, 93-177, 15 September 1993, p. 50.

49. "Phi Ly Va Loi Tho," *Nhan Dan*, 17 September 1993, p. 4.

50. Hanoi Voice of Vietnam Network in Vietnamese, 0015 GMT, 18 September 1993, *FBIS-EAS*, 93-180, 20 September 1993, p. 57.

51. Hanoi Voice of Vietnam in English, 1000 GMT, 28 September 1993, *FBIS-EAS*, 93-187, 29 September 1993, p. 62; Hanoi Voice of Vietnam Network in Vietnamese, 1430 GMT, 28 September 1993, *FBIS-EAS*, 93-188, 30 September 1993, p. 41.

52. Hanoi Voice of Vietnam in English, 1000 GMT, 27 September 1993, *FBIS-EAS*, 93-186, 28 September 1993, p. 40; Hanoi Voice of Vietnam Network in Vietnamese, 1430 GMT, 27 September 1993, *FBIS-EAS*, 93-186, 28 September 1993, pp. 41–42.

53. Hanoi Voice of Vietnam in English, 1000 GMT, 20 September 1993, *FBIS-EAS*, 93-181, 21 September 1993, p. 53; "Du Luan My Bat Binh Voi Quyet Dinh Keo Dai Lenh Cam Van Chong Viet Nam," *Nhan Dan*, 18 September 1993, p. 4; "Du Luan My Bat Binh Voi Quyet Dinh Keo Dai Lenh Cam Van Chong Viet Nam," *Nhan Dan*, 24 September 1993, p. 4; "Hay Bat Tay Voi Viet Nam Luc Nay," *Nhan Dan*, 20 September 1993, p. 4.

54. Hanoi Voice of Vietnam Network in Vietnamese, 1400 GMT, 7 September 1993, *FBIS-EAS*, 93-173, 9 September 1993, p. 53; Nguyen Ngoc Truong, "Suy Nghi Ve Mot Chinh Sach," *Quan He Quoc Te*, August 1993, p. 4.

55. *Izvestiya*, 30 October 1993, p. 3.

56. See Hanoi Voice of Vietnam in English, 1000 GMT, 8 October 1993, *FBIS-EAS*, 93-195, 12 October 1993, p. 59; Hanoi Vietnamese News Agency in English, 1423 GMT, 9 October 1993, *FBIS-EAS*, 93-195, 12 October 1993, p. 59; See Hanoi Voice of Vietnam in English, 1000 GMT, 13 October 1993, *FBIS-EAS*, 93-196, 13 October 1993,

pp. 55–56. For Vietnamese comments on the 25th and 26th Joint Investigations, see Hanoi Vietnamese News Agency in English, 1547 GMT, 6 October 1993, *FBIS-EAS*, 93-193, 7 October 1993, p. 56; Hanoi Voice of Vietnam in English, 1000 GMT, 26 October 1993, *FBIS-EAS*, 93-205, 26 October 1993, p. 57.

57. Hanoi Vietnamese News Agency in English, 1457 GMT, 5 October 1993, *FBIS-EAS*, 93-191, 5 October 1993, p. 48. Also see "Statement of H. E. Phan Van Khai at the 48th Session of the United Nations General Assembly," 6 October 1993.

58. Hanoi Voice of Vietnam in English, 1000 GMT, 6 October 1993, *FBIS-EAS*, 93-192, 6 October 1993, p. 52.

59. Hong Kong AFP in English, 0947 GMT, 7 October 1993, *FBIS-EAS*, 93-193, 7 October 1993, p. 56; Susumu Awanohara, "Hole in the Road," *Far Eastern Economic Review*, 14 October 1993; Jason DeParle, "Mysteries Circle Vietnamese at the Center of Brown Inquiry," *New York Times*, 10 October 1993, p. 24.

60. Hanoi Vietnamese News Agency in English, 1504 GMT, 14 December 1993, *FBIS-EAS*, 93-239, 15 December 1993, p. 66; Hanoi Voice of Vietnam Network in Vietnamese, 1430 GMT, 15 December 1993, *FBIS-EAS*, 93-239, 15 December 1993, pp. 66–67.

61. Hanoi Voice of Vietnam Network in Vietnamese, 1430 GMT, 14 December 1993, *FBIS-EAS*, 93-238, 14 December 1993, p. 68.

62. "Doan Research Group Tham Viet Nam," *Nhan Dan*, 15 January 1994, p. 1; Hanoi Vietnamese News Agency in English, 1619 GMT, 12 January 1994, *FBIS-EAS*, 94-008, 12 January 1994, p. 49.

63. "Tong Bi Thu Do Muoi Tiep Doan Uy Ban Nang Luong va Tai Nguyen Thuong Nghi Vien My Tham Viet Nam," *Saigon Giai Phong*, 10 January 1994, p. 1; "Khach Tham," *Nhan Dan*, 17 January 1994, p. 4.

64. "Cac Thuong Nghi Si My Ken Goi Bo Cam Van Va Lap Quan He Ngoai Giao Voi Viet Nam," *Nhan Dan*, 10 January 1994, p. 4; "Tong Bi Thu Do Muoi Tiep Doan Uy Ban Nang Luong Va Tai Nguyen Thuong Nghi Vien My," *Nhan Dan*, 10 January 1994, p. 4; "Thuong Nghi Si Gion Ke-ri: Cong Chung My Can Biet Rang Viet Nam Hop Tac Day Du Voi My Trong Van De MIA," *Nhan Dan*, 17 January 1994, p. 4.

65. Hanoi Voice of Vietnam Network in Vietnamese, 1430 GMT, 13 January 1994, *FBIS-EAS*, 94-011, 18 January 1994, p. 51; "Doan Tieu Ban Quoc Phong, Uy Ban Chuan Chi Thuong Vien My Tham Viet Nam," *Nhan Dan*, 15 January 1994, p. 4.

66. "Thu Tuong Vo Van Kiet Va Chu Tich QH Nong Duc Manh Tiep Thuong Nghi Si J. Keri," *Nhan Dan*, 17 January 1994, pp. 1, 3.

67. "Do Doc My Sac-Lo La Xon Den Chao Chu Tich Nuoc Le Duc Anh," *Nhan Dan*, 18 January 1994, pp. 1, 4; Hanoi Vietnamese News Agency in English, 1429 GMT, 17 January 1994, *FBIS-EAS*, 94-011, 18 January 1994, pp. 53–54.

68. Hanoi Vietnamese News Agency in English, 1000 GMT, 17 January 1994, *FBIS-EAS*, 94-011, 18 January 1994, p. 54; "Dien Bien Quan He Viet-My," *Nhan Dan*, 5 February 1994, p. 3.

69. Hong Kong AFP in English, 0326 GMT, 28 January 1994, *FBIS-EAS*, 94-019, 28 January 1994, p. 37; Hanoi Voice of Vietnam Network in Vietnamese, 1430 GMT, 27 January 1994, *FBIS-EAS*, 94-018, 27 January 1994, p. 44; Hanoi Voice of Vietnam Network in Vietnamese, 1000 GMT, 28 January 1994, *FBIS-EAS*, 94-020, 31 January 1994, p. 51; "Thuong Nghi Si My Gion Ke-ri: Bay Gio La Luc My Can Bai Bo Lenh Cam Van Buon Ban Doi Voi Viet Nam," *Nhan Dan*, 27 January 1994, p. 4; "Thuong Nghi Vien My Thong Qua Nghi Quyet Uong Ho Huy Bo Cam Van Doi Voi Viet Nam,"

Nhan Dan, 29 January 1994, pp. 1, 4; *Congressional Record*, 26 January 1994, vol. 140, no. 2, pp. S.131–S.174.

70. Hanoi Voice of Vietnam in English, 1000 GMT, 3 February 1994, *FBIS-EAS*, 94-023, 3 February 1994, p. 55.

71. Hanoi Voice of Vietnam Network in Vietnamese, 2300 GMT, 2 February 1994, *FBIS-EAS*, 94-023, 3 February 1994, p. 57.

72. Reuter Transcript Report, Clinton/Vietnam announcement, 3 February 1994 (17:57 02-03), p. 5.

73. "Bo Ngoai Giao Ta Ra Tuyen Bo Ve Viec Tong Tuong My Quet Dinh Bo Cam Van Doi Voi Viet Nam," *Nhan Dan*, 5 February 1994, p. 1.

74. Murray Hiebert and Susuma Awanohara, "Lukewarm Welcome," *Far Eastern Economic Review*, 17 February 1994, pp. 14–17.

75. "Hoc Bao Quoc Te," *Nhan Dan*, 5 February 1994, pp. 1, 4; Hanoi Voice of Vietnam Network in Vietnamese, 1100 GMT, 4 February 1994, *FBIS-EAS*, 94-024, 4 February 1994, pp. 40–41; Philip Shenon, "Vietnam Welcomes U.S. Decision on Embargo," *New York Times*, 5 February 1994, pp. 1, 5.

Chapter Seven

1. H. Bruce Franklin, *MIA or Mythmaking in America* (New York: Lawrence Hill, 1990), pp. 60–74.

2. Patrick Tyler, "Perot Told U.S. to Soften Policy on Vietnamese," *New York Times*, 5 July 1992, pp. 1, 14; "Excerpts from Perot's Letter to Reagan in 1987," *New York Times*, 5 July 1992, p. 14.

3. Tyler, "Perot," p. 1; Susumu Awanohara, "Perot's Patriot Games," *Far Eastern Economic Review*, 18 June 1992, pp. 12–13; "Was Perot Looking for More Than GIs in Vietnam?" *Business Week*, 15 June 1992, pp. 37–38.

4. Hanoi Voice of Vietnam Network in Vietnamese, 1400 GMT, 6 April 1992, *FBIS-EAS*, Serial BK0704150892; Vientiane KPL in English, 0914 GMT, 12 April 1994, *FBIS-EAS*, 94-072, 14 April 1994, p. 27.

5. Hong Kong AFP in English, 0531 GMT, 12 August 1993, *FBIS-EAS*, 93-154, 12 August 1993, p. 39.

6. "Tong Bi Thu Do Muoi Tiep Doan Nghi Si Va Cuu Binh My," *Nhan Dan*, 2 June 1993, p. 4; Phan Van Khai, "Tinh Hinh Dat Nuoc Tiep Tuc Chuyen Bien Tot, Nhung Chua Vung Chac, Con Nhung Mat Yeu Va Kho Khan Lon Phai Khac Phuc," *Nhan Dan*, 17 June 1993, p. 2; Quan Doi Nhan Dan Viet Nam, Tong Cuc Chinh Tri (Thong Bao Noi Bo), "Tinh Hinh The Gioi, Trong Nuoc Va Luc Luong Vu Trang," June 1993, pp. 10–11, and May 1993, pp. 13–15. Also see Hanoi Voice of Vietnam Network in Vietnamese, 2300 GMT, 5 August 1993, *FBIS-EAS*, 93-153, 11 August 1993, pp. 57; and Hanoi Vietnamese Television Network in Vietnamese, 1200 GMT, 5 August 1993, *FBIS-EAS*, 93-151, 9 August 1993, p. 57.

7. Nguyen Phu Trong, "Nhan Quyen-Dao Ly Viet Nam," *Nhan Dan*, 14 May 1993, p. 3.

8. Douglas Pike, *PAVN: People's Army of Vietnam* (Novato, Calif.: Presidio Press, 1986), pp. 95–96; Larry J. O'Daniel, *Missing in Action: Trail of Deceit* (New York: Arlington House, 1979), pp. 223; Thanh Tin, *Nguoi Hung My Chong Mat* (Hanoi: Nha Xuat Ban Thanh Nien, 1974), p. 9–10; Bui Tin's testimony before the Senate Select Committee on POW/MIA Affairs, Hearing to Receive Testimony on

POW/MIA Investigation Policy and Process, 7 November 1991, pp. 63–64, 69, 75, 92, 94, and 113. Also see the following documents in Department of Defense, *Uncorrelated Information Relating to Missing Americans in Southeast Asia*, vol. 14, 15 December 1978: DTG 150700Z December 1973, from DAO SEA AOSOF-IS-R to DIA Washington D.C., Report Number Z 724 3432 73, Project 0710-11, pp. 61–62; DTG 180701Z January 1974, from DAO SGN RVN AOSOP-ISM concerning the 4th Detention Camp in the Chau Son Area, Hoai Nhon District, Binh Dinh Province, pp. 125–28; "Mission of Proselyting Section of Quang Ngai Province," 6 029 3113 68, 28 January 1969, which transmits a translation of a Military Region Five document on the standard operating procedures of the Agency RL, pp. 326–37; "Interrogation of U.S. Prisoners of War," 6 028 1964 69, 18 February 1969, which transmits information from an undated document on the interrogation of U.S. POWs at a detention camp in the Tri-Thien-Hue Military Region, pp. 341–68; "Responsibilities and Regulations for PW Camps of Tri-Thien-Hue Military Region," 6 028 2361 69, 29 March 1969, which transmits a translation of a 10 April 1968 circular from the Troop and Enemy Proselyting Office of the Tri-Thien-Hue Military Region, pp. 369–71; "Military Proselyting Plan for Binh Dinh Province Region," 6 029 0963 68, 21 November 1968, pp. 379–88; "Handling of Prisoners of War, Quang Ngai Province Party Committee, Military Region Five," 6 028 0600 70, 19 July 1970, pp. 399–411; and Combined Document Exploitation Center Document Loc No 06-1907-70, "Circular to Subordinate V Military Proselyting Sections (Through V Current Affairs Committee)," pp. 412–14. I profited from discussions on this subject with Robert Destatte, Defense Intelligence Agency.

BIBLIOGRAPHY

Vietnamese Periodicals

Hanoi Moi
Lao Dong
Nghien Cuu Quoc Te
Nhan Dan
Quan Doi Nhan Dan

Quan He Quoc Te
Saigon Giai Phong
Tap Chi Cong San
Tuoi Tre

Vietnamese-Language Papers (published outside of Vietnam)

Hoa Thinh Don Viet Bao
Phu Nu Viet Nam
Thu Do Thoi Bao

Tu Do
Xay Dung

English-Language Periodicals

Asian Wall Street Journal
Department of Defense POW/MIA Newsletter
Far Eastern Economic Review
Foreign Broadcast Information Service: Daily Report

Joint Publications Research Service: Southeast Asia
National League of Families Updates
New York Times
Soldier of Fortune
Washington Post
Washington Times

Congressional Testimony (Chronologically)

U.S. Congress, Senate Committee on Foreign Relations. *Vietnam 1976: A Report to the Committee on Foreign Relations by George McGovern*. Washington, D.C.: U.S. Government Printing Office, 1976.
U.S. Policy Toward Indochina Since Vietnam's Occupation of Kampuchea. Hearings before the Subcommittee on East Asian and Pacific Affairs of the Committee on Foreign Relations, House of Representatives, 97th Cong., 1st sess., 15, 21, 22 October 1981.
Americans Missing in Southeast Asia. Hearings before the Committee on Veteran's Affairs, U.S. House of Representatives, 100th Cong., 1st sess., 5 August 1988.

U.S. Policy Toward Indochina. Hearing before the Subcommittee on East Asian and Pacific Affairs of the Committee on Foreign Relations, U.S. Senate, 101st Cong., 1st sess., 2 October 1989.

POW/MIAs in Indochina and Korea. Hearing before the East Asia Subcommittee of the House Foreign Affairs Committee, House of Representatives, 101st Cong., 28 June 1990.

Richard Solomon. "Vietnam: The Road Ahead." Testimony before the Senate Foreign Relations Committee Subcommittee on East Asian and Pacific Affairs, 25 April 1991.

Resolving the POW/MIA Issue: A Status Report. Hearings before the Subcommittee on East Asian and Pacific Affairs of the Committee on Foreign Relations, House of Representatives, 102d Cong., 1st sess., 17 July 1991.

General John Vessey. "Opening Statement to the House Foreign Affairs Subcommittee on Asian and Pacific Affairs," 17 July 1991.

American POW/MIAs in Southeast Asia: The Questions Remain. Hearings before the Subcommittee on East Asian and Pacific Affairs of the Committee on Foreign Relations, House of Representatives, 102d Cong., 1st sess., 31 July and 2 August 1991.

POW/MIA Policy and Process. Hearings before the Select Committee on POW/MIA Affairs, U.S. Senate, 102d Cong., 1st sess., on the U.S. government's efforts to learn the fate of America's missing servicemen, 2 parts, 5–7, 15 November 1991.

Questions Regarding American POWs in the 1970s.. Hearings before the Select Committee on POW/MIA Affairs, U.S. Senate, 102d Cong., 1st sess., on the U.S. government's efforts to learn the fate of America's missing servicemen, 21–22 January 1992.

Testimony of the secretary of defense before the Senate Select Committee. Reprinted in *Defense '92* (January/February 1992).

Update on U.S.–Indochina Policy and Other Matters. Hearings before the Committee on Foreign Relations, U.S. Senate, 102d Cong., 2d sess., 31 March 1992.

Hearings before the Select Committee on POW/MIA Affairs, U.S. Senate Hearing on Americans Missing or Prisoner in Southeast Asia. DoD Accounting Process, 25 June 1992.

Hearings before the Select Committee on POW/MIA Affairs, U.S. Senate. Hearing on Americans Missing or Prisoner in Southeast Asia. DoD Accounting Process, 22 September 1992.

Report of the U.S. Senate Select Committee on POW/MIA Affairs, 13 January 1993.

Report of the U.S. Senate Select Committee on POW/MIA Affairs, Appendices, 13 January 1993.

U.S. Policy Toward Vietnam. Hearing before the Subcommittee on East Asian and Pacific Affairs of the Committee on Foreign Relations, U.S. Senate, 103d Cong., 1st sess., 21 July 1993.

Congressional Record, 26 January 1994, vol. 140, no. 2, S.131-S.188.

Miscellaneous Reports and Studies (Chronologically)

U.S. Four Party Joint Military Team (FPJMT). *Conditions in PRG Areas Permit Search for MIA Information*, no date.

Project Contemporary Historical Examination of Current Operations (CHECO) Southeast Asia Report. *The USAF Response to the Spring 1972 Offensive: Situation and*

Redeployment. HQ PACAF, Directorate of Operations Analysis, CHECO/Corona Harvest Division, 10 October 1972.

White House press conference of Henry Kissinger, assistant to the president for national security affairs, 16 December 1972.

"Restoring Peace in Vietnam: Basic Documents on Ending the War and Restoring Peace in Vietnam with a Commentary by Dr. Henry A. Kissinger," 28 January 1973.

"Ending the War and Restoring the Peace in Vietnam." *Weekly Compilation of Presidential Documents,* 29 January 1973, pp. 39–82.

Text of the message from the president of the United States to the prime minister of the Democratic Republic of Vietnam, 1 February 1973.

Project Contemporary Historical Examination of Current Operations (CHECO) Southeast Asia Report. *Linebacker: Overview of the First 120 Days.* HQ PACAF, Directorate of Operations Analysis, CHECO/Corona Harvest Division, 27 September 1973.

Republic of Vietnam Military Delegation to the Central Two-Party JMC. *One Year after the Paris Agreement: Statement of the RVN Military Delegation to the Central Two-Party JMC at the Meeting on 15 January 1974.*

History of the US Delegation, Four Party Joint Military Team, 31 March 73–30 April 75, pp. 7–12.

Project Contemporary Historical Examination of Current Operations (CHECO) Southeast Asia Report. *Joint Personnel Recovery in Southeast Asia,* 1 September 1976.

The Presidential Commission on Americans Missing and Unaccounted for in Southeast Asia: Report on Trip to Vietnam and Laos, 16–20 March 1977.

Recent Reports of U.S. PWs and Collaborators in Southeast Asia. DDI-2430-9-77, prepared by Resources and Installations Division, Directorate for Intelligence Research, Defense Intelligence Agency, 1 April 1977.

Office of the Assistant Secretary of Defense/Public Affairs. "Services to Resume Status Reviews on U.S. Servicemen Unaccounted for in Southeast Asia," 16 August 1977.

Department of Defense. *Uncorrelated Information Relating to Missing Americans in Southeast Asia.* Vol. 14, 15 December 1978.

Department of Press and Information, Ministry of Foreign Affairs, *On the Question of Americans Missing in the Vietnam War,* 1980.

Inspector General Memorandum of Inspection — Office of POW/MIA Branch (DI-E2 and DC), U-202-83/IG, 24 March 1983.

Report of Investigation on Allegations of Wrongdoing by DIA Agents in the POW/MIA Division in the Directorate of Collection Management, U-073-85/IG, 27 February 1985.

DB Examination of DC-2 PW/MIA Division of the Directorate for Collection Management, U-37.745/DB-3C, 15 March 1985.

Director's POW/MIA Task Force Review of PW/MIA Division (VO-PW), 18 March 1986.

The Tighe Task Force Examination of DIA Intelligence Holding Surrounding Unaccounted for United States Military Personnel in Southeast Asia, 27 May 1986.

Office of the Assistant Secretary of Defense for International Security Affairs. "Progress on the POW/MIA Issue," October 1987.

National League of Families of American Prisoners and Missing in Action in Southeast Asia. "Meetings with Vietnamese and Lao Over the Past 12 Months," June 1988.

"The U.S. Side Must Bear Full Responsibility for Impediments in the Pace of Solving the MIA and Other Humanitarian Issues." Hanoi, 12 August 1988.

The Indochina Policy Forum. *Recommendations for the New Administration on United States Policy Toward Indochina*, The Aspen Institute, November 1988.

Final Interagency Report of the Reagan Administration on the POW/MIA Issue in Southeast Asia. Washington, D.C., 19 January 1989.

Department of State. *Vietnam's Humanitarian Concerns: American NGO Activity.* May 1989.

The Future of U.S.–Indochina Relations: An International Symposium. New York: Asia Society, 8–9 September 1989.

The Future of U.S.–Indochina Relations: An International Symposium. New York: Asia Society, October 1989.

Office of the Assistant Secretary of Defense/Public Affairs. "POW/MIA Significant Events," 7 July 1990.

U.S. Department of State. "Vietnam Vice Premier Thach's Visit to Washington," 15 October 1990.

"Interim Report on the Southeast Asian POW/MIA Issue." U.S. Senate Committee on Foreign Relations Republican Staff, 29 October 1990.

"Joint Casualty Resolution Center Operations, 1973–75," February 1991.

Statement by Tracy E. Usry, special investigator, Senate Foreign Relations Committee Minority Staff, before the Minnesota State Senate Veterans Affairs Committee, 6 February 1991.

The Aspen Institute. *The American-Vietnamese Dialogue.* Conference report, 11–14 February 1991, pp. 4–5.

The Aspen Institute. *The Challenge of Indochina: An Examination of the U.S. Role*, 19–21 April 1991.

"An Examination of U.S. Policy Toward POW/MIAs." Senate Select Committee on Foreign Relations Republican Staff, 23 May 1991.

Note from the Ministry of Foreign Affairs of the Socialist Republic of Vietnam to the U.S. Department of State, the U.S. Department of Defense, and the U.S. Special Emissary General John W. Vessey, Jr., 19 July 1991.

Report of the congressional delegation trip to Southeast Asia, 3–11 August 1991.

Office of the Assistant Secretary of Defense/Public Affairs. "POW/MIA Significant Events," 7 August 1991.

Office of the Assistant Secretary of Defense for International Security Affairs. "Subject: POW/MIA Data," 25 October 1991.

U.S. Department of State, Office of the Assistant Secretary, Public Affairs. "U.S.-Vietnam Talk," 21 November 1991.

Pacific Basin Studies Program, Research Institute for Peace and Security. *Normalize Relations with Vietnam Now.* Recommendations by American and Japanese analysts, January 1992.

"Press Release: Kalugin's Statement Denied." Socialist Republic of Vietnam Permanent Mission to the United Nations, 01/BC, 4 January 1992.

"Note of the VNOSMP to the U.S. MIA Office in Hanoi." Socialist Republic of Vietnam Permanent Mission to the United Nations Press Release, 05/BC, 19 February 1992.

Senate Select Committee Forum Report on the Recent Trip to Southeast Asia, 30 April 1992.

The Aspen Institute. *The Challenge of Indochina: An Examination of the U.S. Role*, 2–8 May 1992.

"POW/MIA Agreements Between the U.S. and SRV, February 1982–Present." National League of Families, June 1992.

"Background: Paris Peace Accords." Senate Select Committee on POW/MIA Affairs, circulated in August 1992.

Policy Related Events, Decisions, Comments from 1973 Onward Concerning Unaccounted for American POWs and MIAs in Southeast Asia. Prepared by the Office of the Vice Chairman of the Senate Select Committee on POW/MIA Affairs, 21 September 1992.

U.S. Department of State, Office of the Assistant Secretary, Public Affairs. "Joint Statement," 19 October 1992.

"Summary of DIA Photo Analysis," 28 October 1992.

The Aspen Institute. *The American-Vietnamese Dialogue*, 8–11 February 1993.

The Aspen Institute. *The Challenge of Indochina: An Examination of the U.S. Role*, 30 April–2 May 1993.

Center for National Policy. *A New Look at U.S.–Vietnam Relations*, June 1993.

Office of the White House Press Secretary. "Renewal of the Trading with the Enemy Act and U.S. Policy Toward the Embargo Against Vietnam," 13 September 1993.

Department of Defense. *POW-MIA Fact Book*, June 1984, July 1987, July 1988, July 1989, July 1990, July 1991, October 1992.

"General Summary," undated U.S. government chronology.

English Language Books

Brown, Frederick. *Second Chance: The United States and Indochina in the 1990's*. New York: Council on Foreign Relations Press, 1989.

Cayer, Marc. *Prisoner in Viet Nam*. Translated from the French by Stuart Rawlings. Washington, D.C.: Asia Resource Center, 1990.

Chanda, Nayan. *Brother Enemy: The War After the War—A History of Indochina Since the Fall of Saigon*. New York: Harcourt Brace Jovanovich, 1986.

Cima, Ronald, ed. *Vietnam: A Country Study*. Washington, D.C., U.S. Government Printing Office, 1989.

Clarke, Douglas. *The Missing Man: Politics and the MIA*. Washington, D.C., National Defense University, 1979.

Dillard, Walter Scott. *Sixty Days to Peace: Implementing the Paris Peace Accords, Vietnam 1973*. Washington, D.C.: National Defense University, 1982.

Dunham, George R., and David A. Quinlan. *U.S. Marines in Vietnam—the Bitter End, 1973–1975*. Washington, D.C.: History and Museum Division, Headquarters, USMC.

Galluci, Robert L. *Neither Peace Nor Honor*. Baltimore: Johns Hopkins University Press, 1975.

Goodman, Allan. *The Lost Peace: America's Search for a Negotiated Settlement of the Vietnam War*. Stanford, Calif.: Hoover Institution Press, 1978.

Issacson, Walter. *Kissinger: A Biography*. New York: Simon and Schuster, 1992.

Jensen-Stevenson, Monika, and William Stevenson. *Kiss the Boys Good Bye*. New York: Dutton, 1990.

Kalb, Marvin and Bernard. *Kissinger*. New York: Little, Brown, 1974.

Mather, Paul. "The MIA Story in Southeast Asia," manuscript, 1990.

Pike, Douglas. *PAVN: People's Army of Vietnam*. Novato, California: Presidio Press, 1986.

_____, ed. *The Bunker Papers: Reports to the President from Vietnam, 1967–73*.

Vol. three. Institute of East Asian Studies, University of California at Berkeley, Indochina Research Monograph Number Five, 1990.

————. *Report from Vietnam: 1991.* Berkeley, Calif.: Indochina Studies Project, 1991.

Porter, Gareth. *A Peace Denied: The United States, Vietnam and the Paris Agreement.* Bloomington: Indiana University Press, 1975.

Smith, Garry. *Searching for MIAs.* Spartan, South Carolina: Honorarian Press, 1993.

Stern, Lewis M. *Renovating the Vietnamese Communist Party: Nguyen Van Linh and the Programme for Organizational Reform, 1987–1991.* Singapore: Institute of Southeast Asian Studies, 1993.

Turley, William. *The Second Indochina War: A Short Political and Military History, 1954–1975.* New York: New American Library, 1986.

Turner, Robert F. *Vietnamese Communism: Its Origins and Development.* Stanford, Calif.: Hoover Institution Press, 1975.

Zasloff, Joseph, and MacAlister Brown. *Communist Indochina and U.S. Foreign Policy.* Boulder, Colo.: Westview Press, 1978.

English Language Articles and Papers

Armitage, Richard L. "Time to Turn Page in U.S.–Vietnam Ties." *The Straits Times,* 5 February 1994.

Avery, Dorothy. "Vietnam in 1992: Win Some, Lose Some." *Asian Survey* (January 1993): 67–74.

Awanoharo, Susuma. "Perot's Patriot Games." *Far Eastern Economic Review,* 18 June 1992, p. 13.

Bac, Tran Minh. "Key Issues of Normalization in U.S.–Vietnam Relations." In *The American-Vietnamese Dialogue,* pp. 25–27. The Aspen Institute, 11–14 February 1992.

————. "The U.S.–Vietnam Normalized Diplomatic Relations Meets the Practical Requirements of the Situation." Paper presented to the Vietnamese-American Dialogue, sponsored by the Aspen Institute, Hawaii, 8–11 February 1993.

————. "Normalization of Diplomatic Relations Between the U.S. and Vietnam: Fulfilling Practical Requirements of the Relationship." In *The Challenge of Indochina: An Examination of the U.S. Role,* pp. 55–57. The Aspen Institute, 30 April–2 May 1993.

Bhichai Rattakul. "Negotiating with Vietnam." *The Nation,* 16 February 1985, pp. 4–5.

Binh, Le. "Vietnam–U.S. Relations in the Post-Cold War Era." In *The American-Vietnamese Dialogue,* pp. 47–49. The Aspen Institute, 11–14 February 1992.

Blumenthal, Sidney. "The Mission: Ross Perot's Vietnam Syndrome." *The New Republic,* 6 July 1992, pp. 16–23.

Bresnan, John. "What Should the United States Do About Vietnam?" In *The Challenge of Indochina: An Examination of the U.S. Role,* pp. 19–26. The Aspen Institute, 2–8 May 1992.

Brown, Frederick. "U.S. and Vietnam: Time to Move On." *Indochina Issues,* November 1984.

————. "Normalization of Relations with Vietnam." In *The Challenge of Indochina: An Examination of the U.S. Role,* pp. 29–32. The Aspen Institute, 19–21 April 1992.

————. "The Persistence of a Bitter Past: Impediments to U.S.–Vietnam Normalization." In *The Challenge of Indochina: An Examination of the U.S. Role*, pp. 35–42. The Aspen Institute, 30 April–2 May 1993.

Broyles, William. "The Ghosts of Vietnam." *Newsweek*, 14 February 1994, p. 30.

Chanda, Nayan. "Puzzling Blast from Hanoi." *Far Eastern Economic Review*, 26 November 1976.

———. "Vietnam: Breakthrough in Aid." *Far Eastern Economic Review*, 1 April 1977.

———. "No More Bones to Pick." *Far Eastern Economic Review*, 19 September 1985, pp. 42–43.

———. "Indochina Today: Reform and Paralysis." *The Challenge of Indochina: An Examination of the U.S. Role*, pp. 17–21. The Aspen Institute, 19–21 April 1992.

———. "Research and Destroy: Origins of Vietnam POW Document Remain Obscure." *Far Eastern Economic Review*, 6 May 1993, pp. 70–71.

Co, Tran Quang. "The Future of Vietnam's Relations with Countries of the Asia-Pacific Region and Implications for Vietnam's Economic Development." Presented to George Mason University–East/West Center Conference, Arlington, Virginia, 22 May 1992.

Colbert, Evelyn. "Problems of Normalization: U.S.–Vietnam Relations Since 1975." In *The American-Vietnamese Dialogue*, pp. 5–9. The Aspen Institute, 11–14 February 1992.

Cross, Coy F. "Operation Homecoming: MAC's Finest Hour." Military Airlift Command Office of History Monograph. Scott Air Force Base, Illinois, September 1990.

Crossette, Barbara. "Hanoi Official Sees MIA Searches as Spying." *The New York Times*, 9 August 1992, p. 17.

Downs, Frederick, Jr. "Humanitarian Issues." In *The Challenge of Indochina: An Examination of the U.S. Role*, pp. 23–28. The Aspen Institute, 19–21 April 1992.

Duiker, William. "Is It Time to Recognize Vietnam?" In *The World*, July 1988, pp. 116–21.

Elliot, David W. P. "U.S.–Vietnam Relations: The Past, the Present and the Future." In *The Challenge of Indochina: An Examination of the U.S. Role*, pp. 43–51. The Aspen Institute, 30 April–2 May 1993.

Franklin, H. Bruce. "The POW/MIA Myth: How the White House and Hollywood Combined to Foster a National Fantasy." *The Atlantic*, December 1991, pp. 45–81.

Goldich, Robert R. "POWs and MIAs in Indochina and Korea: Status and Accounting Issues." Congressional Research Service Issue Brief, IB88061, 17 April 1990.

Goodman, Allan E. "U.S. Vietnam Security Issues." Conference on Regional Security in Asia and the Pacific. Washington, D.C., 26 January 1989.

———. "Normalizing Relations with Vietnam: What's in It for Us?" In *The Challenge of Indochina: An Examination of the U.S. Role*, pp. 43–48. The Aspen Institute, 30 April–2 May 1993.

———. "Vietnam's Post-Cold War Diplomacy and the U.S. Response." *Asian Survey*, August 1993, pp. 832–47.

"Hanoi Mixed on Prospects for U.S. Ties after Solomon Visit." *FBIS Trends*, 18 March 1992, pp. 39–41.

Jensen-Stevenson, Monika, and William Stevenson. "Legacy of Covert War—The Boys We Left Behind." Washington Post, 28 October 1990, p. C1.

Jordan, William. "Americans Missing in Southeast Asia: Perceptions, Politics and Realities." U.S. Army War College, 8 May 1990.

Karniol, Robert. "Vietnam Forgets Its Missing POWs." *Jane's Defense Weekly*, 2 May 1992, p. 742.

Kenney, Henry. "American Interests and Normalization with Vietnam." *American Quarterly* (Summer 1992): 38–61.

Khoa, Pham Ngoc. "Vietnam and the Question of Human Rights." *The Challenge of Indochina: An Examination of the U.S. Role*, pp. 53–54. The Aspen Institute, 30 April–2 May 1993.

Larson, Charles. "POW/MIA: Seeking the Answers—The Joint Task Force—Full Accounting Story." 1 July 1993.

Lord, Winston. "POW/MIA Update: Finding the Answers." *U.S. Department of State Dispatch*, 20 September 1993, pp. 638–41.

Mai, Le. "Normalization of U.S.–Vietnamese Relations: The Best Way." *The American-Vietnamese Dialogue*, pp. 11–13. The Aspen Institute, 11–14 February 1992.

Meyers, J. Michael. "How Vietnam Negotiates: A Personal Glimpse." *Indochina Issues* (September 1981).

Morely, James W. "Key Issues of Normalization." In *The American-Vietnamese Dialogue*, pp. 15–24. The Aspen Institute, 11–14 February 1992.

Morris, Stephen J. "Quangmire." *The New Republic*, 31 May 1993, pp. 18–19.

_____. "The '1205' Document: A Story of American Prisoners, Vietnamese Agents, Soviet Archives, Washington Bureaucrats, and the Media." *The National Interest* (Fall 1993).

"Moscow, Hanoi Rebut Charges on American Prisoners of War." *FBIS Trends*, 15 January 1992, pp. 4–6.

Ngoan, Le Thi. "Vietnamese-Americans and the U.S.–Vietnam Relations." In *The Challenge of Indochina: An Examination of the U.S. Role*, pp. 63–66. The Aspen Institute, 30 April–2 May 1993.

Ngoan, Vu Huu. "Renovation in Vietnam and Vietnam–U.S. Relations." In *The American-Vietnamese Dialogue*, pp. 37–40. The Aspen Institute, 11–14 February 1992.

Norland, Irene, Jonas Palm, and Stig Rasmussen. *Libraries in Laos and Vietnam*. A Report from a Consultant Mission on the Library Sector in Laos and Vietnam, NIAS, May 1991.

"On the Question of Americans Missing in the Vietnam War." *Vietnam Courier* 7 (1980): 3–7.

Pike, Douglas. "U.S.–Vietnam Security Relations." Conference on Regional Security in Asia and the Pacific. Washington, D.C., 26 January 1989.

Richburg, Keith B. "Vietnam Finds Itself on the Other Side of MIA Issue." *Washington Post*, 28 September 1989, p. 42.

Romberg, Alan D. "U.S.–Vietnam Relations: Looking at Each Other." In *The American-Vietnamese Dialogue*, pp. 41–46. The Aspen Institute, 11–14 February 1992.

"Security Ministry Disclosure May Foster POW/MIA Progress." *FBIS Trends*, 5 August 1992, pp. 1–3.

Sheehan, Neil. "Prisoners of the Past." *New Yorker*, 24 May 1993.

Sutter, Robert. "Vietnam–U.S. Relations: Issues for U.S. Policy." Congressional Research Service, 86-35F, 10 February 1986.

_____. "Vietnam–U.S. Relations: The Missing in Action (MIAs) and the Impasse Over Cambodia." Congressional Research Service, 20 May 1988.

_____. "Vietnam in Transition: Implications for U.S. Policy." Congressional Research Service, CRS 89-177F, 4 March 1989.

_____. "Vietnam–U.S. Relations: The Missing in Action and the Problem of Cambodia." Congressional Research Service Issue Brief, IB87210, 16 April 1990.

_____. "A Settlement in Cambodia: U.S. Interests, Options and Policy Debate." In *The Challenge of Indochina: An Examination of the U.S. Role*, pp. 9–12. The Aspen Institute, 19–21 April 1992.

_____. "What Would Constitute the Fullest Possible Accounting of POW/MIAs: Current Issues and Possible Approaches for U.S. Policy." In *The Challenge of Indochina: An Examination of the U.S. Role*, pp. 27–34. The Aspen Institute, 2–8 May 1992.

_____. "Vietnam–U.S. Relations: The Debate Over Normalization." Congressional Research Service, January 1994.

_____, and Jeffrey D. Young. "Indochina and Southeast Asia Under Change: Congressional Interests and Options." Congressional Research Service Report for Congress, 31 January 1992.

Thayer, Carlyle. "United States Policy Toward Revolutionary Regimes: Vietnam, 1975–1983." Conference on United States Foreign Policy Adjusting to Change in the Third World, Aspen Institute, Racine, Wisconsin, 2–5 February 1984.

Thien, Ton That. "The Deadly Trap: How Hanoi Negotiates." *Indochina Report* (July–September 1987).

Tombaugh, William W. "Some Thoughts on Negotiating with the North Vietnamese." *National Security Affairs Forum* (Spring/Summer 1975): 49–58.

Turley, William S. "Domestic Issues and Implications for the American-Vietnamese Relationship." In *The American-Vietnamese Dialogue*, pp. 29–36. The Aspen Institute, 11–14 February 1992.

"U.S.–Indochina: Vietnam, Cambodia React to MIA Photograph." *FBIS Trends*, 24 July 1991, p. 14.

"Vietnam–U.S.: Hanoi Sees Little Hope for Normalizing Relations." *FBIS Trends*, 12 February 1992, pp. 43–44.

"Vietnam–U.S.: Hanoi Criticizes U.S. Embargo Decision, Presses on MIA Issue." *FBIS Trends*, 29 September 1993, pp. 60–61.

Vietnamese Language Books

Ban Chap Hanh Dang Bo Dang Cong San Viet Nam Tinh Dong Nai. *Dong Nai: 30 Nam Chien Tranh Giai Phong (1945–1975)*. Dong Nai: Nha Xuat Ban Dong Nai, 1986.

Mai Van Bo. *Tan Cong Ngoai Giao Va Tiep Xuc Bi Mat*. Thanh Pho Ho Chi Minh, Nha Xuat Ban Thanh Pho Ho Chi Minh, 1985.

Bang Giang, et al. *Ban Roi Tai Cho May Bay B.52*. Hanoi: Nhan Xuat Ban Quan Doi Nhan Dan, 1978.

Hai Nam Thi Hanh Hiep Dinh Paris, Ngay 27-01-1973. Saigon: Viet Nam Cong Hoa Bo Ngoai Giao, 1975.

Hoang Van Khanh. *Danh Thang B.52*. Hanoi: Nha Xuat Ban Quan Doi Nhan Dan, 1993.

Luu Van Loi and Nguyen Oanh Vu. *Tiep Xuc Bi Mat Viet Nam Hoa Ky Truoc Hoi Nghi Pa-Ri*, Hanoi: Vien Quan He Quoc Te, 1990.

Nguyen Xuan Mau. *Bao Ve Bau Troi*. Hanoi: Nha Xuat Ban Quan Doi Nhan Dan, 1982.

Mien Dong Nam Bo Khang Chien, 1945–75. Hanoi: Nha Xuat Ban Quan Doi Nhan Dan, 1990.

Muoi Tam Nam Chong My Cuu Nuoc Thang Loi. Hanoi: Nha Xuat Ban Quan Doi Nhan Dan, 1974.

Bo Quoc Phong, *Cuoc Chien Tranh Xam Luoc Thuc Dan Moi Cua De Ouoc My O Viet Nam.* Hanoi: Vien Lich Su Quan Su, 1991.

Bo Quoc Phong, Vien Lich Su Quan Su. *Lich Su Khang Chien Chong My Cuu Nuoc (1954–75).* Vol. 2. Hanoi: Nha Xuat Ban Su That, 1991.

Nguyen Viet Phuong. *Van Tai Quan Su Chien Luoc Tren Duong Ho Chi Minh Trong Khang Chien Chong My.* Hanoi: Tong Cuc Hau Can, 1988.

Quan Khu Ba: Lich Su Khang Chien Chong Thuc Dan Phap. Hanoi: Nha Xuat Ban Quan Doi Nhan Dan, 1990.

Quan Khu Ba: Thang Loi Va Nhung Bai Hoc Trong Khang Chien Chong My. Hanoi: Nha Xuat Ban Quan Doi Nhan Dan, 1981.

Quang Ngai: Lich Su Chien Tranh Nhan Dan 30 Nam (1945–1975). Quang Ngai: Nha Xuat Ban Tong Hop Nghia Binh Bo Chi Huy Quan Su Nghia Binh, 1988.

Su Doan Sao Vang. Hanoi: Nha Xuat Ban Quan Doi Nhan Dan, 1984.

Su Doan 304. Hanoi: Nha Xuat Ban Quan Doi Nhan Dan, 1990.

Hoang Van Thai. *May Van De Ve Tong Ket Chien Tranh Va Viet Lich Su Quan Su.* Hanoi: Vien Lich Su Quan Su, 1987.

Tai Lieu Tham Khao: Nhat Ky Tac Chien Phong Khong, Quan Khu IV, Tu 1964–1973.

Dong Thong and Le Kim. *Nhung Hoat Dong Pha Hoai Lat Do Cua CIA O Viet Nam.* Hanoi: Nha Xuat Ban Cong An Nhan Dan, 1990.

Thanh Tin. *Nguoi Hung My Chong Mat.* Hanoi: Nha Xuat Ban Thanh Nien, 1974.

_____. *Hoa Xuyen Thuyet.* Calif.: Saigon Press, 1991.

_____. *Mat That: Hoi Ky Chinh Tri Cua Bui Tin.* Calif.: Saigon Press, 1993.

Nguyen Duy Trinh. *Mat Tran Ngoai Giao Thoi Ky Chong My Cuu Nuoc, 1965–1975.* Hanoi: Nha Xuat Ban Su That, 1979.

Vu Thong Tin Bao Chi, Bo Ngoai Giao Cong Hoa Xa Hoi Chu Nghia Viet Nam. *Ve Van De Nguoi My Mat Tich Trong Chien Tranh O Viet Nam.* Hanoi, 1980.

Vietnamese Language Articles

Nguyen An. "Bo Cam Van." *Xay Dung* (U.S.), 10 February 1994, pp. 18–24.

"Bao Tang Quan Doi Viet Nam." In *Cac Bao Tang Quoc Gia Viet Nam.* Hanoi: Vien Kinh Te Thong Tin (1990): 65–76.

"Bo Ngoai Giao Ta Ra Tuyen Bo Ve Viec Tong Tuong My Quet Dinh Bo Cam Van Doi Voi Viet Nam." *Nhan Dan*, 5 February 1994, p. 1.

"Bo Truong Ngoai Giao Nguyen Co Thach Gui Thu Cho Dac Phai Vien Tong Thong My-Tuong Gion Vet Xi." *Nhan Dan*, 31 August 1988, pp. 1, 4.

"Cac Thuong Nghi Si My Ken Goi Bo Cam Van Va Lap Quan He Ngoai Giao Voi Viet Nam." *Nhan Dan*, 10 January 1994, p. 4.

Nguyen Manh Cam. "Tren Duong Trien Khai Chinh Sach Doi Ngoai Theo Dinh Huong Moi." *Quan He Quoc Te* (April 1993): 2–5.

_____. "Dae Phai Vien Tong Thong My, Dai Tuong Vecri Tra Loi Phong Van." *Quan He Quoc Te* (February 1992): 8–9

"Chu Tich Le Duc Anh Tiep Thung Nghi Si Gion Ke-ry." *Nhan Dan*, 17 May 1993, pp. 1, 4.

"Dai Hoi Dai Bieu Toan Quoc Hoi Cuu Chien Binh Viet Nam Lan Thu Nhat Thanh Cong Tot Dep." *Quan Doi Nhan Dan*, 22 November 1992, pp. 1, 4.

"Dai Su Trinh Xuan Lang Tiep Dai Dien To Chuc Giai Phau Dem Lai Nu Cuoi Cho Cac Em." *Nhan Dan*, 13 February 1989, p. 4.

"De Cuong Phat Bieu Tai Cuoc Gap Doan Tro Ly Thuong-Ha Vien My Sang Tim Hieu Tinh Hinh Giai Quyet Van De Nguoi My Mat Tich O Viet Nam," 21 July 1991.

"Dien Bien Quan He Viet-My." *Nhan Dan*, 5 February 1994, p. 3.

"Do Doc My Sac-Lo La Xon Den Chao Chu Tich Nuoc Le Duc Anh." *Nhan Dan*, 18 January 1994, pp. 1, 4.

"Du Luan My Bat Binh Voi Quyet Dinh Keo Dai Lenh Cam Van Chong Viet Nam." *Nhan Dan*, 24 September 1993, p. 4.

Thuy Giao. "Chinh Quyen Clinton Va Van De Viet Nam." *Xay Dung* (U.S.) (March 1993): 8–13.

"Hay Bat Tay Voi Viet Nam Luc Nay." *Nhan Dan*, 20 September 1993, p. 4.

Vi Hoang. "Tam Giac Chien Luoc Xo-My-Trung Da Hinh Thanh Nhu The Nao." *Quan He Quoc Te* (April 1993): 16–17.

"Hoc Bao Quoc Te." *Nhan Dan*, 5 February 1994, pp. 1, 4.

V.K. "Can Co Hinh Phat Nghiem Khac Hon Doi Voi Nhung Ke Pham, Toi Dao Boi Mo Ma." *Saigon Giai Phong*, 12 September 1990, p. 4.

"Khach Tham." *Nhan Dan*, 17 January 1994, p. 4.

Phan Van Khai. "Tinh Hinh Dat Nuoc Tiep Tuc Chuyen Bien Tot, Nhung Chua Vung Chac, Con Nhung Mat Yeu Va Kho Khan Lon Phai Khac Phuc." *Nhan Dan*, 17 June 1993, p. 2.

"Ket Luan Cua Nha Trang: Khong Co Bang Chung Nao Cho Thay Tu Binh My Con Song O Viet Nam." *Nhan Dan*, 22 January 1989, p. 4.

Hoang Lan. "Phi Cong My Bi Ban Roi Dau Tien O Mien Bac Viet Nam Tro Thanh Nha Vat Phim Tai Lieu." *Nhan Dan*, 25 April 1993, p. 1.

"Hoat Dong Doi Ngoai." *Quan He Quoc Te* (August 1993): 3.

"Hoat Dong Doi Ngoai." *Quan He Quoc Te* (September 1993): 2.

Dinh Nho Liem. "Tien Toi Xay Dung Ly Luan Ngoai Giao Viet Nam." *Quan He Quoc Te* (September 1993): 7.

Hoang Linh. "Lua Dao Tren Nhung Bo Xung Nguoi." *Tuoi Tre Chu Nhat*, 27 June 1993, p. 13.

Vu Duy Linh. "Cuoc Song Moi Cua Mot Nguoi Linh Cu." *Nhan Dan*, 30 April 1993, p. 3.

Quang Loi. "Mot Kieu Kinh Doanh Tren Noi Dau Nguoi Khao." *Quan Doi Nhan Dan*, 12 September 1993, p. 4.

Ca Van Luong. "Ve Cuoc Tong Tien Cong Va Noi Day Dong Loat Tet Mau Than." *Nghien Cuu Lich Su*, 1/266 (1993): 1–6.

Phan Doan Nam. "Van De Phoi Hop Giua An Ninh, Quoc Phong va Ngoai Giao Trong Giai Doan Cach Mang Moi." *Tap Chi Cong San* (March 1991): 31.

Nguyen Duy Nien. "Tien Toi Mot Dong Nam A Trong The Ky 21." *Quan He Quoc Te* (April 1993): 13–15.

"Oa Sinh Ton Phe Phan Hanh Dong Khien Khich Cua Mot So Tu Nhan My Chong Cac Nuoc Dong Duong." *Nhan Dan*, 18 February 1989, p. 4.

Quan Doi Nhan Dan Viet Nam, Tong Cuc Chinh Tri (Thong Bao Noi Bo), "Tinh Hinh The Gioi, Trong Nuoc Va Luc Luong Vu Trang," April, May, June, and July 1993.

Vu Oanh. "Trach Nhiem Va Tinh Nghia Sau Nang Voi Nhung Nguoi Con Trung Hieu Cua Dat Nuoc." *Nhan Dan*, 31 March 1993, p. 3.

"Phi Ly Va Loi Tho." *Nhan Dan*, 17 September 1993, p. 4.

Phan Van Son. "Cuoc Song Moi Cua Nguoi Linh Cu." *Nhan Dan*, 30 April 1993, p. 3.

Dinh Khoi Sy. "Ke Chuyen Truyen Thong: Hai Ngay Ban Roi 5 May Bay, Bat Song 5 Giac Lai." *Quan Doi Nhan Dan*, 15 July 1990, p. 2.

"Thong Bao Cua Co Quan Viet Nam Tim Kiem Nguoi Mat Tich." *Lao Dong*, 12 August 1993, p. 1.

"Thong Bao Cua Van Phong Co Quan Viet Nam Tim Kiem Nguoi Mat Tich." *Nhan Dan*, 6 January 1989, p. 4.

"Thu Tuong Vo Van Kiet Va Chu Tich QH Nong Duc Manh Tiep Thuong Nghi Si K. Keri." *Nhan Dan*, 17 January 1994, pp. 1, 3.

"Thuong Nghi Si Gion Ke-ri: Cong Chung My Can Biet Rang Viet Nam Hop Tac Day Du Voi My Trong Van De MIA." *Nhan Dan*, 17 January 1994, p. 4.

"Thuong Nghi Si My Gion Ke-ri: Bay Gio La Luc My Can Bai Bo Lenh Cam Van Buon Ban Doi Voi Viet Nam." *Nhan Dan*, 27 January 1994, p. 4.

"Thuong Nghi Vien My Thong Qua Nghi Quyet Uong Ho Huy Bo Cam Van Doi Voi Viet Nam." *Nhan Dan*, 29 January 1994, pp. 1, 4.

"Tong Bi Thu Do Muoi Tiep Doan Nghi Si Va Cuu Binh My." *Nhan Dan*, 2 June 1993, pp. 1, 4.

"Tong Bi Thu Do Muoi Tiep Doan Uy Ban Nang Luong Va Tai Nguyen Thuong Nghi Vien My." *Nhan Dan*, 10 January 1994, p. 4.

"Tong Bi Thu Do Muoi Tiep Doan Uy Ban Nang Luong Va Tai Nguyen Thuong Nghi Vien My Tham Viet Nam." *Saigon Giai Phong*, 10 January 1994, p. 1.

"Tong Bi Thu Do Muoi Tiep Thuong Si Et Mon Mot-xki." *Nhan Dan*, 6 April 1993, pp. 1, 4.

"Tong Cao Cua Co Quan Viet Nam Tim Kiem Nguoi Mat Tich." *Tin Phat Tren Cac Dai, Bao, VTTH, Doi Noi Va Doi Ngoai*, 5 December 1992.

"Tong Thong My B. Clinton: Chinh Phu Viet Nam Thanh Thuc Hoc Tac Trong Van De POW/MIA." *Nhan Dan*, 26 April 1993, p. 4.

Nguyen Phu Trong. "Nhan Quyen Dao Ly Viet Nam." *Nhan Dan*, 14 May 1993, p. 4.

Nguyen Ngoc Truong. "Dac Phai Vien Tong Thong My, Dai Tuong Vecxi Tra Loi Phong Van." *Quan He Quoc Te* (February 1992): 8–9.

_____. "Suy Nghi Ve Mot Chinh Sach." *Quan He Quoc Te* (August 1993): 4–6.

Le Tho Tuong. "Y Kien Ban Doc: Can Xet Xu That Nghiem Vu Nguyen Bach Nhan Kinh Doanh Xuong Nguoi." *Saigon Giai Phong*, 21 August 1990, p. 2.

"Ve Quan He My-Viet Nam." *Nhan Dan*, 3 April 1993, p. 4.

Declassified U.S. Government Memoranda and Cables (Chronologically)

Headquarters, U.S. Military Assistance Command, Vietnam (MACV). *Command History 1965*. Prepared by the Military History Branch, Office of the Secretary, Joint Staff, MACV (declassified).

Headquarters, U.S. Military Assistance Command, Vietnam (MACV). *Command History 1966*. Prepared by the Military History Branch, Office of the Secretary, Joint Staff, MACV (declassified).

Headquarters, U.S. Military Assistance Command, Vietnam (MACV). *Command*

History 1967. Vol. 2. Prepared by the Military History Branch, Office of the Secretary, Joint Staff, MACV (declassified).

Headquarters, U.S. Military Assistance Command, Vietnam (MACV). *Command History 1968*. Vol. 2. Prepared by the Military History Branch, Office of the Secretary, Joint Staff, MACV (declassified).

Headquarters, U.S. Military Assistance Command, Vietnam (MACV). *Command History 1970*. Vol. 2. Prepared by the Military History Branch, Office of the Secretary, Joint Staff, MACV (declassified).

Headquarters, U.S. Military Assistance Command, Vietnam (MACV). *Command History January 1972–March 1973*. Vol. 2. Prepared by the Military History Branch, Office of the Secretary, Joint Staff, MACV (declassified).

U.S. Military Assistance Command, Vietnam (MACV). Memorandum for Record. "Subject: After Action Report—Prisoner of War Release 18 December 1968-2 January 1969," 4 January 1969 (declassified).

Central Intelligence Agency, Telegraphic Dissemination, Foreign Intelligence Report. "Exploitation of American POWs in North Vietnam," 12 January 1970 (declassified).

Central Intelligence Agency, Telegraphic Dissemination, Foreign Intelligence Report. "Ministry of Public Security Responsibility for the Handling, Interrogation and Detention of American Prisoners of War in North Vietnam," 6 February 1970 (declassified).

Memorandum for William Sullivan, deputy assistant secretary of state for East Asian and Pacific Affairs, from the Office of the Director, Special Assistant for Vietnamese Affairs, Central Intelligence Agency. "Subject: Report on Vietnamese Communist Treatment of U.S. Prisoners," 31 March 1970 (declassified).

Message, State 066715, DTG 020045Z May 1970. "Subject: Congressional Hearings on PWs" (declassified).

Central Intelligence Agency, Telegraphic Dissemination, Foreign Intelligence Report. "Personal Views on Possible North Vietnamese Refusal to Comply Fully with Terms of Prisoner Exchange Agreement," 3 November 1970 (declassified).

Central Intelligence Agency, Telegraphic Dissemination, Foreign Intelligence Report. "Public Display of U.S. POWs in North Vietnam," 4 November 1970 (declassified).

Central Intelligence Agency, Telegraphic Dissemination, Foreign Intelligence Report. "Exploitation of U.S. POWs," 3 December 1970 (declassified).

Central Intelligence Agency, Telegraphic Dissemination, Foreign Intelligence Report. "Evacuation, Escape Attempts, Illnesses and Detention of American POWs," 10 December 1970 (declassified).

Message, Saigon 30322, DTG 091103Z May 1971. "Subject: Dang Tan" (declassified).

Message, Director 138762, 10 May 1971. "Subject: Dang Tan" (declassified).

Message, Saigon 30400, DTG 110238Z May 1971. "Subject: Dang Tan" (declassified).

Message, Saigon 30422, DTG 111035Z May 1971. "Subject: Dang Tan" (declassified).

Message, Saigon 30444, DTG 111139Z May 1971. "Subject: Dang Tan" (declassified).

Message, Saigon 30504, DTG 121200Z May 1971. "Subject: Dang Tan" (declassified).

Message, Saigon 7347, DTG 121035Z May 1971. "Subject: Press Conference by North Vietnamese Defector Dang Tan" (declassified).

Memorandum for Henry A. Kissinger, assistant to the president for National Security Affairs, from the Office of the Director, Central Intelligence Agency. "Planned Surfacing in Saigon of North Vietnamese Army Rallier Knowledgable of North Vietnamese Prisoner Handling Policies," 10 May 1971 (declassified).

Memorandum of conversation between Henry Kissinger and Xuan Thuy, Paris, France, 16 August 1971 (declassified).

Memorandum of conversation between Henry Kissinger and Nguyen Van Thieu, Saigon, 17 August 1972 (declassified).

Memorandum of conversation between Henry Kissinger and Le Duc Tho, Essonne, France, 26 September 1972 (declassified).

Memorandum to General Haig from Henry Kissinger, 27 September 1972 (declassified).

Memorandum of conversation between General Haig and President Thieu, 2 October 1972 (declassified).

Cable from General Haig to Colonel Guay in Paris, 20 October 1972 (declassified).

Message in the name of the prime minister of the government of the DRV in reply to the message of the President of the United States, 20 October 1972, 21 October 1972 (declassified).

Washington Special Actions Group. "Subject: Steps for Implementation of a Southeast Asia Agreement," 30 October 1972 (declassified).

Washington Special Actions Group. "Subject: Vietnam Planning Summary of Conclusions," 8 November 1972 (declassified).

Memorandum for the assistant to the president for National Security Affairs from the secretary of defense. "Subject: Essential Negotiating Points," 10 November 1972 (declassified).

Memorandum for General Haig from Colonel Guay, Paris, France, 14 December 1972 (declassified).

Cable from Henry Kissinger to Ambassador Bunker, DTG: 112000Z January 1973 (declassified).

Washington Special Actions Group. "Subject: Vietnam Planning Summary of Conclusions," 29 January 1973 (declassified).

Cable from General Scowcroft to Colonel Guay, DTG: 311630Z, 31 January 1973 (declassified).

Cable from Colonel Guay to General Scowcroft, 1 February 1973 (declassified).

Cable from Colonel Guay to General Scowcroft, DTG: 021118Z 2 February 1973 (declassified).

National Security Council Memorandum for Mr. Kissinger. "Subject: Minutes of the Washington Special Actions Group meeting of 13 March 1973," 16 March 1973 (declassified).

Memorandum for the president from Henry Kissinger. "Subject: Response to Continued North Vietnamese Infiltration and Logistics Activity in the South, 14 March 1973 (declassified).

Memorandum for the secretary of defense from Acting Assistant Secretary Eagleburger. "Subject: Status Report on Return of POWs/Accounting for MIAs," I-3548/73, 19 March 1973 (declassified).

Wire from Brent Scowcroft to Colonel Guay, 20 March 1973 (declassified).

Memorandum of conversation between Henry Kissinger and Le Duc Tho, St. Nom La Breteche, France, 23 May 1973 (declassified).

Memorandum for the assistant to the president for National Security Affairs from the secretary of defense. "Subject: U.S. POW/MIA Personnel in Laos," 28 March 1973 (declassified).

Memorandum for the assistant to the president for National Security Affairs from the secretary of defense. "Subject: U.S. POW/MIA Personnel in Laos," I-35174/73, 28 March 1973 (declassified).

INDEX